Praise

In a world where we seem to be more divided than ever, Lana reminds us of our common humanity as holistic people who ultimately have one common goal–build a world where our children can grow to become healthy, kind, fulfilled adults. This is the book that every school leader and every teacher needs to read. Whether you are new to SEL or you are a seasoned SEL practitioner, this book will enhance your journey and your goals. When school leaders and teachers have asked me, "Where do I begin this SEL journey, and where do I go for additional resources when I have questions?" this is the book that I wished I could have given them–now it's here!

Dido Balla
Educator, Speaker, Leader; Florida

'Relationships before rigor' is one of the many quotes from Lana that resonated with me. Lana has perfected the playbook for SEL education. The book's easy-to-follow structure, common sense strategies, and actionable steps make it a valuable resource for school districts, principals, and teachers. Each chapter concludes with a CALL TO ACTION, urging educators to implement these essential practices immediately. My CALL TO ACTION after reading this book: If you want educators and students to be kind, empathetic, anxiety-free, and achieve top test scores, dive into Lana's Blueprint and apply its principles.

Joni Strama
Teacher and Coach; Charlotte Meck

Every school leader would benefit from reading *Unlocking SEL*! This book offers a road map for creating a community of wellness and care that is an essential foundation for a well-rounded education. This book brilliantly establishes the importance of adults internalizing mindfulness as the base structure for creating a school community of care and emotional regulation for adults and students.

Mary Pearson
School Principal; Portland Public

What a lovely journey this book takes the reader on! Lana's relatable stories and insightful reflections captivate the reader from the very beginning. I would love to use this book as a tool to open the school year with my staff. It helps me to be a more empathetic, thoughtful leader. It also allows me to care for myself and maintain my SEL to model healthy behavior for my team!

Mary Melvin
Regional Director; LAUS

Unlocking SEL by Lana Penley offers a comprehensive, practical approach to integrating social emotional learning into the classroom. With clear strategies, real-world examples, and actionable insights, Penley helps educators support students' emotional and social development. This book is an invaluable resource for creating an inclusive and supportive learning environment.

Kim Cain
Principal; Glen Dale, WV

One of the standout features of the book is its recognition of how trauma can impact behavior, offering thoughtful insights within an SEL framework. By equipping educators with tools to create safe and supportive environments, *Unlocking SEL* helps mitigate student dysregulation and address behavioral challenges effectively. For anyone interested in creating emotionally intelligent classrooms, this book is a must-read. Lana Penley guides readers through practical steps to transform classrooms and schools into nurturing environments where both children and adults can thrive and learn together.

Kristie Lindholm
Executive Director of Schools and Learning; Vancouver School District

Unlocking SEL is exactly what is needed today in education. It is a must read for both teachers and administrators whether they are new to their positions or veterans. The personal anecdotes are relatable, funny, and inspirational. This book will guide a school's journey to unite the entire school through intentional strategies that emphasize communication, inclusivity, and shared goals.

Barb Jepson
High School Principal; LAUSD

Unlocking SEL by Lana Penley is a valuable gift to educators. As a retired principal, this book would have been a game-changer for me and my staff as we navigated the trials of implementing social emotional learning practices in our school. I am grateful that such a resource now exists for current and future educators. Whether you read this book alone, with a team, or as a full staff, I encourage you to crack it open and get started. Lana's personal experience and expertise are shared in a clear and accessible way that will leave you grateful for her insights.

Lori Clark
Retired Principal; Portland Public

Unlocking SEL

The 5 Keys to Transform Schools Through Social and Emotional Learning

You are here!

01 BUILD THE FOUNDATION

02 CENTER ADULT SEL

03 COME INTO THE CLASSROOM

04 SCALE SCHOOL WIDE

05 DESIGN A CYCLE OF SUCCESS

TeacherGoals Publishing

Unlocking SEL

© 2024 by Lana Penley

All rights reserved. No part of this publication may be reproduced in any form or by any means—electronic, photocopying, recording, or mechanical means, including information storage and retrieval systems without permission in writing from the publisher, except by a reviewer who may quote brief passages in a review. For more information regarding permission, contact the publisher at publishing@teachergoals.com. For bulk purchases go to teachergoals.com/bulk.

Published by TeacherGoals Publishing, LLC, Beech Grove, IN
www.teachergoals.com
Cover Design by: Tricia Fuglestad
Interior Design by: Heather Brown
Edited by: Carrie Turner and Heather Brown

Library of Congress Control Number: 2024939291
Paperback ISBN: 978-1-959419-22-8
ASIN: B0D4CCYT9T

First Printing September 2024

Dedication

To Marysville School,

In the halls of this remarkable school, a story unfolded – one that has shaped not just these pages but who I am as a person. This book is a tribute to our journey, a reflection of the enduring spirit and resilience that Marysville embodies. Here, I discovered more than just knowledge.

I found inspiration, strength, and a community that forever altered the course of my life.

With deepest gratitude and affection, I dedicate this book to Marysville School – a place where stories are born, futures are forged, and lives are transformed.

Thank You

♥ **Marysville School:** I served as the principal of Marysville K-8 school in southeast Portland for over a decade. The journey of Marysville rising from crisis was not a solo flight but a collective endeavor. I remember Diana, our long-serving, wonderful secretary saying, "We have a lot of miracles that happen here. We call them Marysville Miracles." These miracles were brought to life by committed teachers, custodians, secretaries, administrative staff, teacher assistants, parents, and neighbors. If you've ever worked at, "The Ville" or are currently working there, thank you, and Go Lions!

♥ **Portland, Oregon:** Between the time of the destruction of our school and the opening day of our surrogate school, the city of Portland rallied around us. Everyone pitched in to help get the new school ready in record time: Portland Public Schools, Superintendent Carole Smith, the neighborhood of Rose City Park, Nike, and many others deserve credit for meeting this moment with kindness and grace. I am forever grateful for how the people of Portland.

♥ **Friends:** I want to give a special shout-out to some incredible individuals. Their unwavering support has been invaluable, especially during the aftermath of a fire. Some of these special people are Carla Welker, Leynise Bible, Joni Strama, Lori Clark, Kristie Lindholm, Linda McCann, Dana Jacobs, Mary Melvin, Jennifer Patterson, Cathy Murray, Jerrie Perkins, Diana Christensen, and many others.

♥ **In addition, I want to thank my family:** First, to my mom and dad. You instilled in me the values of hard work, persistence, and belief that dreams can come true. Without you, this book would not have been possible. You are the kindest, most supportive parents someone could be born to. You gave me the grounding of a loving home while also encouraging me to fly high. I hit the parent lottery. Another thank you goes to my three brothers. Thank you for caring for your only sister and never giving her any slack on the basketball court.

♥ **And** finally, I want to thank my **life partner:** Dian Smith. It was she who believed in me even when I didn't yet believe in myself. For nearly 20 years, she has been there for me and cheering me on. She is my foundation, our company's co-founder, and the rock on which I stand as I stretch for my dreams. I love you.

Table of Contents

Introduction

The Fire	1
Resiliency Bounce	6
The Pandemic is Your Fire	8
The Question this Book Answers	9
An Invitation to a Journey	10

1st Key: Build the Foundation

Chpt. 1	Putting Fundamentals First	15
Chpt. 2	Setting the SEL Vision	25
Chpt. 3	Organizing the Work	31
Chpt. 4	Building the SEL Team	39
Chpt. 5	Incorporating Mindfulness	47

2nd Key: Center Adult SEL

Chpt. 6	Creating a Community of Care	63
Chpt. 7	Being Aware of the Adult Impact	71
Chpt. 8	Demystifying Stress	79
Chpt. 9	Seeking Joy	93

3rd Key: Come into the Classroom

Chpt. 10	Prioritizing Relationships	105
Chpt. 11	Modeling Mindfulness	113
Chpt. 12	Tending to Classroom Space	121
Chpt. 13	Beginning with a Soft Start	129
Chpt. 14	Doing Daily Mindful Moments	135
Chpt. 15	Using a Trauma-Informed Lens	143
Chpt. 16	Teaching Explicit SEL Lessons	151
Chpt. 17	Creating a Peace Corner	159

4th Key: Scale Schoolwide

Chpt. 18	Tending to Schoolwide Space	173
Chpt. 19	Implementing an Anchor Curriculum	183
Chpt. 20	Building a Common SEL Block	193
Chpt. 21	Following an SEL Scope and Sequence	201
Chpt. 22	Creating a Common Language	209
Chpt. 23	Building Belonging	217

5th Key: Designing a Cycle of Success

Chpt. 24	Aligning Resources	229
Chpt. 25	Leveraging Staff Meetings	237
Chpt. 26	Monitoring the Progress	247
Chpt. 27	Planning for Mistakes	255
Chpt. 28	Celebrating Wins	228

Final Thoughts

Hope	271
Rebuild Update	273
Afterword	275
Appendix: A: Lana Professional Development Offerings	*276*
Appendix B: Resource Reminders	*277*
Appendix C: The 5 Habits of a Mindful Educator	*278*
Appendix D: The Big 8-Classroom SEL Strategies	*279*
References	*280*

Free Book Resources

For a copy of the Unlocking SEL Blueprint *and other free resources to complement your experience through this book, scan the QR code below.*

Connect with Lana

If you're looking to bring meaningful, lasting transformation to your school, I can help. With a proven track record in SEL implementation and mindful leadership, I offer hands-on strategies to foster well-being and success for both educators and students. Together, we can create a compassionate, thriving school culture where both adults and students can thrive.

Lana offers professional development through:
- Keynote Speaking
- Core SEL Series – a multi-series training for schoolwide SEL implementation
- Mindful Leader Network – multi-session work for school leaders
-

Scan QR code below to connect.

Foreword

When I first walked into Marysville K-8 school in SE Portland, it didn't take long to realize there was something really special happening within the walls of the schoolhouse. Hearing Principal Lana Penley tell the story, it was clear that the opportunity to rebuild the school in the aftermath of a school fire provided fertile ground for the school to regenerate and to heal. With heart and determination, Lana set forward on a journey that would not only restore Marysville's sense of community, but it would set the school on a trajectory for success.

An outlier among other neighboring Title 1 schools, Marysville's school culture became marked by high engagement, strong staff retention, joyful children, strong academic outcomes, and involved community. News of Marysville's magic started spreading, and soon, Lana and her team were leading school learning walks and helping to inspire others to adopt mindful practices as the anchor for belonging, safety, learning, and positive culture. Lana's story and leadership remind everyone that there is no more powerful tool than social and emotional learning practices to transform a school.

Lana Penley offers her own personal story and compelling framework–a powerful tool to help us all approach our roles with greater presence, patience, and empathy. This book is a practical guide, rich with strategies, exercises, and insights designed specifically for K-12 educators. Offering a road map, reflective prompts, and real-world examples, it is accessible for educators at all levels of experience.

In the rapidly evolving world of education, where the demands on both educators and students seem to grow each year, the need for grounded presence, connection, and care has never been more pressing. This book comes at a crucial juncture, offering a timely and much-needed resource for teachers and school leaders seeking to cultivate a more centered, calm and holistic learning environment.

Lana boldly invites us to transform the way we teach and lead, offering this book as a beacon of guidance and inspiration to support us in the work we do each day. Together, Lana reminds us that we have the key to unlocking mindful schools where every child and educator has the opportunity to thrive.

Jennifer Patterson
Assistant Superintendent
Oregon Department of Education

Introduction

The Fire

On Tuesday, November 10, 2009, our school burned down. Much like a Phoenix, our school, and this book, rose from those ashes. This book is a testament to the transformative journey our school embarked upon, guided by the principles of social and emotional learning (SEL), and viewed through the lens of mindfulness.

As the principal of Marysville K-8 in Portland for over a decade, the crisis affected me personally. I knew that we would have to rally in a whole new way, which led us into an immersive social and emotional learning journey.

That fateful Tuesday morning unfolded like any other day at the school. I was in a meeting with a teacher when the piercing sound of the fire alarm sliced through the air. As the principal, I was always in the loop about scheduled fire drills, yet this caught me off guard. Stepping out of my office, I approached our secretary with a mix of confusion and concern.

"Why are we having a fire drill today?" I asked.

Her response, a direct and equally puzzled, "I don't know, I didn't schedule it either," sent a chill down my spine.

As the words she spoke sunk in, the reality of the situation began to dawn on me. My stomach held a potent blend of anxiety and dread as I wondered if it could be real. I imagined raging flames devouring our walls. Indeed, it was no drill.

The fire was real. With it, my life and the trajectory of our school took an irreversible turn. That day marked the beginning of an extraordinary odyssey—a journey punctuated by survival, resilience, and a steadfast commitment to healing and rebuilding.

"Surely this is a false alarm," I muttered to the secretary as we walked out of the office. Then, I rounded the corner, and in the blink of an eye, everything changed.

Chaos erupted as the deafening alarm echoed throughout our hallways, piercing my ears as smoke billowed through the classroom doors. The smoke was thick like a deep fog, and it was getting darker by the second. The smell was pungent—a cocktail of burning wood and chemicals. The terrible scent seared itself into my memory, as the bitter stench hung at the back of my throat, prickling my eyes, and making every breath a challenge.

© Penley Consulting 2023

As I made my way around the corner, I saw where the fire was most powerful, in the kindergarten and first grade wings. Flames were shooting out of a room into the hallway, blocking any escape in that direction. Panic began to engulf the school. There were screams, yells, and cries that sounded far away and yet were right in front of me. Confusion filled the halls as we tried to orient ourselves to the moment at hand.

Amid this mayhem, our staff stood up tall, gathered their wits, and maintained a sense of calm. They assumed the responsibility of ensuring the care of the students. Guiding them out of the classroom and sometimes through nearly suffocating corridors, teachers led students to safety, hearts pounding with every step.

As the fire raged and began to overtake the school, students and staff spilled out of the building, evacuating rapidly, making their way to their usual line-up spots. I looked around at each line doing a quick mathematical calculation hoping that I would find each classroom line filled. I froze.

OH MY GOD! We were missing children. There were empty spaces in our lines!

Fear gripped me like a vice, but I knew this was not the time to panic as we were facing the unimaginable. We had to go back into the burning building to ensure everyone was safe and out of harm's way.

With several of the staff beside me, I went back inside. We made our way through thick, gray smoke that covered the hallway like a curtain.

We must find the missing students was the only thought coursing through my brain. An intense smell made my chest constrict, and I was overwhelmed with coughing. Dense smoke obscured my vision, but what was that I heard in the distance?

The faint cries of terrified students filled me with terror. I fought an internal battle between my survival instincts—to run to safety—and the duty and moral responsibility to help others. The burden of leadership had never been more salient as I wondered if I was about to die. Oddly enough, I remember thinking, "Who would tell my mom?" **But none of that mattered if the kids didn't make it.**

Adrenaline surged through my veins, sharpening my senses. I quickly snapped out of fear and back into the moment. I could hear another teacher at the other end of the hall calling to the students. She was encouraging them to run to her so she could lead them out safely. We ushered them outside, trying to quell their fears. To this day, her bravery amazes me.

Once no one else was inside, we ran out of the building. I coughed, panting—my lungs felt as if they might burst. My eyes watered. A strange sensation traveled down my face as I realized my nose was bleeding.

There was no time to relax. I turned and had my first look at the school. One side was totally consumed in flames as the fire raged through the building. The devastation threatened to paralyze me. Then, the flames shot higher, and I wondered if the building might blow up.

"We have to get out of here!" someone shouted behind me. It was no longer safe to stay close to the building. **We had to evacuate to our secondary safety location.**

Nearly 500 students and more than 50 educators walked—well, it was more like ran—the short distance to the neighborhood public library. Once we were there, the library welcomed us with open arms.

In retrospect, my mind was bombarded with questions: How did they know we were coming? Did they see the fire? Did someone call them? The truth is, I don't know. What I do know is that their support was amazing, and I have a lasting memory of their goodwill that I will carry with me for the rest of my life. (*Thank you, Holgate Library!*)

Once inside, we still had to make sure everyone was accounted for. We began the process of checking names. The students were told to line up quickly by homeroom. One by one, the teacher checked the roll and called each student's name. I heard things like "Jacob?"

"Here."

"Juan?"

"Here."

"Angelina?"

"Here."

We all held our collective breath, hoping each person would be accounted for. We waited, trying to remember to breathe as tension hung in the air.

Finally, we got word that everyone was safe and accounted for. We cheered. My eyes began to water as I finally exhaled. Relief washed over me, extinguishing the wave of anxiety that had raged within. We all began hugging whomever we could find. Our community had survived.

With all the students accounted for, we focused next on calming the children's fears. They were safe now, and we wanted their little bodies to not hold the trauma of the moment one minute longer than they had to.

After a very short time, we were faced with the **reunification process as we paired children up with their families.** It was a glorious sight to witness the hugs and tears of joy as parents realized their children were safe.

As fewer and fewer students were eventually left, the school and district leaders started to huddle around a stack of books. The question became, *what do we do now?*

Many ideas were thrown out.

"Could we divide up the students to go to other schools?" someone asked.

I immediately said, "No. I don't think that is a good idea. We have to stay as a community." I didn't know the way forward, but I did know it was important to keep us together.

Then came the question, "How quickly could we get the students back in school?"

I felt a jump in the pit of my stomach and looked at the person with a startled expression.

Did I really just hear that?* I wondered. *Are you freaking kidding me? We just survived a burning building; I think we need a minute.

Now, before we jump on the amazing insensitivity of the question, we must remember the times. This was in 2009, before the era of SEL (social and emotional learning) and trauma-informed care.

Hours later, I numbly made the drive home. There would be no sleep that night as my body was still in fight or flight mode. That night, I laid in bed trying to slow my breathing as tears streamed down my face and I considered what had happened. It was a strange juxtaposition, as right along with that sadness, I was filled with gratitude that everyone made it safely out.

For the more than three years that we were removed from our school while it was rebuilt, a lot happened, and many things shifted. I knew we had a window of opportunity that few schools ever experience. We had the ability for a re-do. A do-over. We had to take advantage of our second chance, to create a new and better school, a **Marysville 2.0!**

During the aftermath of our school tragedy, I immersed myself in exploring how to cultivate a nurturing school culture. The task was clear: to heal and foster well-being, acknowledging the emotional scars we all carried.

I recognized the need to transform my leadership approach, moving from enforcing inflexible rules and prioritizing academic outcomes to truly nurturing our community and building strong, enduring relationships.

Personal growth came through the duality of therapy and incorporating mindfulness. I learned to better navigate my emotions and decisions with grace, consideration, and self-compassion. This personal evolution was not just for my sake. It was crucial for my effectiveness as an educator and ability to lead our school through trauma. It underscored the profound truth that self-care is paramount to caring for others. Embracing this, I aimed to be a more authentic and empathetic leader, ensuring my own well-being to better serve both my school, and loved ones.

On a school level, I wondered, "How do we heal?" I didn't know much about SEL at the time, but I knew it was about two necessary things: community and connection. As I began to research SEL, it became clear that it could shift our school into a healthier place, which was exactly what we needed.

Our initial steps toward reinventing our school culture began with the introduction of a student-oriented SEL program, championed by a colleague with positive experiences in his own school. Yet, it quickly surfaced that while the program was impactful, it alone could not catalyze the deep transformation we sought.

We expanded our approach to include mindfulness, for the students and the adults, recognizing its profound influence in education. This dual focus on SEL and mindfulness fostered a novel ethos for our community, equipping us with the necessary tools and mindset to nurture and sustain our reimagined school environment.

As we delved deeper into this comprehensive strategy, embracing both SEL and mindfulness, we embarked on a transformative journey that not only equipped us with tools for growth but also laid the groundwork for resilience in the face of adversity—a journey encapsulated by the concept of resiliency bounce.

Resiliency Bounce

I'm sure many of you have had defining moments in your life, those times when the situation was so intense that it served as a sort of dividing line. When that happens, you begin to know your life in two parts: part one, before the crisis and part two after the crisis. That was me. I was changing, and even though the pain of that fateful day was there, it coexisted with the hope for something better.

You may have heard of something called a **resiliency bounce.** It is the idea that when bad things happen to us, there's one of two ways that we can go. In the first way, the traumatic situation can take our energy, joy, and happiness, robbing us of our well-being for a long time, if not forever.

But there's another way. It is the idea that, over time, we can take the situation that happened to us and use it to bounce us forward and help us become something better than we could've been before, had the situation not occurred. I realized that resiliency bounce was an opportunity to build a positive school culture for us during a traumatic time. The key to our resiliency would be **Unlocking SEL.**

It wasn't as easy as simply deciding it, however. Building a positive school culture was easier said than done, as there was little guidance on how to do that. In the words of Rumi: **"As you start to walk on the way, the way appears."** That is what we did. We stepped out on the way and began the journey of total school transformation. We were all committed to doing things differently from the moment we entered our rebuilt school building. We became committed to building a community focused on wellness through SEL and the lens of mindfulness.

Though we wouldn't see the full results until years later, the outcome was nothing short of remarkable. While some changes manifested rapidly, the most significant transformations emerged from the accumulation of countless small, daily decisions, behaviors, and mindset shifts. Together, these elements compounded over time into a comprehensive transformation.

Over time, we observed the following long-term results:
- Office referrals went down nearly 75%
- Suspension days drastically decreased by nearly 50%
- Huge gains in teacher retention and teacher satisfaction were reported
- We became the highest performing Title I School in both math and reading in our school district.

Marysville Data Post Fire

Decrease
- **75%** Office Referrals went down nearly 75%
- **50%** Suspension days decreased by nearly 50%

Increase
- Marysville School became the highest performing Title 1 School in Portland Public for both Math and Reading.

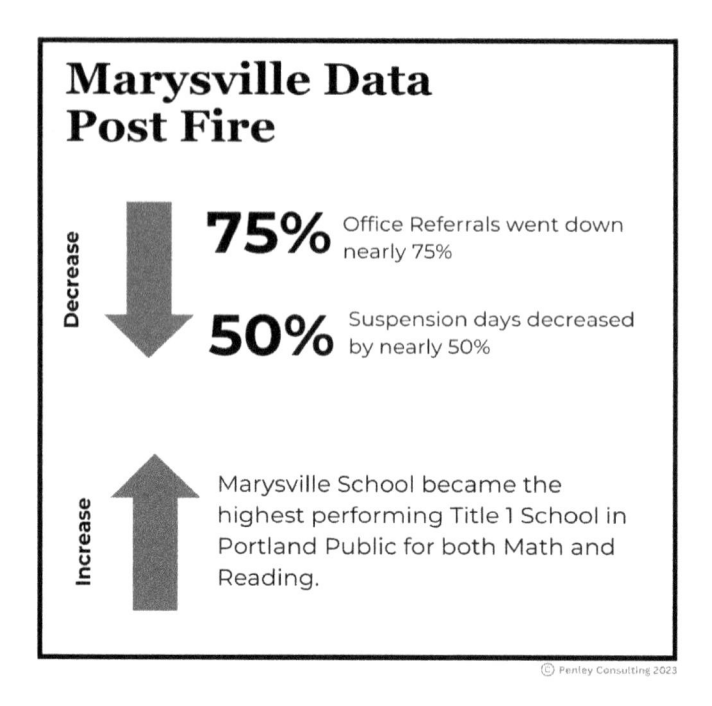

© Penley Consulting 2023

The transformation we witnessed was truly extraordinary: what once stood as a site of profound tragedy evolved into a shining example of hope and pioneering advancements in education. Our journey, marked by an unwavering resilience and the strength of our community, showcased the transformative power of SEL.

The Pandemic is Your Fire

Our school rising from the ashes of a devastating fire became a story about growth and renewal, a testament to the strength of social and emotional learning. Today, this story takes on a broader significance as schools worldwide grapple with the universal upheaval caused by the COVID-19 pandemic. While differing in scale and context, the parallels in disruption and the need for resilience are similar.

Educational systems are navigating uncharted waters with significant drops in academic performance and heightened emotional distress. This signals a pivotal moment of need for revolutionary change in education. As the National Center for Education Statistics (2022) notes, this period is marked by declining test scores, increased anxiety, and widespread discontent. It's clear that the pre-pandemic approaches no longer suffice; instead, a radical shift in our educational practices is required.

The fire we overcame and the global pandemic, though distinct, both demanded swift, adaptive responses to profound challenges—be it embracing remote learning amid technological divides and mental health crises or rebuilding from literal ashes. These crises dismantled old routines. They highlighted the urgent need for community solidarity, mental wellness, and innovative teaching methods.

Post-pandemic, the mental health crisis looms large, with students missing out on critical aspects of their educational and social experiences. The digital divide has also exacerbated inequalities, hitting students from low socio-economic backgrounds the hardest. Teachers and principals are overwhelmed, and many are considering leaving the field all together. In this context, the pandemic has been a universal 'fire,' in its devastating effects. But it's also created a rallying call for educators, students, and communities to exhibit resilience, to **'bounce back better.'**

The Question This Book Answers

In navigating the post-pandemic educational landscape, this question looms large: How can we leverage the challenges of the pandemic to revolutionize our approach to teaching and learning? This book provides a strategic BLUEPRINT for enacting such change.

We'll discuss evidence-based, actionable strategies that address the pervasive stress and disconnection in today's schools. If you recognize the current struggle and sense that social and emotional learning may hold the key but are uncertain about implementation—this is your companion and guide.

Within these pages lies the 'how', I call it a **"How to with Humanity."** This book contains the steps you can take to integrate SEL into the fabric of your educational practice. As you adopt these strategies, you'll see tangible changes unfold. Your classroom or school will transform into a robust community characterized by enduring relationships and comprehensive education. This shift, grounded in intentional action, demonstrates the substantial impact of purposeful change.

How This Book is Organized

The SEL Blueprint consists of five **KEYS**. Think of these keys as the steps to Unlocking SEL. Within each of the Five Keys, there are **CHAPTERS** that break down each key into specific steps to take.

Additionally, there will be **Teacher Tips** and **Principal Points** that help delineate ideas into a more position-specific lens. Each section closes with a **Call to Action.**

I recommend reading the book chronologically. Though the chapters can stand alone, they are meant to build upon each other for a cumulative effect.

Each chapter is structured to move you from the 'why' to the 'how,' ensuring that the principles come off the page and into the pulse of your daily life as an educator. The aim is to equip you with a toolkit that is both thought-provoking and actionable, transforming theory into practice with clarity and ease.

An Invitation to a Journey

Over the past five years, my journey extended beyond the border of Marysville School. Eventually, I left the principalship to take my message of school transformation to a broader audience. I have delved into a deep study of SEL. I've had the pleasure of helping schools, teachers, and leaders integrate SEL solutions into their environment.

My travels and collaborations with numerous schools nationwide have revealed a diverse landscape. While some classrooms excel in implementing SEL, others grapple with its concept, and most schools find themselves somewhere in between, hovering in the intermediate space.

This book is my effort to construct bridges over the gaps I've encountered. Consider this your personal invitation to join the forefront of the educational revolution.

Our shared mission is clear: to seed positive atmospheres in our schools through the nurturing lens of SEL, enriching the lives of students and educators alike. While SEL isn't an instant panacea for all educational challenges, it holds the power to alleviate stress, bolster academic success, and, crucially, weave a fabric of communal care. This book is a clarion call to all principals, teachers, educators, parents, and community members—to embark on this voyage. Together, let's shift the dialogue from diagnosing the ills of education to forging life-changing solutions.

I subscribe to the "Ladder Theory of Change," the belief that we thrive by learning from those just a few steps ahead on the journey. I hope to be that guiding light for you. Picture this book as your ladder, with me a few rungs up, extending a hand to assist you in your ascent toward impactful SEL implementation. As we scale these rungs collectively, our teamwork will empower the transcendent capabilities of SEL. And one day, you may extend your hand to aid the next climber. Our adventure begins at the very base, the solid foundation—where every enduring edifice must start.

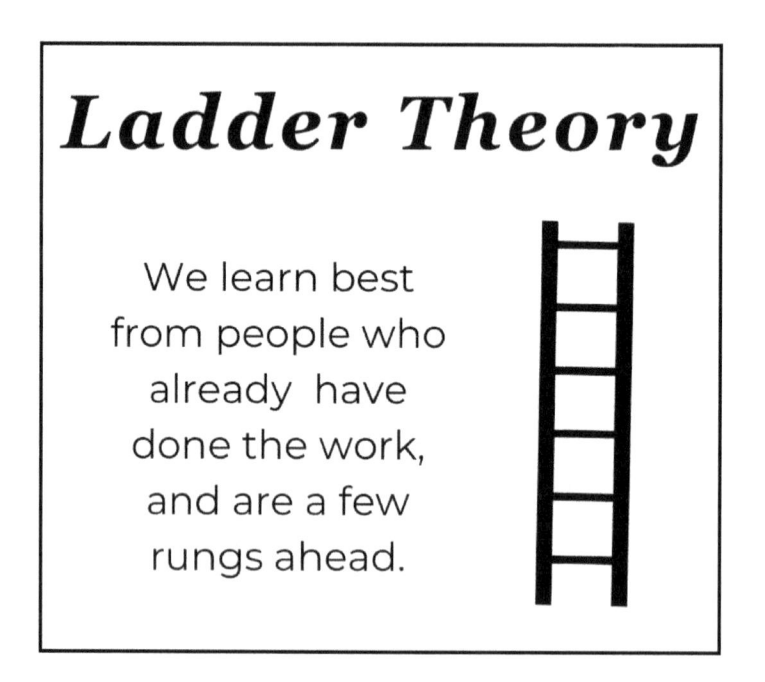

Ladder Theory

We learn best from people who already have done the work, and are a few rungs ahead.

For resources from the book, go to www.unlockingsel.com/blueprint

The First Key:
Build the Foundation

You are here!

01 BUILD THE FOUNDATION
02 CENTER ADULT SEL
03 COME INTO THE CLASSROOM
04 SCALE SCHOOL WIDE
05 DESIGN A CYCLE OF SUCCESS

Can you Fix my Schools?

"Help!" Peter, an assistant superintendent, called me one day, sounding desperate. "I need you!" he said. "Can you help me fix my schools?" He told me that his schools were struggling with dysregulation, high anxiety, and an overall negative vibe. "We are using some sort of SEL curriculum, but I am not sure how it is being implemented and with what fidelity. All I know is we are in a mess."

Trying to empathize with Peter, I began to get curious, asking questions like, "What does your current SEL program look like? What does your suspension and referral data tell you? Do you have an adult SEL component? What is your teacher turnover rate?"

If Peter's story sounds familiar, you are not alone. Many classrooms, schools, and districts have implemented bits and pieces of an SEL program. They may see incremental improvements, **but small is not the goal.** *Unlocking* SEL involves wholesale, full-on, total transformation. To do that, we need to have a deep understanding of the basics of social and emotional learning.

In order to build a strong house that will last for the ages, you must start with the foundation. Any builder or homeowner knows this to be true. The foundation will provide the support as you move toward building a positive school and classroom environment.

Chpt. 1: Putting Fundamentals First

"I fear not the man who has practiced 10,000 kicks once, but for the man who has practiced one kick 10,000 times."
– Bruce Lee

The Lesson of Pickleball

I'm learning how to play pickleball. As a former college athlete, I thought, "How hard can this be?" Boy was I wrong! You see, what I tried to do was just jump into the middle of a game with people who have been playing for a while, and I got spanked. The truth was, I lacked the fundamentals.

I backed up and took a few lessons, talked to experts, and watched videos. I practiced the basics. Here I am a year later with a much better grasp of the sport, and I can lean on my newly gained knowledge to help make me a better player.

Frequently, the root cause of something malfunctioning is simply a lack of basic skills. Without a grasp of the fundamentals, it is challenging to initiate change, articulate the need for it, and analyze problems effectively.

This chapter is about focusing on the basics, building up our foundational skills, and then practicing these skills over and over again. That type of understanding of the fundamentals of SEL is the impetus for what can become an amazing classroom, school, or district. Let's get started.

The Basics of SEL

Social and emotional learning (SEL) is the process through which children and adults understand and manage their emotions, set and achieve positive goals, feel and show empathy for others, establish and maintain positive relationships, and make responsible decisions. It's about equipping people with needed skills for success. SEL empowers individuals to handle themselves, their relationships, and their decisions both effectively and ethically.

In schools, SEL can be used to teach crucial lessons to build lifelong skills. Sometimes, a school may adopt a student-focused SEL curriculum, and mandate that teachers teach the lessons. Oftentimes this comes with very little instruction, preparation, or oversight. Sometimes the teacher receives zero training in the content area. (Raise your hand if you have ever been told to teach something you have had no training on. I'm raising mine right now!)

While I fully acknowledge the importance of student-focused SEL curriculums, as highlighted in the Third Key, it's crucial to understand that SEL encompasses much more. It's not just about teaching students explicit lessons; it's also about supporting the students AND the adults. I view SEL as a dynamic, continuous action–a verb, if you will–that creates conditions conducive to the success of everyone in the educational ecosystem.

Think of SEL as an umbrella term that covers a broad spectrum of educational domains. Under this umbrella are nestled the best practices in education, including restorative approaches, exemplary classroom management, inclusive equity work, and the nurturing of a constructive school culture and climate.

Now that we have determined what SEL is, let's examine some common misconceptions:

Misconceptions of SEL

Misconception #1. SEL is political.
SEL is not political; full stop. This is a time of high tension in our country, and divisiveness can have a significant negative impact on the atmosphere and functioning of schools as people bring varying political beliefs into the educational environment. This can lead to tension, disagreement, and in some cases, conflict.

Additionally, school policies, resources, rules, and regulations can be influenced by local political leanings. This is one of the nuanced challenges of schools and begs the question, "How do we foster a respectful environment, where diverse views are welcomed and constructive dialogue is encouraged, while remaining focused on education and overall development of students?" Doing this effectively requires compassion, perspective taking, and open communication. The irony here is that these are exactly the characteristics that SEL advances. The heart of SEL is kindness. **Surely, we can all get behind the idea that more kindness is needed in schools today.**

> *Surely, we can all get behind the idea that more kindness is needed in schools today.*

Kindness plays a crucial role in fostering a positive, inclusive learning environment. It encourages empathy and understanding among students, helping them appreciate and respect the diverse backgrounds and perspectives of their peers. Kindness enhances students' social and emotional well-being. But it also contributes to a more conducive learning environment. Promoting kindness in schools is not just about creating a pleasant ambience but equipping students with emotional intelligence and social skills necessary for success in our world.

SEL is not a way to teach students any specific political ideology but rather, a way to support well-being for all. *If we believe that SEL is about creating healthy schools, students, and staff through a community in which everyone thrives, then perhaps we can agree that SEL is vital educational component.*

Misconception #2. SEL is for affluent schools.
SEL is an educational necessity, not a luxury reserved for a specific group, race, or socio-economic class. Everyone deserves the right to cultivate healthy social and emotional skills. Regrettably, the implementation of SEL tends to be skewed, favoring schools in wealthier areas as those less affluent regions may lack the required resources. This uneven distribution is a pressing issue that we must strive to rectify.

I learned it the hard way a few years ago when I worked with a Title I school. The school had been neglecting crucial aspects of education like implementing SEL, fostering intentional relationships, and understanding the pervasive impact of anxiety and dysregulation. Staff and administration found themselves continuously battling behavior issues, grappling with disciplinary actions with limited resources, leaving them extremely overwhelmed. Imagine if they were able to redirect some of their efforts upstream: prioritizing relationships, teaching SEL lessons explicitly and establishing an SEL framework. These strategies would dramatically transform the school's climate.

Ironically, at the same time, I was working with another school whose large PTA had raised hundreds of thousands of dollars: They were able to fund, resource, and roll-out an effective SEL program. The primary obstacle preventing many schools from making this shift, like the Title I school I mentioned, is finances. We need to tackle these barriers and ensure all schools have the resources necessary to foster a nurturing environment that promotes social and emotional growth.

SEL must transcend socio-economic barriers to become a standard in all schools, not a privilege for the few. The discrepancy in SEL access across different economic backgrounds is an injustice to our youth and a challenge that demands immediate action. Ensuring every child receives the benefits of SEL is not just an educational imperative, but a commitment to a more equitable future.

Misconception #3. SEL is about controlling others.
Some people tend to misconstrue the true essence of social and emotional learning, viewing it as a method of managing, controlling, or even coercing students. However, this interpretation couldn't be further from my experience. Effective SEL teaches students about their own body and

brain, providing them with the tools to understand and build self-agency. When they understand their emotions, thoughts, and reactions, they are empowered to take ownership of their actions. They learn to respond, not react, to make informed decisions, handle stress effectively, empathize with others, and forge healthy relationships. This renewed self-agency extends beyond the classroom, as students can navigate the world's complexities with confidence and responsibly. **SEL is not about control, but rather, empowerment!**

I still remember the time when SEL empowered an unsuspecting student much to my surprise. Corey was one of those students we have all had, the ones you love so much but also push you to the brink through their behavior choices. From distracting others, to constantly calling out in class, Corey was a handful.

He was also a pitcher on his baseball team. One morning, I saw him in the hallways.

"Ms. Penley," he said with excitement in his voice, "I have to tell you something. You would be so proud of me. Last night, when I was playing baseball, I used my calming breath."

"Oh, tell me more," I said eager to hear the whole story.

"The bases were loaded," he replied. "It was the bottom of the seventh and I was on the mound. I had thrown three straight balls to this batter. I knew that if I threw another ball, I would walk in the winning run." He continued, "So I paused and became aware of how nervous my body was feeling. I stepped off the mound and took three deep breaths and calmed myself down."

I could not believe the words coming out of his mouth. Corey was a student who seemed to struggle to understand the importance of mindfulness or breathwork, but the truth was that **I had underestimated him.**

The story goes on with Corey stating, "I threw a pitch right down the middle. I struck him out!"

A huge smile took over his face. I felt so incredibly proud of him and how he used the strategies he was learning at school. He learned the value of pausing, checking in with the body, using breath to calm himself, and then performing to his potential. IT WAS SELF-AGENCY IN ACTION!

Misconception #4 SEL is a distraction from learning.
SEL is not a distraction from learning; instead, it is an integral part of a comprehensive and holistic education experience. It's not a matter of academics *or* SEL. The two aren't mutually exclusive, and, in fact, we can and should do both.

As educators, we know learning extends far beyond just acquiring and regurgitating facts. True education encompasses the development of the whole individual. That includes social skills, setting goals, listening ability, and focus over an extended period of time. A strong SEL program targets these components. Moreover, research has consistently shown that students who participate in SEL programs tend to perform better academically as the students learn skills to manage stress and focus on their learning. They're better able to maintain healthy relationships with their peers and teachers, creating a more conducive learning environment.

SEL is not an either/or decision. In fact, it makes academic work stronger. Most teachers know this, as a recent survey by Education Research (2022) showed. It found that **83% of teachers say SEL improves academics.** So, why don't we take it from the experts doing the work in the classrooms? SEL works in tandem with an academic curriculum, rounding out a school's focus, and cultivating a positive school environment conducive to rigorous academic work.

But Why Do We Need SEL?

Students are struggling. COVID-19, anxiety, and social distancing left many of our students feeling disconnected. The years-long lack of solid routine, and general feelings of instability caused students to experience levels of anxiety that we educators had not yet seen. Recently, I spoke with Jen, a second grade teacher, and she shared with me how much her students were struggling both academically and socially. She put it this way, "My second graders feel like kindergarteners emotionally and academically." This makes sense given how much of their academic life was disrupted.

In fact, a survey by Pew (2019) found that ***70% of teens say anxiety and depression is a major problem for them (Horowitz & Graf, 2019).*** The concerns about mental health cut across gender, as well as racial and socio-economic lines. And before we write this off as typical teen angst, we must note that these numbers are rising. According to a meta-analysis of 29 studies, the percentage of kids experiencing anxiety has nearly doubled to since before the pandemic (Benton et al., 2021).

At the greatest risk of anxiety are our underserved populations. According to The Trevor Project's *National Survey on LGBTQ Youth Mental Health*, 73% of LGBTQ+ youth reported experiencing current symptoms of anxiety, and 45% said they had seriously considered attempting suicide in the past year (Paley, 2022). The senior research scientist said this of our LGBTQ+ students, "Although our data continues to show high rates of mental health and suicide risk among LGBTQ young people, it is crucial to note that these rates vary widely based on the way LGBTQ youth are treated."

And for students of color, the numbers are staggering. A study from the National Institutes of Health found that approximately **34% of Black students** reported feeling "so depressed in the last year it was difficult to function" (Chen et al., 2019). That is one out of every three students. This anxiety isn't just for the teens—it has slipped down into the little ones. Teacher after teacher talks about students as young as five displaying high anxiety and significant behavior concerns.

Data on SEL

Why am I confident in SEL's transformative power? My belief stems from direct experience in my own life. SEL totally transformed our school—a once underperforming school—which rose to the top performing Title I school in the Portland Public Schools system. The gift of the fire gave us space to pause and reimagine school as a place of healing. Behavior improved as students became more regulated and more focused. We grew stronger at holistically supporting our students. Furthermore, we shifted more of our energies to the front end, building proactive systems that focused on care and compassion rather than the back end of compliance and consequences.

Perhaps most importantly, adults (staff and teachers) stayed in their positions much longer, and most thrived. I was one of them. Though the job was never easy, people enjoyed coming to work and it showed in the way staff cared for themselves, each other, and the kiddos.

Well, you could argue, "Good for you, but that is just one story. What does the research tell us about SEL?" I have some good news for you—the evidence is clear. In multiple empirical studies, SEL has been found to promote positive outcomes for schools.

Two large-scale reviews focus on the findings of SEL programs. There were 213 studies in 2011 (Durlak, et al., 2011) and 82 studies in 2017 (Taylor et al., 2017). The data below illustrates how much better off a student body is over a period of time when an SEL program is offered compared to the lack of such a program (Durlak & Mahoney, 2019). More specifically, these studies showed that with SEL programs:

- **27% more students** improved their academic performance
- **57% more** gained in their skills levels
- **24% more** improved social behaviors and lower levels of distress
- **23% more** improved attitudes
- **22% more** showed fewer conduct problems.

Before the pandemic, SEL had a stronger focus on behavior management, but now, there is a much broader vision which includes self-regulation, compassion, inclusion, and the added component of mental health.

Part of the support in implementing both SEL and mental health is thanks to productive staff meetings where SEL is emphasized. It's no wonder really. It's amazing what a group of educators can do when they come together.

Staff Meetings Reinforce the SEL focus

Since staff meetings are vital platforms for reinforcing SEL, it's important that they're prioritized. Likewise, how administration and faculty approach these meetings play a crucial role in creating a school's climate. They are prime opportunities for educators and staff to align their understanding and approach towards SEL, build on their fundamental knowledge, and ensure consistency in schoolwide implementation.

When we dedicate the time to reinforce our shared focus on SEL, our actions underscore the importance not just for students but also for the educators. This consistent focus fosters a shared vision which is essential for creating an inclusive school and classroom culture.

Furthermore, using staff meetings to emphasize SEL on an ongoing basis benefits educators' professional and personal growth. This is because one of the important components of adult learning is continuing to develop a singular focus in an ongoing manner. In other words, it's not a 'one and done' training.

🎯 PRINCIPAL POINTS

One effective approach I have witnessed in the integration of SEL is through dedicated monthly staff meetings. These regular gatherings provide a structured and recurring opportunity for educators and staff to deeply engage with SEL principles. During these meetings, staff members delve into various SEL topics, discuss strategies for implementation, and share experiences about how these practices are impacting their interactions with students as well as their classrooms. This ongoing commitment ensures that SEL remains a dynamic and evolving part of the school's culture, rather than a static, one-time initiative.

💡 TEACHER TIPS

In your journey as an educator, you'll likely encounter various misconceptions about SEL. Some may view it as an additional task on an already full plate or as a detour from academic instruction. However, it's essential to share your experiences and the tangible benefits you've observed. Emphasize how SEL can streamline classroom management and enhance learning. Detail how it has fostered a sense of belonging and support within your classroom, and how it has led to improved classroom environment.

Chapter Summary

Now that we've discussed the critical nature of foundational skills in Social and Emotional Learning, I hope you can see how pivotal they are. SEL is non-political, essential for all schools irrespective of socioeconomic status, and it's aimed at empowering rather than controlling students. SEL can build a supportive, inclusive school culture that fosters emotional intelligence and addresses the broader vision of mental wellness.

We must commit to equip our schools with SEL resources, since fostering social and emotional competencies is integral to education. What we need is systemic SEL implementation, and we can find that united focus in staff meetings to reinforce its value for the betterment of the entire school community.

Call to Action

- **Learn the basics:** To build a strong foundational knowledge, grow your skills and understanding of the basics of SEL.

- **Dispel the misconceptions:** It's important to allow space to hear other perspectives and speak to misconceptions about SEL.

- **Review the data**: Familiarize yourself with research-based benefits of SEL that you can share with others.

Chpt 2: Setting the SEL Vision

*"A vision is not just a picture of what could be:
it is an appeal to our better selves,
a call to become something more."*
— Rosebeth Moss Kenter

Hiking Misadventures

When I lived in Portland, I remember waking up one day wanting to go on a hike. I quickly googled "Hikes Close to Portland" and found one I wanted to try. All I knew was that the hike was somewhere nearby, was of moderate difficulty, and had a beautiful view from the top of Mount Hood. It was a rare sunny spring day, and flowers had just started to bloom. I was excited and off I went, but I was totally unprepared!

You see, I didn't plan it out. I just started hiking. I brought very little water with me, no compass, and no map. There are enough news stories, movies, and books that cover what happens when setting off in that manner! My journey had disaster written all over it. I wasn't long into the hike when I realized a "moderate" hike in the Pacific Northwest was a code word for "DIFFICULT." Quickly, I became dehydrated, lost, and completely regretted my decision.

While on the hike, I came to a crossroads. I had no idea which way to go, seeing as many paths converged in that spot. There was no visible signage anywhere. For a few hours, I meandered around, looking for any way forward. Eventually, I passed other hikers. Fortunately, they were able to tell me how to get to where I needed to go. When we reached the top, it wasn't even that beautiful of a view. In fact, it was mostly blocked with trees.

Though I did get a good bit of exercise, what I didn't do was have a well-planned hike. The day could have gone much better if I had a vision of where I wanted to go and an effective plan to get there and back. I learned lessons from that experience: First, plan. Set a vision for where you are going. Second, take more water. Third, don't trust moderate hikes in the Pacific Northwest. ☺

Principal Champions the SEL Vision

As you might guess from my hiking experience, vision changes everything! It's the answer to "What do you want the future to be like?"

As the leader of the school, the principal is posed a similar question. They're charged with creating their school's vision that can be used as a tool for strategic planning and decision making. People want their leader to be clear and concise with where they are headed, which is just one more reason a specific vision is necessary. A vision can be helpful to school leaders in a myriad of ways, such as:

- **Uniting a community:** We know what we're going to do and what we're going to focus on. There's a synergy that comes with that. **It's more than just *my* focus or *your* focus. It's *our* focus *together*.**

- **Providing opportunities for innovation:** Innovation can help schools be engaging, relevant, and a future-facing organization—a bit more like the company Apple and a bit less like 'A is for Apple.'

- **Establishing the focus:** This focus sets the direction, allows for the prioritization of efforts, guides decision-making, and reduces confusion and general overwhelm.

Prioritize and Resource SEL

Prioritizing the vision of social and emotional learning with a dedicated allocation of time and resources is crucial. It's essential to understand that educators often experience fatigue from constant introductions of new initiatives. This is known as "initiative overload," and it should be considered. As we approach SEL implementation, we should do it in a way that acknowledges and respects these challenges.

Since the data tells us consistently that SEL contributes to better academic outcomes, improves students' emotional skills, attendance, and the strength of peer relationships, it is essential that we support SEL with time and resources. Supporting SEL with time may look like ensuring that we have time in the schedule designated for SEL which we will discuss more later. In addition, it will look like making decisions that allocate resources to support schoolwide SEL implementation.

Committing to SEL is not just about setting intentions; it's about actionable steps that embed it within the school's culture. This includes dedicated time for SEL curriculum and activities, professional development for educators, and financial investment in materials and training.

By integrating SEL into the school day and budget, a clear message is sent about its value. When SEL becomes woven into the fabric of daily practice, rather than an add-on, it ensures that it becomes a lived experience for students and staff alike. This strategic prioritization enables SEL to flourish, becoming as fundamental to schooling as any core academic subject.

Implement SEL Schoolwide

Building a robust foundation for SEL ideally calls for a schoolwide approach. But why? Does going schoolwide really matter? Let's explore some of the reasons it is best to go schoolwide, if possible:

- **Unified strategy:** A schoolwide approach ensures coherence across the school. For instance, it eliminates the disjointedness in which classroom A follows one method, while classroom B follows another, and yet others may not implement it at all. We must remember that schools function as dynamic ecosystems where each element influences, and is influenced by, others. Recognizing this interconnected nature of schools underscores the effectiveness of a schoolwide implementation of SEL. It fosters a consistent learning environment for all students.

- **Cultural shift:** Implementing SEL across the entire school also fosters a cultural shift, building a common language and set of practices. It contributes to a positive, inclusive school culture. This cultural shift also allows for collective growth, where students and staff can support each other's emotional and social development.

- **Equity driver**: A schoolwide SEL program ensures that all students have equal access to the benefits of SEL. This equity can help close gaps in achievement and well-being that often correlate with race, socioeconomic status, and other demographic factors.

- **Integration:** Since SEL isn't just an add-on, it should be integrated into all areas of the curriculum. This holistic integration helps students make connections between their emotional skills and academic content.

- **Data and accountability:** Schools can track outcomes related to SEL, such as reductions in disciplinary incidents or improvements in academic performance. With this information, schools can pivot and adjust as needed.

- **Sustainability and scale:** Starting with a pilot is a good testing ground, but the goal is to scale up to a schoolwide model as we are talking about driving big changes. It's critical to implement SEL into all spaces so that it doesn't rely on the presence of specific individuals. This way, it lasts long term.

****There is, however, one caveat. As we know, school change is nothing if not complicated. We must acknowledge that starting with the schoolwide approach may not always be feasible. In cases where buy-in is limited or the best implementation strategy is uncertain, it may be sensible to begin with a pilot classroom. This smaller scale initiation allows for the gathering of evidence on the effectiveness of SEL, building a case for its broader implementation. By demonstrating success and benefits in trial classrooms, it becomes easier to gain support and expand SEL practices across the entire school. This ensures a more unified, effective approach to schoolwide transformation through SEL.

🎯 PRINCIPAL POINTS

You know, the old saying of don't put all your eggs in one basket? Well, in this situation, that's exactly what I'm suggesting. Put all your "educational eggs" in this basket. Commit to SEL. SEL is about building positive relationships and a positive school culture, and that supersedes everything else. Let your staff know that all your eggs are in the SEL basket, and commit to it for several years. This commitment will ebb and flow, but the focus on creating a culture of SEL and unlocking its benefits cannot wane. This laser-like focus will pay off down the line.

💡 TEACHER TIPS

What happens if you are ready to move forward with SEL and your principal is not? Do your best to not let that stop you. Hopefully, you can build a case with evidence of awesomeness in your classroom. Start small by incorporating SEL practices into your classroom in manageable ways. Include activities like mindful exercises, student check-ins, and direct SEL instruction into your existing curriculum. Document the impact of these practices on student engagement, behavior and belonging. Seek allies with other teachers who are interested in SEL. **In other words, YOU be the visionary, and hopefully later, your administrator will join you.**

Chapter Summary

Having a clear vision for SEL is pivotal to strategic educational planning. The principal plays a critical role in shaping and championing this vision, which should be supported with dedicated time and resources to avoid initiative fatigue among educators.

A schoolwide implementation of SEL ensures consistency, fosters a supportive culture, and addresses equity, making SEL an integrated part of every student's experience. The emphasis is on prioritizing SEL not just in policy but in practice, which involves a collective commitment from the entire school community to sustain and scale SEL initiatives effectively.

📢 Call to Action

- **Be the champion:** To build consensus around SEL it's important to have people that are champions.

- **Commit resources:** If we believe SEL can make a significant impact on positive school culture then we must commit resources, time, and money.

- **Roll out SEL schoolwide**: SEL needs to be in every classroom. This greatly increases the potential impact to making significant positive change for students and staff.

Chpt. 3: Organizing the Work

"Forget about goals. Focus on systems."
– James Clear

Initiative Overload

In the heart of the outer southeast stood our well-intentioned Marysville K-8 school. With its ambitious administration and dedicated faculty, our school had become a laboratory of education initiatives. Eager to improve student outcomes, we had adopted more than thirteen different programs, ranging from literacy enhancements to sophisticated middle school projects.

However, our office, which should have been full of the sounds of collaborative learning, at times resonated more with a cacophony of confusion. Staff burdened with the weight of multiple initiatives found themselves caught in a tangle of overlapping objectives and methods. We were overwhelmed and struggled to find coherence. The enthusiasm that had fueled the various adoptions began to wane. As fatigue set in, our once promising initiatives ran together often indistinguishable from one another in their rushed implementation.

Does this sound familiar?

If you've been in education for any period of time, my guess is you can relate. It is rare to work with a school or district that is not in some way struggling with this issue of "Initiative Overload."

Often, I see weak, scattered, unclear systems in schools. The purpose of this chapter is not to lay blame at the feet of anyone. That cannot be overstated. My goal is merely to point out a problem that needs to be addressed. Sometimes, we try to do too many things in education. Schools are doing a lot of things and trying hard to be good at each of them. The problem, of course, is that it's impossible to be great at everything. It is better to be great at a few things than mediocre at many. **After all, mediocrity will not transform any classroom or school.**

What I have found is that poor results have less to do with goals and more to do with the systems that are set up to achieve them. As Clear said, "It's not that goals are completely useless. They're good for setting direction, but systems are the best for making progress."

In other words, if we want to have a strong and successful SEL system, we need to organize the work! Let's see what needs to be done to make that happen.

Synthesize to Synergize

In every school, there pulses a constant stream of activity, the lifeblood of the institution's daily operations. To forge a path ahead for a robust SEL framework, it is essential to first understand the school's current modus operandi. The next step is crafting a workflow that achieves the necessary outcomes while also fostering cohesion among all stakeholders. This process, which I like to call "Synthesize to Synergize," is about creating a harmonious, efficient system that aligns with SEL objectives, transforming independent efforts into a symphony of collaborative achievement.

To embody this approach, we must first deconstruct our current practices, examining each thread of our school's tapestry of workflows. This careful dissection allows us to identify redundancies, eliminate unneeded obstacles, and spotlight areas ripe for integration. From this vantage point, we can construct a streamlined workflow, one that is not only efficient but also collaborative. By strategically aligning our processes, resources, and people, we transform individual efforts into a collective rhythm, each part synchronized with the others. This harmony in action creates a dynamic where the whole is greater than the sum of its parts, ultimately amplifying our capacity to foster an SEL environment that resonates with purpose and connectivity.

Think of it like a **workflow audit.** To have a proper workflow audit, you need to do two important things: list out all you do, and then reduce it by half. Here's what it looks like:

List out all you do: Take a moment and gather your staff and/or leadership team together. Then, collectively begin to write down all the objectives your school is doing. Just get it all out. Look under every nook and cranny. You may be surprised by your number of initiatives. When we did this, I certainly was! Our school was doing 13 things! How could you *ever* do 13 things well? You can't! Attempting to excel in 13 different initiatives can stretch a school's resources and attention too thin, leading to diminished effectiveness in all areas. There's a limit to the focus and energy that staff and students can maintain, and overcommitment can lead to burnout and a decline in quality.

Moreover, with so many concurrent projects, the clarity of each initiative's goals and the measurement of their success can become muddled, making it challenging to achieve any lasting impact. Juggling 13 initiatives is like a school trying to tap dance, cook a gourmet meal, and solve a Rubik's Cube all at once. It may be an impressive act to attempt, but it's likely you'll end up with a confused audience, a burnt dinner, and a very mixed-up cube. Best to pick one dance and wow the crowd with that.

Now, reduce by half: Eliminate about half of that flow. By that I mean put guard rails on your work. Remember, you are trying "all eggs, one basket" and your basket will hold only so many eggs. In other words, you're going to have to say no to some things.

I remember one time when our city's professional basketball team was doing a reading giveaway. Students had to read a certain number of books, and in return, they got tickets to a game. We were excited about free tickets, but we soon realized it came with a lot of red tape. And the truth was we just had a very limited amount of energy, so we decided to pass. The problem was that I was a total sports lover. So, saying no to anything that had to do with basketball was like a sugar addict saying no to chocolate. But it had to be done.

It was hard to do, but it was worth the struggle because it felt amazing to see our plan come into place. But listing and cutting weren't enough. Next, it was time to categorize.

Categorize Work Into Buckets

As a school, we wanted to excel in areas that would most significantly impact our community. We took decisive action, trimming our list of initiatives by half to ensure quality over quantity. The initiatives that made the cut were then meticulously categorized into four or five core groups we referred to as "buckets." These were not just random assortments but strategic focal points that encapsulated our mission. Each bucket represented a vital area of our concerted efforts, a pillar of our collective ambition. These refined initiatives became our beacons, guiding our concentrated efforts with unwavering precision. Like a laser focusing its beam to cut through steel, we would channel our energies to carve out excellence in our "few but mighty" educational endeavors.

An example of our schoolwide buckets were: Student SEL, Equity, Behavior Support, and Teaching and Learning. Though our goal was for everything to be intertwined, it was also helpful to categorize and label our work. Everything we did had to fit in one of those buckets. If it didn't, we either paused or stopped it completely. We began to envision our school not as a jack-of-all-trades but as a master of the essentials, where excellence is not just an aspiration but a tangible reality to help us build our synergy toward greatness and away from mediocracy. (We will circle back to these buckets of work in our 5th Key-*The Process Pyramid.*)

Each bucket within our framework is assigned a dedicated leader, ensuring focused and effective management. This ensures that action items within each bucket are not only managed but championed by someone with a vested interest and expertise in that particular domain. The leaders are thus empowered to breathe life into their areas of focus, fostering a sense of ownership and dedication that is contagious throughout the school community.

For example, when the principal spearheads adult SEL initiatives, they model the practices that bolster staff morale and effectiveness. Conversely, the assistant principal champions equity, becoming the standard-bearer for inclusivity, and weaving it into the fabric of our institutional identity. The behavior coach tailors intervention strategies, transforming challenges into opportunities for student growth, while the counselor nurtures the school's heart by ensuring each child's socio-emotional landscape is tended to with care. The academic coach, steering the teaching and learning bucket, becomes the architect of intellectual discovery, ensuring that the pedagogy resonates with both teachers and students.

By embedding these leadership roles into our meeting structures, we synchronize our collective efforts, ensuring that each gathering, whether a staff briefing or a grade-level huddle, orbits around these core areas. It transforms meetings from mundane administrative necessities into dynamic strategy sessions focused on tangible outcomes. This approach allows for cross-pollination of ideas, ensuring that every initiative is enriched by diverse perspectives, and every meeting becomes a stepping stone towards achieving our goals.

Now let's revisit our earlier umbrella graphic. Now we take the bottom layer and make them into buckets. Hopefully, the flow of school transformation through social and emotional learning is becoming clearer.

🎯 PRINCIPAL POINTS

As the guiding force of our school, it's vital to acknowledge that the mantle of leadership does not demand that we personally oversee every detail. The breadth of modern educational leadership has grown; the job has simply become too vast for one person to hold all the reins. Embracing this reality, it's essential to understand that true leadership lies in setting a clear vision, cultivating an environment rich with the necessary time, resources, and inspiration, and then stepping back to empower our capable team. It may feel daunting to delegate, yet it is through this act of trust in the skilled professionals we've chosen that we can truly rise to the heights of great leadership.

💡 TEACHER TIPS

A teacher may aspire to join the school leadership team to have a direct impact on shaping the educational strategies and policies that affect their classroom and community. Being on the leadership team offers a platform to advocate for the needs and ideas of both students and fellow educators, ensuring their voices are heard in decision-making processes. It's also an opportunity for professional growth, gaining insight into the broader administrative functions of the school and to contribute to a positive and productive school culture. Engaging with the leadership team is a way to influence change and innovation in teaching practices and curriculum development, ultimately enriching the learning experience for all.

Chapter Summary

Organizing the work is the critical task of restructuring the bustling hub of a school's initiatives to enhance focus and effectiveness. Anyone who's overwhelmed by the "Initiative Overload" can use James Clear's transformative strategy and the systems-over-goals philosophy. Through a meticulous process dubbed "Synthesize to Synergize," schools begin by auditing its workflow, identifying, and eliminating redundancies, and categorizing remaining tasks into core groups known as "buckets." This refined focus is matched with dedicated leadership for each bucket, embedding a sense of ownership and tailored expertise. The reorganization transcends simple streamlining, fostering a collaborative, goal-oriented culture that prioritizes efficiency, clarity, and the achievement of a cohesive SEL environment.

Call to Action

- **Conduct an audit:** Look at the workflow of your school to gain a good handle on exactly where the energy is going. Reduce this list.

- **Organize activities:** organize the school focus areas that are left over after the audit into defined SEL categories or buckets.

- **Designate:** Decide who is responsible for each bucket.

Chpt. 4: Building the SEL Team

"Alone we can do so little. Together we can do so much."
– Helen Keller

From Solitude to Strength: The Power of Co-Leading

In the quiet hum of my new office, the sense of isolation was palpable. As the new principal, my office walls seemed to echo back the silence. The staff was friendly, smiles were exchanged, and polite conversations peppered the hallways, but the camaraderie that comes from time spent together, shared experiences, and forged bonds was absent for me. I was a long way from my previous job in North Carolina to this new one in Oregon. I had left my family, friends, and a place I loved to move across the country and start this new role.

The weight of the principalship rested on my shoulders like an old, heavy coat, woven with the threads of responsibility, expectations, and a relentless pressure to raise test scores. Each decision no matter how small carried mighty repercussions. Assuming the role of a new principal felt akin to being seated at the center table of a bustling restaurant, where every eye, seated far way in their own private booth, occasionally glances in your direction, appraising, judging your every move.

That evening, long after the bell rang and most people had left the building, the hallways stood empty, as if they were holding their breath, waiting for guidance and action. I sat alone as the sun streamed in through my office window while I contemplated the enormity of what lay ahead. The vibrant energy of the day, with its laughter and learning, began to fade away as the silence pressed in. It was a stark reminder that at the end of the day I was alone in this leadership, and I did not like the feeling. It wasn't good for me, nor my school. I knew I had two choices: I could either learn to carry the heaviness alone or find a way to share the load with those willing to walk with me.

I made a decision: I would create a leadership team that would co-lead with me. It was one of the best decisions I ever made as a principal. That decision changed the trajectory of my life and our school.

I learned that school transformation cannot be shouldered by the leader alone. It's not good for the leader or the school. Transforming a school is like assembling an intricate puzzle; the task is overwhelming for just one person. Every piece, representing the insights and efforts of the entire school community, is essential to complete the picture of change. This puzzle is just too big, too many pieces for one person to manage.✱

> ***Transforming a school is like assembling an intricate puzzle; the task is overwhelming for just one person. Every piece, representing the insights and efforts of the entire school community, is essential to complete the picture of change.***

Ensure a Diverse SEL Leadership Team

This load of leadership is best managed by the SEL leadership team. This should not just be a group of individuals who are in positions of authority but a diverse and representative mix of the school's population, including members from different backgrounds, areas of expertise, and skill sets, reflecting the diversity of the staff and students. This diversity is key to ensuring that a wide range of perspectives is considered in decision-making, which fosters a more holistic and inclusive approach to school transformation.

A diverse leadership team brings several advantages. Let's unpack a few of them:

- **Different perspectives**: Different perspectives can lead to more innovative solutions, a broader understanding of the needs of the school community, and more effective strategies for engaging and motivating staff and students. This variety of viewpoints is not only crucial for internal dynamics, i.e the interactions, relationships and processes that occur within an organization. It also ensures better representation of different demographics, improving a school's ability to understand and meet the needs of their stakeholders.

- **Stronger support**: A leadership team with varied levels of expertise and skills can provide support in areas where a single leader may lack experience or knowledge, making the process of school transformation more efficient and effective.

- **Feels inclusive**: Having a group of highly skilled and trusted people drives change in a way that is more inclusive, widening the circle of power.

Let's say you're a diverse K-8 school trying to decide on what student SEL curriculum to use. Having an SEL team brings with it a multitude of perspectives, ensuring that the chosen curriculum is inclusive and addresses the various needs and cultural backgrounds of all students. They can evaluate each option through a comprehensive lens, considering the developmental appropriateness for different age groups and the nuances of social and emotional learning dynamics in a mixed environment.

Furthermore, a team approach allows for the incorporation of insights from different stakeholders—teachers who understand their students' day-to-day challenges, counselors who recognize the emotional landscape, and parents who can offer a broader viewpoint. This collaborative method not only democratizes the decision-making process but also promotes buy-in from the entire school community. When done well, it paves the way for a more effective and seamlessly integrated SEL curriculum.

In essence, the creation of a diverse leadership team is not just a strategic move, but a necessity for meaningful and lasting school transformation. It alleviates the pressure on the principal, fosters a collaborative and inclusive culture, and ensures that the school's journey towards change is guided by a rich tapestry of insights and experiences, truly reflecting the community it serves.

What do you call this team? One idea would be to call them the **Superstar Superspecial Support Team Superheroes.** Ok, well that might be a bit much. How about just **The Support Team**. They are just that: a group of people who support the school, support the teachers, and support the staff. Look for people who have a passion for SEL, are highly skilled, and are willing to model mindful strategies. If there aren't additional supports outside of the classroom, school leaders may need to meet with folks after the school day or see if the budget allows for paying substitutes to cover the classes to allow for the team to meet.

Your Support Team is here.

© Penley Consulting 2023

Set up Team Logistics

There are several key logistical areas that are important to unpack:

1. **Meeting times**: SEL teams should meet consistently, weekly if possible, to ensure the smoothest workflow. This regular gathering serves as a crucial platform for team members to discuss ongoing projects, share updates, and collaborate effectively. By coming together on a consistent basis, the SEL team fosters communication and coordination, while promoting a culture of accountability. Ultimately, it leads to more efficient, successful outcomes in their work.

2. **Consistent location**: Choose a professional and consistent location. Too often we ask teachers to meet in student desks in the spaces that in no world would business executives be asked to meet in. I realize that many schools struggle with adult spaces, but we must do better in education and find places that encourage professionalism and inspire great work.

3. **Communication plan**: Ensure that there is a two-way communication plan. Having information flow both ways will ensure that there is clarity and understanding among all members. With open channels of communication, information is not only disseminated, but can be clarified reducing the likelihood of misunderstandings. When staff feel there is a method for them to express views and contribute to discussions, they'll feel more valued and involved, leading to a greater sense of ownership and commitment to the initiative. This is crucial for finding feedback and continuous improvement. It will create a feedback loop whereby staff can offer suggestions allowing the school to adapt and refine system policies based on input.

For our school, this looked like a meeting of our Support Team every Monday for 1.5 hours. To allow for focused, uninterrupted time, we had various people manage the building. For example, we were able to provide a blank space in a special teacher's schedule so she could cover.

We started with a breathing exercise to ground ourselves in the present moment, not worrying about the past or projecting to the future, just being in that moment. Next, we moved to some sort of connection activity like a gratitude circle, and then it was on to planning, strategizing, and calibrating.

THIS WEEKLY SUPPORT TEAM MEETING IS THE SECRET SAUCE TO A WELL-RUN SCHOOL. Though it was a sacrifice to make this meeting happen each week, the laser-like focus on systems planning led to a much more organized and thus calmer schooling experience for all.

Perhaps you're wondering how that would look when it's laid out. Below is an example of one of our meeting schedules. As you review it, consider what you would tweak for your school.

Support Team Meeting Agenda Example

Time	Item	Notes
8:45-8:55	Opening Grounding Exercise	Do a 5-minute breathwork exercise to ground us in the present moment.
8:55-9:00	Connection Activity	Use a prompt to build connections. Try something like, "Share something you are grateful for in your life."
9:00-9:15	Digging Deeper	Research article, poem, etc.
9:15-9:30	School Calendar	Long- and Short-Term Planning: What's coming up in the next two weeks?
9:30-10:00	Meat of the Meeting	Review and calibrate action plans for upcoming events.
10:00-10:05	Task Assignment	Ensure there is a task list with clear delineation.
10:00-10:15	Positive Close	Close the meeting with one positive take-away.

For a PDF of the Support Team meeting, go to
www.unlockingsel.com/blueprint

🎯 PRINCIPAL POINTS

I realize there are schools that do not offer much leadership support. I've worked at some of them. There may be no one outside of the classroom except the school principal. This thin model of leadership is not the most effective model. It's not fair to the school or the school leader. That said, if that is your situation, see if you can figure out a creative way to pull a few teachers to meet and be a part of an SEL leadership team. A few compensation options may be to pay teachers to meet after school or provide them a 1/2 day sub once a quarter.

And, just as a reminder, if we are going to ask people to show up as highly skilled professionals, then there needs to be a professional space for them to meet. It is best to have a room that is set aside for the adults to do adult work. This could include a round table that everybody can gather around, adult seating and plenty of supplies. The space should have good technology, be clean and organized. And a little chocolate won't hurt. :)

💡 TEACHER TIPS

What happens if your school does not have an SEL team? Don't let that stop you. ***You were born for brilliance.*** *Begin to integrate more and more SEL into your classroom to showcase its transformative power. Continue to advocate for SEL by raising awareness with your colleagues and administration by sharing your work, research, and evidence on the benefits of SEL. And finally, seek out professional development opportunities. This will show you are not alone! There are many SEL champions out there. Find your peeps.*

Chapter Summary

There is a need for collective leadership in school transformation. The moment I chose to share the lift with a diverse and dedicated SEL leadership team changed everything. That single move would become one of the best decisions I made for personal growth and my school's progress. Your team, a microcosm of your school's rich diversity, can bring an array of perspectives to the table, which is vital for meeting the multifaceted needs of a school. The emphasis is on inclusivity and collaboration, with the goal of fostering an SEL environment that echoes the school's commitment to a comprehensive education.

📢 Call to Action

- **Form an SEL leadership team:** Ensure the team is diverse and meets weekly.

- **Implement a communication plan:** Determine how the team communicates with the staff and the staff to the team.

Chpt. 5: Incorporating Mindfulness

"You can't stop the waves, but you can learn to surf."
– Jon Kabat-Zinn

Mrs. Parker's Morning Magic

The morning clamor of the schoolyard tapered off as the ring of the bell sent waves of students scurrying into their classroom. Their little feet pattered on the tiled floors, a bustle of early morning excitement and the day's potential bubbling in their conversations. Mrs. Parker, their Kindergarten teacher, stood by the doorway, her smile a steady beacon amidst the flurry. She had always found the first few minutes of the school day to be a rodeo of wrangling energies. Some students bounced like pinballs, while others seemed lost in a morning fog. How to start school each morning was a daily puzzle.

However, all of this changed once she implemented mindfulness. Potential solutions began to take shape in her mind. Ms. Parker learned the nuances of the developing brain, how the prefrontal cortex and the amygdala affected learning. She also saw the power in teaching her young students to tune into their bodies and notice how they are feeling. With newfound understanding, she introduced the 'mindful minute' at the start of each day.

During this short but impactful quiet interlude for children, she invited them to close their eyes, sit quietly, and tune into the rhythm of their breathing. This simple practice became a cornerstone of their daily routine, transforming chaos into calm and beginning each learning chapter with a collective breath of readiness.

"This has been a lifesaver. It's like magic," Mrs. Parker would often say, watching her students settle into a harmonious quiet group of 5-year-olds. Ready for the day.

When I ask you to picture a mindful person, what image comes to mind? Perhaps you envision a yogi, infused with the earthy scent of patchouli, serenely seated in a lotus position on a cushion. That was certainly my initial perception. I used to believe that mindfulness, while intriguing, was beyond my reach—especially for someone like me, a girl hailing from the humble mountainous backdrop of Appalachia. However, I couldn't have been more mistaken. Embracing mindfulness has been a transformative journey in my life, and it holds the potential to revolutionize yours as well!

> *Mindfulness has changed my life, and it can change yours, too!*

I regard my ten-year journey with mindfulness as one of the most important experiences of my life. Through my studies, talking with others, taking classes, attending seminars, and reading books, I have learned many life lessons from mindfulness, yet I still feel like I have so much more to learn.

Consider this scenario: Sleep had always been an elusive treasure for me, especially exacerbated by the aftermath of the fire incident. Before discovering mindfulness, my days blurred into nights, carrying the weight of school matters home with me. Leading the school felt like an unsolvable puzzle, perpetually dangling just out of reach.

Home became more like an extended school day, as my mind incessantly wandered back to school affairs. Conversely, when at school, I yearned for the comfort of home. My existence felt fractured, with my mind and body often not in the same place. Multitasking became a misguided pursuit, a false badge of honor.

Yet, through mindfulness, I unearthed a profound truth: the essence of life lies in embracing the present moment. I gradually learned to compartmentalize work and cherish moments of rest. Through meditation and delving into neuroscience, I honed techniques to soothe my frayed nerves, employing regulated breathwork to calm my racing thoughts. Mindfulness nurtured a heightened self-awareness, allowing me to observe my thoughts without being ensnared by them, fostering a deeper understanding of myself and others through compassionate acknowledgment of feelings. Consequently, mindfulness has **improved my sleep quality** and helped **enhance my interpersonal relationships**. Most importantly, it helped me **develop a greater sense of gratitude** for the wonderful life I have around me.

The *gift* of the fire set me on the path of mindfulness as a way to heal. And look at some of the gifts I have received: stress reduction, self-awareness, enhanced personal relationships, and a stronger sense of gratitude.

Witnessing the transformative power of mindfulness extends beyond my personal journey; it has also enriched the lives of others. Recently, I had the privilege of leading the Unlocking SEL's Mindful Leaders Network (MLN) for former school principals and superintendents from the State Department of Hawaii. Initially apprehensive about how the message of present-moment awareness would resonate, we delved into the essence of mindfulness, exploring its research-backed benefits, particularly in stress reduction. Together, we navigated practical strategies to integrate mindfulness into both personal and professional spheres.

As the course concluded, I eagerly awaited the feedback, and to my delight, 100% of the participants reported a positive impact from the mindfulness training. Their testimonials revealed how mindfulness had empowered them to navigate challenging situations with grace, from calming their nerves before pivotal meetings to embracing the power of pause in moments of tension. It was a humbling experience, reaffirming the profound impact mindfulness can have on collective well-being. In facilitating their journey, I found myself learning anew, inspired by their resilience and openness to growth.

Mindfulness can be defined as being in the present moment with kindness. It means being aware: being aware of what you are feeling, being aware of what's happening inside of you, and aware of what's happening around you. Present-moment awareness can serve as an antidote to the busyness that often takes over schools and serves to help us move from our head to a more heart-centered place. Over time, these small moments add up.

So, just imagine the impact mindfulness can have on an entire staff. It's a transformative approach that holds immense promise for the well-being and success of educators and students alike.

As we navigate the complexities of modern education, it becomes increasingly evident that fostering a supportive learning environment goes beyond textbooks and lesson plans. It requires nurturing the holistic development of teachers, who serve as the cornerstone of the educational experience.

By equipping educators with mindfulness practices, we empower them to cultivate resilience, manage stress, and foster emotional intelligence not only within themselves but also among their students.

Mindfulness for Staff

Let's unpack four reasons why teaching mindfulness to educators is not just beneficial but essential for creating thriving learning communities:

- **Enhanced well-being**-Teaching mindfulness to teachers can significantly improve their overall well-being. By equipping them with the right techniques, they can better manage stress, avoid burnout, and cultivate resilience in the face of daily challenges. This is crucial, because when teachers prioritize their own well-being, they are better equipped to create a supportive and nurturing classroom environment for their students.

- **Enhanced SEL skills**-Teaching mindfulness to teachers can also enhance their ability to incorporate SEL into their classrooms. By practicing it themselves, teachers can model self-awareness, self-regulation, and empathy for their students. This not only fosters a more positive classroom culture but also equips students with valuable life skills that promote their overall well-being and academic success.

- **Improved classroom management**-Mindfulness training for teachers can lead to more effective classroom management. When teachers are grounded in the present moment and able to regulate their own emotions, they can respond to student behaviors calmly and with greater empathy. This creates a more positive learning atmosphere where students feel understood and supported, ultimately enhancing student engagement and achievement.

- **Building stronger relationships**-Mindfulness empowers teachers to form deeper connections with their students and colleagues. By cultivating present-moment awareness, educators can better understand the perspectives and experiences of those around them. They can come across as a bit softer, kinder, and clearer. This deeper understanding fosters trust, respect, and communication, laying the foundation for meaningful relationships within the school community.

At Marysville, the benefits of teaching mindfulness to our staff manifested in various ways. Picture a classroom where a teacher, equipped with mindfulness techniques, navigates daily challenges with grace and composure. When a student acts out, instead of reacting impulsively, the teacher responds with empathy and understanding, de-escalating the situation, and fostering a positive learning atmosphere. Meanwhile, in the staffroom, or in the hallways and happy hours, colleagues mingle in open dialogue, forging connections and championing each other's well-being. It was a beautiful sight to behold at our school.

As the school leader, I could tell mindfulness was working. Things shifted. It was as if the soft breeze of kindness had blown in, and I never wanted it to go away. Our newfound mindful interactions cultivated a culture of trust and collaboration, where we all felt connected, like we belonged to something special, because we did. We were creating a new, healthier ecosystem not one based on the crisis of the fire but on the promise of a better tomorrow.

What Does the Research Say About Mindfulness in Schools?

I could tell from our new and improved interactions and daily innerworkings that mindfulness was working. To no one's surprise, the research agrees!

For students: Research indicates that incorporating mindfulness in schools offers significant benefits, including:
- Enhanced attention and focus
- Improved emotional regulation
- Greater engagement in learning activities

For educators: Mindfulness also extends remarkable advantages, such as:
- Sharpened attention and emotional regulation
- Heightened compassion
- Reduced levels of stress and anxiety (Source: Mindful Schools, 2023)

These findings align deeply with my experience as an educator and a mindfulness practitioner. I've had the pleasure of witnessing students evolve into more emotionally balanced, engaged, and empathetic individuals. As for us adults, the practice of mindfulness gently steered us towards becoming kinder, calmer, and clearer in our thoughts and actions. This transformation has not only enhanced the learning environment but also fostered a more nurturing and supportive community within our school. Witnessing these changes has been profoundly rewarding, affirming the immense power of mindfulness in shaping positive behaviors and attitudes, both in students and educators.

Use Mindfulness as the Vehicle to Implement SEL

In my experience, mindfulness played a pivotal role in the implementation and success of SEL within our school setting. To understand this relationship, it may be helpful to think of mindfulness as the vehicle that drives us towards our ultimate destination: a healthy school environment. Just as a vehicle is essential for a journey, mindfulness is crucial for navigating the path towards realizing a positive school culture.

As an engine that powers the journey, mindfulness equips students, teachers, and staff with the ability to be present in the moment, aware of their thoughts and feelings, and responsive in a thoughtful, intentional manner. By fostering a mindful attitude, individuals in schools are better prepared to recognize and regulate their emotions, understand, and empathize with others, and engage in positive social interactions.

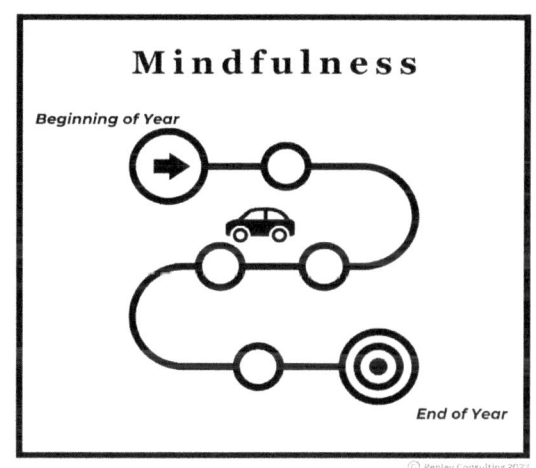

Like a steering wheel, mindfulness guides the school communities through the ups and downs of the school year. It empowers them to navigate complex social dynamics as well as manage stress and anxiety. And finally, like the headlights, mindfulness can shine the path ahead bringing clarity and focus, enabling educators and students to see beyond immediate obstacles and stay aligned with the long-term vision of SEL.

◎ PRINCIPAL POINTS

Many times, we can be more mindful in the way we run our staff meetings. Pre-mindfulness, the school day ended at 3:00 and staff meetings began at 3:15. We would all rush around trying to close our day and perhaps grab a cup of coffee before running into the room to start the staff meeting. Everybody came to the meeting in a frantic space and often with a negative attitude. After mindfulness, we slowed down a moment. We put much more intention into the meetings. We decided to start at 3:30 to allow staff time to transition after the kids left (and to use the bathroom after holding it all day).

Then, we would start our meetings with a moment of breathwork to give everyone an opportunity to slow down, to reconnect our mind and our bodies. Next, we would follow with a non-school related prompt. We'd made suggestions like, "Talk with your partner about your favorite book or movie." It was just a time for us to connect outside of talking about school.

Think of the difference in those two scenarios. Which meeting would you want to attend?

💡 TEACHER TIPS

What if your school isn't implementing mindfulness? Don't let that stop you. If I waited on my school district to make changes, I would still be waiting. Take the steering wheel. One of the strategies I used early in my mindfulness journey was taking a class called, "Mindful-Based Stress Reduction." This class is offered in most cities around the country, and you can find information online. It helped me learn the basics of mindfulness as well as applicable ways to build resilience and learn stress management strategies.

Chapter Summary

Incorporating mindfulness has transformative potential in educational settings. It has a profound impact on an educator's well-being, classroom management, and relationships. By integrating mindfulness techniques into daily routines, educators can cultivate resilience, manage stress, and foster emotional intelligence among themselves and their students, creating a supportive environment conducive to learning and growth. Mindfulness is a catalyst for positive change, steering schools toward a more compassionate and inclusive future.

Call to Action

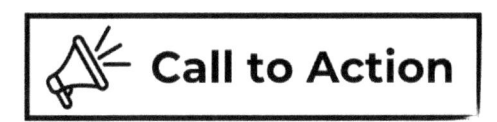

- **Learn the basics of mindfulness:** Look for ways to grow in your foundational knowledge of this practice.

- **Think of mindfulness as a vehicle:** Mindfulness is the vehicle to help your classroom or school implement SEL.

First Key Reflection Questions
Building the Foundation

Question	Answer
What is your definition of SEL?	
How are resources currently allocated in your school or classroom?	
What is the current vision of your school or classroom? How does the vision impact what you do?	
What are your school's existing initiatives? Does it feel like the right amount? Why or why not?	
Do you have a current leadership team? If so, who are the members and how were they chosen?	
Do you have an experience with mindfulness? If so, how do you use it to support your classroom or school?	

For resources from the book, go to
www.unlockingsel.com/blueprint

The 2nd Key: Center Adult SEL

01 BUILDING THE FOUNDATION
02 CENTERING ADULT SEL — You are here!
03 COMING INTO THE CLASSROOM
04 SCALE SCHOOL WIDE
05 DESIGN A CYCLE OF SUCCESS

The Superintendent Showdown

A few years ago, I met with a school superintendent. Let's call him Mr. Brown. Due to his role of overseeing all of the schools, I was slightly intimidated by the prospect of our meeting. I stood up straight, shoulders back and walked in the district office with passion and enthusiasm with my well-prepared proposal in hand.

As I entered the office, I hoped to find a receptive ear, but reality quickly slapped me in the face.

Mr. Brown seemed distracted, and his body language revealed irritation that I was taking up his precious time. He motioned towards a plastic chair and told me to have a seat. At last, he asked, "How can I help you?"

I explained that educators were struggling and shared data on teacher dissatisfaction and high stress levels. Then, I showed how adult SEL could help and why I was the one to deliver it to his school system. I spoke about how we could focus on stress reduction, increase morale, and ultimately, improve student outcomes. When I finished, I thought, "Yes—that felt good. I knocked it out of the park," and breathed a sigh of relief. However much to my surprise, Mr. Brown remained unmoved.

He paused, looked me squarely in the eye, tilted his head, and said, "We cannot spend time or resources on teacher well-being. Our community would never stand for that!" With that, he got up and said, "Thank you for coming." It was clear that was my cue to go.

My Theory of Change

Fortunately, not everyone agrees with Mr. Brown. I have consistently championed the significance of adult SEL, and it's heartening to see the national dialogue beginning to align with this perspective. Increasingly, school districts are recognizing that adults, too, are facing challenges that must be addressed. When SEL interventions are exclusively student-focused, we observe only modest improvements in student outcomes, as these shifts tend to be constrained and minimal.

However, integrating SEL for adults can lead to profound and far-reaching changes, because it not only enhances the effectiveness of educators but also creates a more supportive learning environment for students.

Let's examine the following diagram that illustrates this Theory of Change, highlighting the impact of incorporating adult SEL.

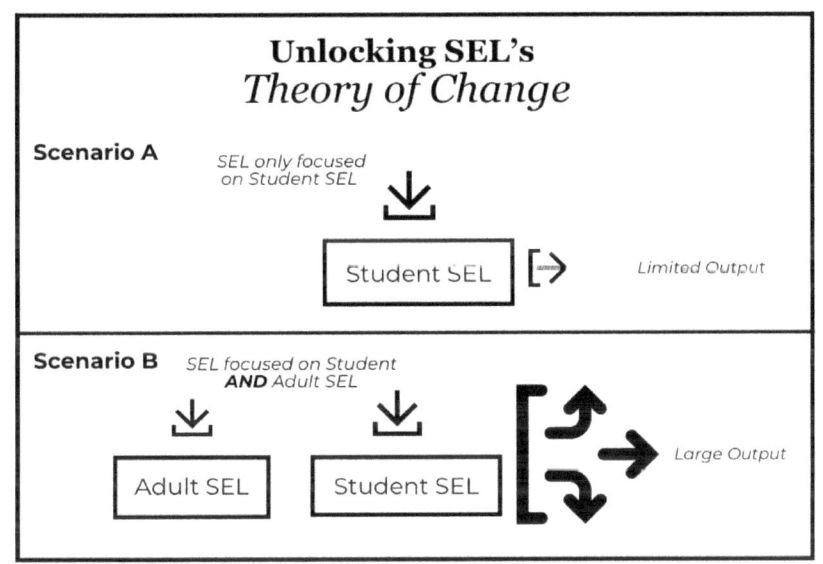

Unlocking SEL's
Theory of Change

Scenario A: SEL only focused on Student SEL → Student SEL → Limited Output

Scenario B: SEL focused on Student AND Adult SEL → Adult SEL + Student SEL → Large Output

© Penley Consulting 2023

Scenario A: SEL Only Focused on Student SEL

- Description: In this scenario, SEL initiatives are targeted exclusively at students.

- Output: The impact on students is limited. This is represented by a single arrow pointing to "Student SEL" with a note of "Limited Output," small increases in social skills, regulation, and academic focus.

- Implication: By only focusing on student SEL, the potential benefits are constrained, resulting in a less significant overall impact.

Scenario B: SEL Focused on Both Student and Adult SEL

- Description: In this scenario, SEL initiatives are extended to include both students and adults (teachers, staff, etc.).

- Output: The impact is significantly greater. This is illustrated by arrows pointing towards both "Adult SEL" and "Student SEL" with a note of "Large Output."

- Implication: By incorporating SEL for both adults and students, the benefits are multiplied, leading to a more substantial and holistic impact on the entire school environment.

Key Takeaway

The diagram underscores the importance of integrating SEL for both students and adults. While focusing solely on students provides some benefits, including adults in the SEL initiatives creates a more robust and effective environment for social and emotional growth, leading to improved outcomes for the entire school community.

In my experience, most schools "implement SEL" by adding only a student SEL curriculum. This, at best, brings small changes, and at worst, adds just another initiative onto the plate of overworked educators. To curate big changes, we have to go big and include the people who have the largest impact on the school and classroom environment—the adults in the building. So how do we do this? How do we broaden the lens of SEL to include the adults? Throughout these chapters, I will introduce different strategies for adult SEL.

One thing to note, as an educator, you're familiar with the term, 'pedagogy,' and have likely been asked to define yours in more staff meetings than you care to count! But have you heard of the term, 'andragogy?' Malcom Knowles, the leading thinker in andragogy, suggested that formal learning required five acknowledgements, including:

- We must let learners know why learning something is particularly important.

- We must show learners how to work through the necessary information.

- We must relate the information back to the learners' experiences.

- People won't learn unless they're ready and motivated to do so.

- Education requires helping learners overcome certain inhibitions, behaviors, and beliefs about the meaning of learning itself.

Adults have lived their entire lives before coming into your school, and they've established their own belief systems and thought processes years ago! To overcome this, you need to show why change is important and how it can help.

Chpt. 6: Creating a Community of Care

"I have never felt as lonely as I had when I was a member of a large school staff. No one knew me beyond what I taught."
– High School Teacher, Texas

Ms. Thompson's Morning Moments

In the bustling halls of Oakwood Elementary, Ms. Thompson was a beacon of warmth and compassion. As a beloved third-grade teacher, she embodied the spirit of the tight knit school community where everyone genuinely cared for one another. Each morning, as she arrived, Ms. Thompson greeted her grade level teaching partners with a smile, showing she was happy to be there. After unloading her bag, she'd make her way up to the office to check mail. On the way there, she'd always see several teachers and greet each one.

When she finally arrived at the office, she would be greeted by the school secretary. "Good morning Ms. Thompson. How are you doing today?"

"I'm doing great," Ms. Thompson would say. "Today's going to be a great day. I'm excited about this lesson that I'm teaching on the metamorphosis of butterflies."

"Oh, I can't wait to hear all about it," the secretary would respond. "I'm sure they're going to be so excited."

Ms. Thompson grabbed her mail and poked her head in the principal's office to say hello. Though the principal, Ms. Smith was always busy, she always stopped and took the time to ask Ms. Thompson a question.

"How did the game go last night?" She'd ask, knowing that Ms. Thompson's son played for the middle school basketball team.

"It went well!" Ms. Thompson said. "We lost, but it was a close one."

"Oh shoot," the principal said. "Well maybe next time." As Ms. Thompson made her way back to class, she felt excited about the day ahead

The contrast between the opening quote of this chapter and Ms. Thompson's warm and engaging entrance into the school day is striking. How can schools cultivate such an environment that prioritizes community and care? Let's explore this concept in detail.

Cultivating Community Care

Humans are inherently social beings, designed to thrive within the framework of a community. Back in the Stone Age, our ancestors formed tribes, which highlighted a deep-seated desire to be part of something larger and more meaningful. Being part of a community bestows a profound sense of belonging, offering a support network that fosters feelings of being understood and supported. This connection allows us to engage with others who share similar interests and values, significantly enhancing our overall well-being and happiness.

Consider the analogy of Wi-Fi connectivity. When disconnected, we often experience frustration and irritation, prompting us to troubleshoot our routers and devices in an attempt to re-establish connection. This longing for connectivity mirrors our innate need to connect with others. Just as a lack of internet connection can hinder our ability to work and communicate, being disconnected from a community leads to a sense of isolation and discontent.

Thus, being part of a community is not just a matter of preference but rather a fundamental aspect of human existence. It's crucial for both our mental and emotional health. In a profession marked by high levels of stress and burnout, a strong sense of community among teachers acts as a buffer, providing emotional support, shared resources, and collective wisdom.

> *...a strong sense of community among teachers acts as a buffer, providing emotional support, shared resources, and collective wisdom.*

Unlocking SEL's
4 Ways to Create a Community of Care

- **Foster meaningful relationships:** Provide opportunities for genuine connections to form. From allowing time at the start of staff meetings to discuss non-educational things to having lunch together, prioritizing relationship building can create a sense of belonging and support that extends beyond the classroom.

- **Prioritize wellness:** Implement initiatives that prioritize the physical, emotional, and mental well-being of staff. Offer wellness programs, mindfulness practices, and mental health resources to support the holistic needs of the school community. By fostering a culture that values self-care and prioritizes well-being, you can create a foundation for resilience, growth, and mutual support within the community.

- **Celebrate diversity and inclusion**: Embrace and celebrate the diversity of backgrounds, experiences, and perspectives within the school community. Foster an inclusive environment where all individuals feel valued, respected, and heard. Promote cultural competency through curriculum integration, diverse representation in school materials, and inclusive practices in decision-making processes. By honoring each person's unique identity and fostering a sense of belonging for all, you can create a community where everyone feels welcome.

- **Embrace our humanity:** It's crucial to acknowledge that educators are more than just professionals; they're real people with real joys, struggles, and lives outside of school. By fostering a culture of support, grace, and compassion, your team can uplift one another through life's challenges and celebrate triumphs together. Don't forget to inject some fun into staff interactions, whether it's through team outings like bowling or pickleball or simply sharing laughter during happy hours. Those moments of camaraderie and shared joy can strengthen bonds and nourish your team's collective spirit.

**4 Ways to Create a
Community of Care**

- Foster Meaningful Relationships
- Prioritize Wellness
- Embrace our Humanity
- Celebrate Diversity and Inclusion

© Penley Consulting 2023

Cultivating Care for Ourselves and Others

Self-care is a term often overused in today's world. It can be thought of as something small, such as spa treatments, massages, or other types of personal treats. Not that there's anything wrong with those things—I love a good massage! However, at times, self-care can be rooted in a consumerist ideology: We're taught that to care for ourselves, we need to purchase something to do so. That's just not the case!

When I use the term self-care, I'm thinking holistically with a focus on wellness. I am referring to all-encompassing strategies such as adequate sleep, work/life balance, relationships, stress management, and joy, all things we need. Such actions involve pursuing a balanced and fulfilled life—making conscious decisions to maintain and improve our lives and recognizing our full potential.

Have you heard of Maslow's Hierarchy of Needs? It is often depicted as a pyramid: On the bottom layer are physiological needs, like food, water, shelter, and clothing. On the next level are safety needs or needs of personal security; then are our love and belonging needs, like the desire to feel cared for and supported by others. On top of these are our esteem needs, or our needs to feel respected and needed. And lastly, we have the need for self-actualization, which includes recognizing who we are and what we need to become our best selves.

Self-care satisfies many of these essential and foundational needs—weighted blankets and candles help us feel safe and warm, and exercise satisfies our health and physiological needs. But they only satisfy foundational needs and don't begin to touch self-actualization.

And it is not just about self-care. It is also about care for others and helping them get their social needs met. Remember, schools are ecosystems with each interaction and person influencing each other. When there are collaborative environments where educators work together as a community and for a common goal, there will be a positive work culture. Caring for colleagues involves valuing them as human beings, building intentional relationships, supporting them in tough times, and encouraging each other's goals and aspirations—in other words, fostering self-actualization.

I remember a few years ago when one of our teachers received a dreaded call that her husband had a medical emergency. I walked down to her room to let her know the news in person. The amazing thing was what happened when the rest of the staff heard the news. They went into "How can I help mode?," from watching her class, to walking out with her, and even taking her home.

This ties back to Maslow's needs. Our team helped her feel safe and protected in a difficult moment. I was profoundly proud of our school. They were the embodiment of empathy in action. When educators feel valued and supported by their colleagues, it creates a healthy oxygen for them to inhale and then exhale into the community around them.

> ***When educators feel valued and supported by their colleagues, this creates a healthy oxygen for them to inhale and then exhale into the community around them.***

Cultivating Systemic Care

We have discussed self-care and care for others. Now let's broaden our lens to discuss school settings: the ecosystem our teams function in. This is what I call the systemic collective care—i.e., care for the school and its educators—by district leaders.

Educational systems bear a significant moral responsibility that extends beyond just meeting basic academic metrics and achieving the bottom-line. This responsibility encompasses prioritizing the well-being of all individuals within the system, including adults. By prioritizing well-being, educational systems demonstrate a commitment to nurturing not only the intellectual but also the personal development of their communities, thereby fulfilling a deeper, more comprehensive moral obligation.

The aim is for the employees to both feel a real sense of being supported by the school and hopefully, by the district. Educators should be encouraged to prioritize their own well-being and self-care practices. They also need to be provided with training and strategies for stress reduction.

Healthy districts recognize that caring for oneself is essential for being able to care for others. When educators feel valued and that the larger system cares for them, they can exhale a bit. Trust is developed as people feel safe to share their struggles and vulnerabilities.

On the other hand, when systemic care is absent from the educational landscape, the responsibility for change and well-being is placed solely on the individual educators. This isolated approach can inadvertently transform self-care into a perilous concept, where teachers and administrators are left to fend for themselves in a sea of stress and burnout.

Self-care, while vital, is not a cure-all for the systemic issues contributing to educator fatigue. When that's all that's offered, it's merely a band-aid on a deep wound. If not done with intention, self-care can imply that the individual is solely at fault for not managing their well-being effectively, disregarding the structural factors that significantly contribute to their stress.

Without an institutionally supported care system, self-care runs the risk of being an overwhelming task that adds to a teacher's burdens rather than relieving them. It's imperative that schools and societies construct a robust framework of support. We must acknowledge the complexities of educational roles and create an environment where self-care is complemented by systemic policies and practices that foster a culture of holistic well-being.

This visual below illustrates the "Circle of Care Model," which emphasizes a tiered approach to creating a caring educational environment.

- **Self-Care**: At the core of the model is self-care. Educators must prioritize their own well-being to be effective in their roles. This includes practices that support mental, emotional, and physical health.

- **Care for Others**: Surrounding self-care is the layer of care for others. This involves educators extending their well-being practices to students, staff, and families. By fostering a supportive and caring atmosphere, relationships within the school community are strengthened.

- **Systemic Collective Care**: The outermost layer represents systemic collective care. This is the overarching support provided by the school and district systems to ensure that the entire community benefits from a culture of care. It includes policies, resources, and practices that promote collective well-being.

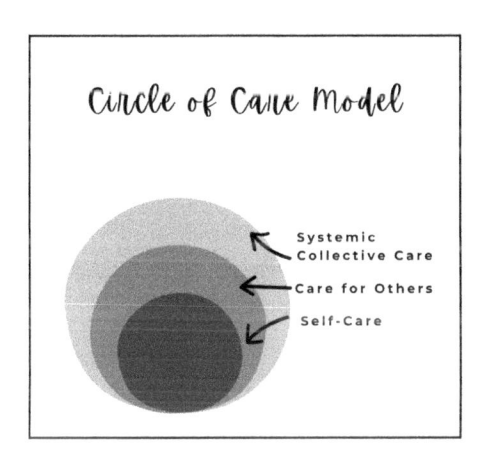

Circle of Care Model

By following this model, schools and districts can create a more nurturing and supportive educational environment, leading to a positive shift in the overall culture of education. **Could you imagine the shift of education if schools and districts followed this model?**

Chapter Summary

It's clear why schools need to be more than just places of learning; they must be spaces where teachers feel connected and supported. Establishing a supportive communal network within schools is crucial to counteract the prevalent loneliness, stress, and isolation that educators often experience.

We can do this by fostering meaningful relationships, prioritizing wellness, embracing diversity, and acknowledging educators' humanity. This elevates the discussion from personal self-care rituals to a systemic embrace of collective care. When done successfully, schools and districts can cultivate a supportive environment that recognizes the interdependence of individual and community well-being.

📣 Call to Action

- **Prioritize building community**: Put energy into creating a support network for you and your colleagues.

- **Practice self-care**: Focus on your own personal wellness, pursuing a life of balance and fulfilled life.

- **Be part of the change**: Discuss with leaders ways in which the system can better practice collective care.

Chpt. 7: Being Aware of the Adult Impact

"I feel as if the weight of the world is on my shoulders."
— *Middle School Principal, Oregon*

Evaluation Overload

Once upon a time in an urban school district, a wave of anticipation swept through the administrative offices as they introduced a new teacher evaluation system. The administrators, full of hope, envisioned a system that would bring clarity and progress to the classrooms. They imagined teachers feeling empowered by clear guidelines and constructive feedback. Furthermore, they viewed themselves as architects of a more efficient and impactful evaluation process. The shiny new document, with nearly 30 pages of meticulous criteria, was handed out with a sense of ceremony, as if it was the key to a secret garden of educational excellence.

But as the leaves turned and the school year plunged into its busiest months, reality set in. Teachers, already juggling the delicate balance of teaching, grading, and life, found themselves lost and overwhelmed by the new procedures. Administrators, their calendars bloated with back-to-back evaluations, saw their days stretch thin. The promise of a value-added system was eclipsed by the reality of its complexity. Meetings that were once filled with the lively exchange of innovative teaching ideas became gripe sessions focused on the cumbersome evaluation tool. The well-intended initiative, designed to streamline and improve, had instead woven a tangled web, ensnaring the very individuals it was meant to help.

❖

I wish the above story was unusual. But it is not. New initiatives, procedures, and processes that are meant to better education, often turn up the level of stress in a building.

What would have happened if someone who was able to make the decision on teacher evaluation, paused, took a deep dive into the document, and determined that it was much too massive? What if they realized the lengthy document might impact both the administration and the teachers negatively? If they had thought about the adult impact, perhaps they would have realized that the process needed simplification for it to be effective and manageable.

We all know, it can be exhausting to be an educator, working well beyond the standard working hours. Preparing lessons, grading assignments and planning activities all consume a significant amount of time and effort. Add on feeling emotionally invested in students' success, doing everything we can to help them succeed, and it's exhausting. This emotional commitment combined with the high workload can be emotionally draining. Furthermore, there is pressure to ensure students perform well on standardized tests. The tension can influence a teacher's performance evaluation and weighs heavily on their shoulders. And while the teachers are battling all this stress, they are doing it with limited resources and support.

This is why we must disrupt the educational cultural norm. We must push back against the misconception that the state of the educator is irrelevant. We must CENTER THE ADULTS ALSO! I'm not saying students aren't the priority, just that we must broaden our view to include the adults who prioritize them.

The thought of centering the adults in school may be controversial—I get it. It seems some people are worried that if we stop to consider the adult impact, adults will somehow take advantage of this, and it will be used to somehow lessen their performance.

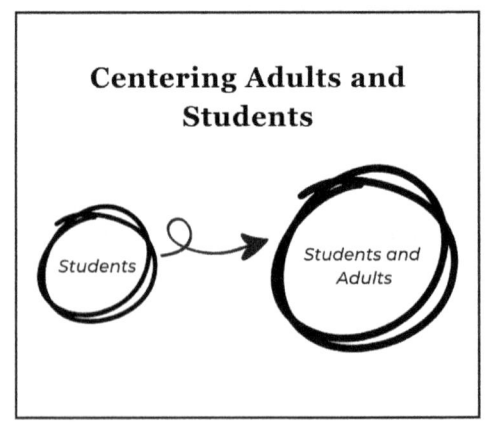

Centering Adults and Students

Students → Students and Adults

This was not my experience. In fact, the opposite was true. When we slowed down, thought about the adults, and were careful about what fell into the lap of teachers, they really appreciated it. It had a positive impact both on our teachers' lives and their performance.

Examine the Impact of Systems and Processes

Take a moment to think of all the current systems and processes in your school. Now, consider how each one of these might be impacting the adults in the building.

When looking at systems, whether the ones already in place or new ones that may be added it can be helpful to ask the following four questions:

4 Key Questions for Gauging the Adult Impact

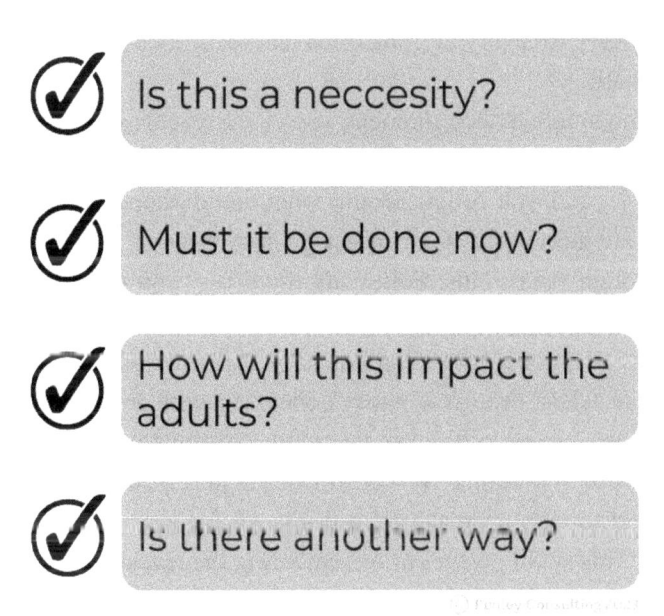

- ✓ Is this a neccesity?
- ✓ Must it be done now?
- ✓ How will this impact the adults?
- ✓ Is there another way?

Reflecting on these questions allows for a deeper understanding of the daily experiences of educators and staff. It's crucial to evaluate whether these systems and processes are facilitating their work or adding unnecessary burdens. By aligning these systems more closely with the needs and realities of the staff, leaders can foster a more supportive, efficient, and positive working environment. Let me share a quick story of what this can look like in real time.

A few years back, we had a new student who struggled significantly with emotional regulation. At times, this would look like the student having a tantrum, grabbing things off the walls, throwing things, screaming, running etc. As this student was new to us, I felt that, over time, we would be able to support the student in becoming more regulated and developing a stronger sense of emotional agency. But, in the meantime, we were dealing with the dreaded room clears.

Those of you in education know what is meant by, "Room Clears." It is when a student has a severe meltdown, is not following directions, and is causing chaos in the classroom. To ensure safety for all students, we may have to call a room clear, which means moving other students out of the room and sending in support for the teacher dealing with the tantrum. This situation is scary for everyone, and often leaves a very stressed-out teacher in its aftermath.

Could you imagine, for a moment, you're the teacher in that classroom? You have a child that has spiraled out of control, whose behavior is unpredictable, and you're left unsure what could happen to you or your students. Your nervous system might go into fight or flight, adrenaline rushing through your veins. Following the crisis, you may need time to regulate yourself again, calm down, and catch your breath.

With that awareness of teacher impact in mind, we added a component to our Room Clear Protocol: always check in with the adult when the situation becomes stable. We ask the adult questions like, "How are you doing? Is there something we can do to support you in this moment? Do you need to take a break, get a drink, go for a walk, or just talk to someone?" This small gesture of remembering the teacher's humanity can have a large impact on his or her overall feeling of support and serve as a buffer to handle difficult situations.

Allocate Resources for Adult Well-being

Pausing and considering the adult impact of systems and processes is important, but it's not enough. We can't stop there. Decisions need to be made to resource both time and money for adults. Too often I have seen schools or districts talk about the importance of adult well-being, but, when you dig deeper, there is no resourcing.

Allocating resources for adult well-being in schools can be likened to ensuring a pilot is in optimal health before flying a plane. In other words, when a pilot is well rested, healthy, and supported, they're better equipped to handle the complexities of flying and responding to unforeseen challenges during the flight. We all believe that the health of the pilot is critical. Nobody wants an overly stressed-out person with our lives in their hands.

However, when it comes to educators, we don't treat their well-being with the same importance. Just as the pilot's well-being is crucial for the safety and successful journey of the passengers, educator well-being is fundamental for the effective learning and development of students. This needs to change. In both cases, the well-being of the individual in charge, the pilot or the educator, has significant implications for those in their care. This makes it not just a personal priority, but a collective one.

By investing in resources such as wellness programs, mental health support, and professional development opportunities focused on self-care and stress management, schools demonstrate a commitment to the holistic health and happiness of their staff. Supporting teacher wellness not only improves job satisfaction and retention but also enhances the quality of instruction and fosters a positive school culture where educators feel valued, respected, and empowered to perform at their best.

One thing to remember: it doesn't always have to be money that's spent. Remember the story of the teacher after the room clear? That didn't cost anything in dollars and cents, just an investment of time and a little compassion.

🎯 PRINCIPAL POINTS

Principals, you should have a line item in your budget for teacher wellness. Yes, there are restrictions on how monies can be spent, so consider donations or use of the PTA. Ask for staff input on ways to spend the monies. Some examples I have seen are: updating the staff lounge, treats, gatherings, class coverages, and stress management PD. Don't underestimate the impact these things can have on morale. Feeling cared for is a key motivator for job satisfaction.

💡 TEACHER TIPS

If you are a teacher of a student who needs Room Clears as a support intervention, talk with your school administration. Explain what the experience is like for you and the effect of Room Clears on your well-being. Ask for what you need—a break, a walk, or a talk—whatever it is to help process the stress of the situation. YOUR well-being matters!

Chapter Summary

It's imperative we consider the impact of systems and processes on educators within the school community. Well-intentioned initiatives can backfire when the adult impact is overlooked, which is why systems and processes must be viewed through the lens of their impact on teacher workload, emotional well-being, and overall job satisfaction. Leaders can prioritize the well-being of educators and staff by allocating resources and support systems.

From implementing protocols for managing crisis situations with empathy to advocating for wellness programs and mental health support, a holistic approach to teacher wellness is required. Ultimately, we need a paradigm shift in education where the well-being of educators is recognized as essential for fostering a positive school culture and enhancing student learning outcomes.

📣 Call to Action

- **Slow down:** When implementing anything new, pause, and consider how it will affect the adults in the building.

- **Allocate resources:** Ensure resources are allocated to support adult well-being.

Chpt. 8: Demystify Stress

"Classroom teaching is perhaps the most complex, most challenging, and most demanding, subtle, nuanced, and frightening activity that our species has ever invented."
– Lee Shulman

Pressure Points: A Principal's Wake-Up Call

In a bustling, large urban city, where the school was the heart of the community, Principal P. was the captain. She navigated the ship through calm and stormy seas alike. However, the relentless stress of meeting academic targets, managing staff, and tending to the endless administrative demands had insidiously taken its toll. Each decision weighed heavily on her shoulders. Every student and parent concern echoed in her mind at night, stealing precious sleep and peace. As the pressure mounted, so did her blood pressure, an invisible but fierce adversary that coursed through her veins, threatening to undermine the very career she had worked so hard to achieve.

It was during a particularly strenuous budget season, as voices around her blurred, that she felt the vice-like grip of hypertension seize. A headache pounded as her heartbeat thundered in her ears. Her chest felt tight, and her stomach churned. This did not feel like a normal illness. This was different. Over time, the feeling passed. But it came back again and again throughout the week.

The next week, Principal P. went to the doctor. The culprit–high blood pressure. When the doctor found out what Principal P. did for a living, she asked, "What strategies are you using to manage your high stress?"

Principal P. laughed as she tried to lighten the moment, "Let's say my favorite stress management strategies are Netflix, red wine, and a delicious donut."

"Not funny," the reflection of the doctor's face told her. Then, the doctor said sternly, "This is serious and you're either going to have to get a grip on your stress or your stress is going to get a grip on you."

Though a frequent topic of conversation, stress often remains an enigmatic presence in our schools. To effectively employ mindfulness and mitigate stress, we must first unpack it—understanding its effects and subtleties. Only then can we truly harness the power of mindfulness and mitigate some of the stress that pervades the halls and classrooms of our institutions.

As you may have guessed, I was Principal P. I was that person who did not know about stress or have any healthy stress management strategies. That conversation with my doctor was the impetus for change I needed. I was determined to learn all I could about stress, what causes it, and what we can do about it. Furthermore, I was dead set on bringing that information to my staff. Because I wasn't the only one who was battling this high stress and the negative health effects that come along with it.

Education is an **incredibly high-stress profession**. Given this reality, isn't it our moral duty to educate about the management and impact of stress? Absolutely, it is!

Let's Look at Some Data

Let's start with the leaders. Principals have never had a more difficult job than they do in today's education climate. Exhausted leaders are trying their best to steady the ship, meet learners where they are, support student and staff mental health concerns, deal with higher student dysregulation and anxiety, and close the learning gap created by more than a year of virtual schooling.

A recent survey by Rand stated that 83% of principals experience frequent stress; the principal populations with the most stress were principals of color, women, and ones in high poverty schools (Superville, 2022).

For teachers, the data isn't much better. The job of teaching was very challenging before the pandemic, but now the stress is off the charts. In studies, 60% of teachers expressed high stress (Will, 2021). And now, as a result, teachers are considering leaving the field in record numbers. According to Ed Week (2023), more than a third of teachers are considering leaving the profession in the next two years. That's a huge piece of the teaching force! What would this mean for our schools if a third of teachers walked out the door tomorrow?

It's not surprising that teaching often comes in as one of the most stressful occupations in the United States. And stress affects teachers' job satisfaction, turnover rate, health, well-being and student outcomes (Greenberg, et al, 2016). This is precisely why adult SEL is critical.

The stark reality that educators grapple with stress cannot be understated, as its ripples are felt across every facet of classroom life. It shapes the environment, colors the educational experiences of students, and even influences the passion that once ignited teacher commitment to this noble profession.

Given this undeniable truth, it's imperative to confront a critical, yet often overlooked question: As a community deeply invested in education, why are we not mobilizing to safeguard the well-being of our educators? **The vitality of our educational system hinges on the health of those at its helm,** and it's time to prioritize and actively support educator wellness with the same vigor we apply to student success.

Likewise, it's necessary to turn a reflective eye upon our educational institutions and ask ourselves why necessary programs are not already embedded into the foundations of our schools. The absence of robust support is more than an oversight; it is a disservice to the very individuals who cultivate the minds of future generations. We must ignite a transformation that not only recognizes the significance of educator wellness but enshrines it as a pillar of educational excellence. If we are to truly enrich the fabric of learning, then the nurturing of teacher well-being cannot be an afterthought; it must be a cornerstone.

> *If we are to truly enrich the fabric of learning, then the nurturing of teacher well-being cannot be an afterthought; it must be a cornerstone.*

In working with educators across the country, I've seen this firsthand. Regardless of whether I am working with schools in California or West Virginia, the message is similar: educators are exhausted. What was a hard job before COVID has become nearly untenable now. We can't afford to continue the profession of schooling in the way we have for decades ignoring the well-being of the adults. The status quo must be disrupted.

Imagine being a factory worker constantly surrounded by dangerously loud noises. In such a scenario, two crucial steps are typically taken for your well-being.

- You're informed about the risks associated with these loud noises.
- You're trained and mandated to use headphones as a protective measure.

This example illustrates a proactive approach: recognizing the hazard and equipping workers with both knowledge and tools to safeguard their health. Contrastingly, in the realm of education, this kind of support is often lacking. Many educators I've encountered are not only unaware of the long-term effects of chronic stress but also lack the necessary resources and strategies to effectively manage it.

So, what does it look like to use mindfulness as a stress reduction strategy? Let's look at three different ways.

Train Educators About the Impact of Stress

Let's look at chronic stress more specifically. Now I'm not talking about just normal, temporary stress, as a little bit of stress can be good for us. (Let's say you've got a big speech coming up that you are nervous about. Stress helps us prepare and meet those moments effectively.)

What I am referring to is chronic stress that becomes that constant low ache in your gut. The prolonged exposure to stress hormones through chronic stress has a detrimental effect on the body and can be associated with sleep disturbances, high blood pressure, weakened immune system, cardiovascular disease, and many other problems. It's no wonder so many teachers walk around like machines with depleted batteries.

The dangers of chronic stress are clear, yet in my more than twenty years in education, I can't remember attending any kind of district sponsored professional development where chronic stress was discussed. I only became aware of this after going to the doctor and discovering that I had high blood pressure.

It is critical that we teach educators about stress because awareness precludes prevention. We cannot change what we don't know. With knowledge, we can take back our power and make preventative decisions. Understanding what causes stress can help us in tending to that stress, change what we can, and minimize the triggers that we cannot change. This leads to better overall health and well-being. Furthermore, learning about stress is the impetus for learning stress management techniques. But first, let's start with a workload conversation.

> *It is critical that we teach educators about stress because awareness precludes prevention. We cannot change what we don't know.*

Normalize Work/Life Balance

Raise your hand if you work most nights. Have your work email on your personal phone? Spend at least one weekend day grading papers? This is the norm for many educators.

Due to an overwhelming workload, teachers and school leaders can feel a pressure to work at night and on the weekends. Research has shown that long working hours and weekend work can cause the deterioration of mental health (Sato et al., 2020).

Without a proper work/life balance, teachers can experience chronic stress with a significant decline in both physical and mental health. Prioritizing work/life balance is crucial both for leaders who want to foster a healthy workplace, and for employees who want to live a healthy life. And who doesn't want that?

One tangible way you can help is leading by example. Principals should model the value they place on their own well-being, prioritize their own personal time, and encourage their employees to do the same. One principal recently told me he never emails his staff at night or on the weekends.

"They need a break," he said, "They don't want to hear from me, and they need to get away from this job, so it doesn't swallow them whole." What great modeling this was for his staff.

One strategy to normalize the conversation around work/life balance is to have a staff meeting where that is the focus. Below is a sample agenda you could use.

Sample Staff Meeting Agenda on Work/Life Balance

The principal or counselor should bring the staff together and explain the meeting's purpose: "Today's meeting is about a very important topic, preventing burnout. One of the key ways to do this is maintaining a work/life balance. So today we will wrestle with this together and dedicate an hour to this important topic."

1. Open with personal story about the importance of work/life balance (5 min)
2. Do a connection activity–How do you feel about your work/life balance? (5 min)
3. Discuss what a work/life balance is and why it matters. (10 min)
4. Discuss signs, and give examples that your work/life balance may need a reset (10 min)
5. Provide time to do a reflection on strategies to increase work/life balance (10 min)
6. Have the teachers get in small groups and invite them to discuss (10 min)
7. Share examples and discuss common agreements on work/life balance (10 min)

In addition, it may also be helpful to create some work/life agreements as a school. Some examples of this could be:

- Administrators do not email staff after 6:00 at night.
- Administrators don't expect staff to check their emails after that time either.
- Taking breaks and time off is encouraged.
- Unplugging from technology is normalized.
- Emails are not expected to be returned immediately (within 24 hours).
- Have honest and open staff conversations around work/life balance.
- Encourage staff to send each other positive emails.
- Bigger, more complicated issues are discussed in person.

Do you have school or district resources such as your counselor, leadership team, or other staff members who have experience/competence in this area? Don't be afraid to look outside for more resources on adult stress management. Our company has a program built just for this. You can email us for more information at lana@unlockingsel.com.

Use Mindfulness as a Tool to Mitigate Stress

A few years ago, I decided to take a downhill mountain biking lesson. My instructor and I were at the top of the mountain looking down at the steep decline, and I thought, "What have I gotten myself into?"

"Do you downhill bike much?" my trainer asked.

"I've ridden a mountain bike plenty of times," I answered, "but I've never ridden a bike down a mountain. I mean the very name of this sport is downhill. This looks much more like a mountain, not a hill."

She laughed. "Don't worry," she said. "I'll keep you safe." Then, my instructor began to coach me. We did a practice run down a flatter part of the mountain. I gritted my teeth, tightened my body, and held on for dear life.

The instructor paused for a bit and then said, "There's something I'm noticing. You're holding the bike too tight, and your legs are too stiff. This doesn't leave you with any ability to be able to manage the bumps as they occur."

"Lean forward a bit," she continued. "But then soften your body, your arms, and your legs. Let the bike move underneath you. This will make it easier to handle the bumps of the path."

Who knew my mountain bike trainer was a Guru! That lesson was a great example of mindfulness in action.

As a new principal, I used to hold everything so tight and rigid, and I felt every bump on my way up the mountain. Over time and through mindfulness, I learned to be flexible, with a little more bend in my knees. I even learned to hold the "bike" a little looser. This led to a much better experience for me and for my school.

> To go over rough terrain, bend in your knees and hold the "bike" a little looser.

If we aren't careful, educators can develop hypervigilance. This comes from navigating a job that requires us to always be at the ready. It is almost like we spend our day bracing for impact–crunching up our shoulders and standing firm.

Though this may make us feel we are ready for anything, it also comes at a cost. The shadow side of that hypervigilance is that it can leave us reverberating at a high level, feeling the intensity of stress responses even if a situation itself does not call for it. I mean, who hasn't lost their cool when a student forgets to bring a pencil to class? But we aren't meant to live in this state of fight or flight for an extended period of time.

On the contrary, mindfulness can offer a bit of an oasis of tranquility in the bustling day. By anchoring ourselves in the present moment through mindfulness, we can gently untangle the web of stress that often accompanies the demands of our profession.

Engaging in deep breathing, guided visualization, or simply being still and aware amidst the classroom's rhythm, teachers can cultivate a sense of calm and clarity. This practice can lower stress levels, soothe the nervous system, and refresh the mind—ultimately fostering a more serene and attentive presence, which radiates through to students and creates a more harmonious learning environment for all.

When we begin to build our mindfulness practice, we can learn how to counteract the physiological effects of stress by focusing on the present moment and learning to activate our parasympathetic nervous system, aka, our relaxation response. Activating this response serves to soothe us and leads to a decrease in heart rate. It creates decreased activity in the amygdala and down-regulates our nervous system. We can learn over time to be a bit softer and a bit less rigid. We'll also feel a ton better!

What Does the Data Say About Mindfulness?

Mindfulness originated thousands of years ago in Eastern traditions. It has long been associated with well-being and reduced stress. A comprehensive meta-analysis of more than 200 studies found that mindfulness "is especially effective for reducing anxiety, depression, and stress" (Khoury et al., 2013).

As I mentioned in the First Key Teaching Tip, I enrolled in a course titled Mindful Based Stress Reduction (MBSR). This research-backed mindfulness intervention program, developed by Dr. Jon Kabat-Zinn, spans eight weeks, consisting of weekly classes interspersed with mindfulness exercises as homework. Studies, such as one conducted by Ito, have demonstrated the effectiveness of MBSR in enhancing self-compassion and promoting better mental health. Personally, I found this program instrumental in my journey towards improved self-regulation, alleviating anxiety, and mitigating stress through the adoption of mindful techniques.

One example that stands out for me was my reduction of sleep disturbances. One of my goals in the class was to increase and improve my sleep— at that time, I was rarely, if ever, sleeping through the night. In retrospect, what was probably going on was that my system was so dysregulated and stuck in fight-or-flight since the fire that I simply could not rest.

Through MBSR, I learned about how we hold stress in our bodies. We learned about body scans, a type of meditation where you bring awareness to every part of your body, slowly scanning from head to toe. You are look ing for tension, tightness, and feelings of discomfort. Then, through breathing, you can release some of that tension. Over time, I was able to calm my body and sleep through the night for the first time since 2009.

So, what role does mindfulness play in stress reduction for educators? It acts as a powerful tool for stress management by altering the way one perceives and responds to stressors, leading to a more balanced and less stress-dominated life. Here are three specific ways mindfulness helps us stress less:

- **Present moment**: Mindfulness trains people to focus on the present moment, shifting away from past worries or future anxieties. It reduces the tendency to perseverate or do the same stressful thing a million times and allows us to be in the present.

- **Emotional regulation**: Mindfulness helps us better regulate our emotions through having a non-judgmental awareness of our emotions. This helps us recognize and be aware of our feelings without getting overwhelmed.

- **Reduce reactivity**: Mindfulness practice helps us reduce our reactivity by not reacting automatically and developing more of a controlled response.

If you are interested in the benefits of mindfulness but aren't quite sure where to start, I suggest starting with just five minutes of morning meditation. Meditating only five minutes a day can make a significant impact on our health and wellness (Lam, 2015).

Are you interested in mindfulness and you're looking for more help? Go to our website www.unlockingsel.com/blueprint, and click on the Center Adult SEL section.

The Five Habits Training

Perhaps you find yourself interested in mindfulness, but you have no idea where to begin. Our core mindfulness framework for adults is entitled The Five Habits of a Mindful Person™ and is a great place to start. This framework is the basis of a comprehensive, multi-part training program I offer to schools and educators. It's aimed at fostering a more mindful, supportive teaching environment.

In the "5 Habits Training", we unpack these five Mindful Habits of Presence, Pause, Movement, Gratitude and Rest. We discuss the definitions, benefits of each practice, and why each is important to live a healthy, happy life. In our educator training, we follow this up with a discussion of an actionable hack that can help us develop these habits.

Let's take a look at each Habit:

Unlocking SEL's
The 5 Habits of a Mindful Person

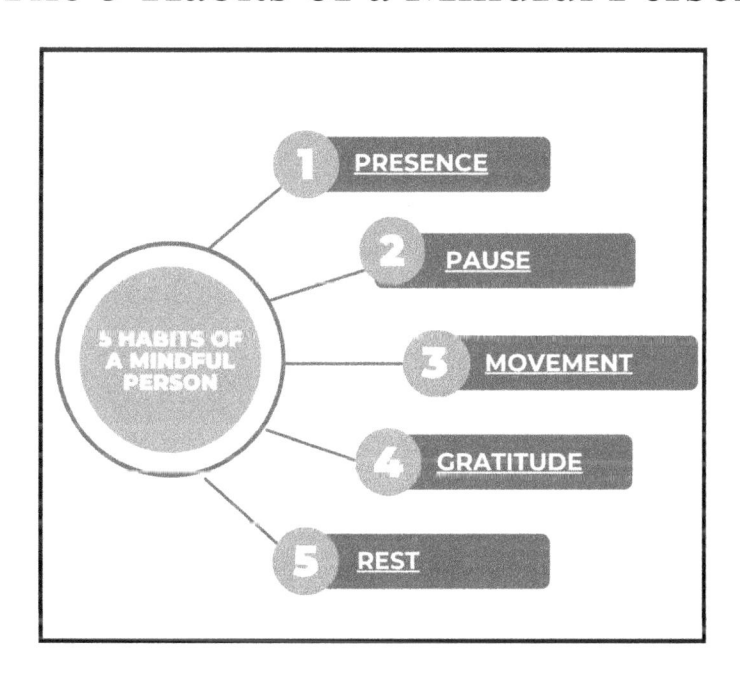

5 HABITS OF A MINDFUL PERSON

1. PRESENCE
2. PAUSE
3. MOVEMENT
4. GRATITUDE
5. REST

For a PDF of Mindful Habits go to
www.unlockingsel.com/blueprint

Presence:
- *Definition*: Presence is the state of being consciously engaged in the current moment, aware of one's thoughts, emotions, and surroundings.
- *Teacher Benefits*: A teacher with a strong sense of presence can better respond to the needs of their students, manage classroom dynamics, and deliver lessons effectively. For instance, when a student asks a challenging question, a present teacher can provide a thoughtful, focused response.

Pause:
- *Definition*: A pause is a deliberate stop in action or speech, used to reflect, gather thoughts, or simply rest before continuing.
- *Teacher Benefits:* Taking intentional pauses can help a teacher regroup during a hectic day. For example, pausing for a few moments of silence after a bustling activity can help transition the class into a more focused state for the next lesson, thereby improving classroom management and student engagement.

Movement:
- *Definition*: Movement refers to physical activity, ranging from simple gestures to complex exercises, that energizes or relaxes the body and mind.
- *Teacher Benefits:* Integrating movement into a teacher's routine can boost energy, reduce stress, and improve overall health.

Gratitude:
- *Definition*: Gratitude is the quality of being thankful and showing appreciation for the positive aspects of life.
- *Teacher Benefits:* Cultivating gratitude can enhance a teacher's well-being by focusing on positive elements of their work, such as progress made by students or supportive colleagues. Acknowledging these can bolster morale and provide motivation, especially on challenging days.

Rest:
- *Definition*: Rest is a period of relaxation, where one ceases work or movement to relax, refresh oneself, and recover strength.
- *Teacher Benefits:* Adequate rest is crucial for a teacher to maintain energy levels and mental clarity. For instance, ensuring they get a good night's sleep or taking short breaks throughout the day can prevent burnout and promote a sustained, high level of teaching performance.

🎯 PRINCIPAL POINTS

I strongly recommend setting limits on when you check your e-mail. One possible way to do this is no email after 6:00 PM and before 6:00 AM. Though this can be hard to establish at first, making it a personal rule can help. When it's a rule, it becomes easier for you to enforce. You can say to people, "Oh, sorry. I don't check my e-mail after 6:00 PM."

Don't worry if you think it makes make you seem like a slacker. In fact, the opposite is true. It will make you seem like a person who has their life together and practices a healthy work/life balance.

The other point of this tip is to remember what the usual outcome is for a principal when we check emails late at night. It is never, "Hello Principal P., I just wanted to tell you what a good principal you are." No, it's a problem or concern they want you to fix. And though it might feel important to them, it's not worth losing your nighttime peace.

💡 TEACHER TIPS

I hope you get started in your mindfulness journey sooner than I did. Don't wait. It can do wonders for your stress level. We can wish all we want that the system of education was more proactive regarding stress management, but we can't wait. Our health is too important. To get started in a mindfulness journey, I recommend MBSR. Check out the latest information for a class near you at www.unlockingsel/blueprint.

Chapter 8 Summary

Tackling the complexities of stress within our educational system is no easy task. Educators carry a heavy burden and overwhelming pressure in today's demanding school climate. As you've seen, alarming statistics reveal high levels of stress among educators. Often, this leads to burnout and even the contemplation of leaving the profession.

What we need is a systemic approach to stress management. Adult social and emotional learning is crucial to build resilience among educators. We need intentional practices like mindfulness, not only to understand and manage stress but to transform the educational environment into a space of calm, focused learning. You can foster well-being and support for yourself and other educators in your orbit, ultimately enhancing the educational experience for all.

Call to Action

- **Learn more about stress:** Study the impact of chronic stress on your overall health.

- **Examine your work/life balance:** Increase your awareness of work/life balance. What is going well in yours? Where do you want to make shifts?

- **Five minutes of morning meditation:** Start small with meditation. Try just five minutes in the morning.

Chpt. 9: Seeking Joy

*"If I asked you what anxiety feels like in your body,
you could probably tell me instantly.
But we forget that joy has a feeling too."*
– Ingrid Lee

The Gift of Joy Hunts

As a principal, I would often find myself swamped with endless responsibilities that stretched the days thin. On stressful afternoons, when the weight of budget decisions seemed too heavy, I always had the same strategy. **Go on a joy hunt**.

I would slip away from my office quietly, walking into the hallways and taking a hard right. Down at the very end of the hallways were the two spaces that made me feel so happy–the kindergarten classrooms.

The moment I crossed that threshold, I was greeted as if I was a rock star. I was consistently met with a symphony of innocent laughter and the vibrant chaos of children engaged in unbridled learning. Sometimes, I would sit in the pint-sized chairs, and a curious 5-year-old would waddle over to give me the best hug ever.

"Hi, Ms. Penley," they would say in that lovely high-pitched tone. Every time, I immediately felt my spirits lifted.

Those visits, though brief, were like a balm to my soul, flooding me with feel-good emotions. They served as vivid reminders of why my work mattered. The tension that had once coiled tightly around my shoulders would begin to unravel as I immersed myself in their tales, saw the spark of pure delight in their eyes, and felt the unguarded grins spread across their faces.

Over the years I've been working with schools, one of the things I've heard over and over and over is that teaching has lost its joy. I'm not surprised when I hear this, but I'm always a bit saddened. Being around children is an innate way to cultivate joy.

But the truth is, the last few years of education, have felt far from joyful for many educators. It's important for leaders to recognize this and focus on the work of rebuilding joy for themselves, their educators, and their students.

Happiness and joy are often used interchangeably, but they're two very different things. Joy can be defined as a broad evaluation of how we feel about where our lives are over time. In contrast, happiness is more how we feel in the moment. With life's ups and downs, happiness can be hard to measure as sometimes we're not even sure how happy we are. However, as educators, we play a crucial role in shaping the lives of students. We want to cultivate joy for them but also cultivate joy in our work and personal lives.

As time marches on, the vibrancy of our youthful joy can become muted under the layers of adult stress and responsibility. It's easy to relegate joy to the margins of our lives, viewing it as a luxury reserved for fleeting moments of leisure—something to look forward to in the evening, over the weekend, or during a summer vacation. Some might even question joy's place in the professional realm.

However, I stand firmly against such notions. Joy is not only essential in the workplace; it's a vital part of it and should never be shelved for 'later.' Embracing joy in our daily work infuses our lives with happiness, sparks our creativity, and fuels innovation. It's a force that enriches us personally and enhances our collective work environment. It also makes us less desperate for the workday to end and helps reduce turnover.

> ***Joy is not only essential in the workplace; it's a vital part of it and should never be shelved for 'later.'***

Joy also belongs in our classrooms and schools as positive emotions are linked to higher levels of engagement, creativity, and motivation all of which are crucial for both learning and retaining information. When students enjoy what they're learning, they are more likely to be curious and attentive in their schooling. A joyful school environment can reduce stress and anxiety and promote social cohesion among students. Just like us, students want to be a part of a joyful community.

Perhaps Judy Willis said it best in her book, *The Neuroscience of Joyful Education*. "The truth is that when we scrub joy and comfort from the classroom, we distance our students from effective information processing and long-term memory storage."

In other words, when joy is removed, bad things happen. Instead of taking pleasure from learning, students become bored, anxious, and anything but engaged. They ultimately learn to feel bad about school and lose the joy they once felt.

If we know we don't want to "scrub joy" for students, wouldn't it stand to reason that we don't want to do the same thing for staff? Instead of taking away joy, why not look for ways to add it to our daily interactions? But how do we do that? I'm glad you asked.

Savor the Good

In an educational landscape filled with challenges, pressures, and high-stakes outcomes, it's important to find balance by savoring the many good moments that occur throughout our days, weeks, and months. These moments, whether in celebration of academic achievements, simple acts of kindness, or student artwork, can serve as refreshing reminders of the inherent beauty and joy in places where children are present. Taking the time to relish in these moments can create for us a reservoir of positive memories that we can later tap into during more demanding times. In addition, it encourages a positive school culture where successes are celebrated. The result is an environment of optimism, resilience, and collective well-being.

When we savor the good moments, we are, in essence, valuing the journey as much as the destination. The conscious act of pausing and relishing the experiences in front of us amplifies joy and provides relief from the pressure and stress that come with adulthood.

In theory, savoring the moment sounds like a great idea, but how the heck do we do it? I'm reminded of a training that I went to a few years back from Dr. Rick Hanson. He discussed a simple practice to help us "hardwire happiness" into the brain. It goes something like this:

Imagine our inputs (things that happen to us) going into a jar. Also, imagine the size of the jar lid helping determine how many positive things can come inside. If we pause and savor for a moment, we increase the size of the opening of the jar to allow more good things to get in.

Make sure our jar lid is wide to allow all of the good to come in.

Over time, this savoring and lingering can change the brain for the better. This is not just positive or unrealistic thinking, it just means seeing the whole reality—the good, the bad, and the neutral, but making sure the good gets equal airtime.

Be Aware of Negativity Bias

Have you ever heard of negativity bias? If not, it may be the most important thing you learn in this chapter. Negativity bias is deeply ingrained in the human brain. You could say it is an evolutionary legacy from our ancestors who had to have a strong focus against perceived threats just to survive.

For example, back in the caveman days, if you were walking around the jungle and heard a sound, there would be a higher chance it was a tiger waiting to eat you than a Door Dash driver bringing you pizza. In other words, people had to pay attention and be hypervigilant.

That type of hardwiring means we're naturally more affected by negative incidences than positive ones. So, a critical comment from a supervisor, a challenging interaction with a student, or a failed lesson can loom much larger in our minds than a successful situation. This survival mechanism may have served our prehistoric ancestors well, but in our modern context, especially for us educators, it can result in an imbalanced perspective that unduly emphasizes the negative aspects of our daily experience and undervalues the positive ones.

This is where savoring the good comes into play. As educators, we can actively cultivate a practice of seeking out and recognizing the positive moments in our day-to-day professional lives. This might involve a deliberate reflection at the end of each day to identify successes, no matter how small, or perhaps maintaining a gratitude journal to record special moments. By intentionally spotlighting the good, we can balance perceptions, build resilience, and create a more positive, appreciative, and joyful school culture.

Prioritize Team Building

One of my most cherished experiences was leisure time with my colleagues outside of work hours. Our routine often involved a monthly happy hour, typically scheduled for the first Friday after payday. Our gatherings were more than just social events. They served as a vital space for us to engage in conversations unrelated to work, allowing us to bond and forge deeper connections. In these relaxed settings, we shared stories, laughed together, and discovered common interests.

Team-building events for teachers can play a crucial role in fostering a joyful and collaborative work environment. These moments help build trust among colleagues and build relationships which are two components vital for successful team dynamics. When teachers trust each other, they're more likely to enjoy their jobs, share resources, and provide support, which in turn can lead to a more enriching educational environment for all. They can break down barriers and reduce feelings of isolation, which is especially important in larger schools where teachers may not interact regularly with others.

◎ PRINCIPAL POINTS

A principal can amplify joy within a school by being the exemplar of positivity and enthusiasm. Start each day with a welcoming smile, greeting both students and staff with genuine warmth, infusing even morning announcements with uplifting messages. Look to celebrate both small victories and major milestones, making sure to recognize the efforts of teachers and students alike.

Create spaces for joy to flourish, like a "Good News" bulletin board in the staff room. Encourage classrooms to share a happy moment from their day during assemblies. You could also prioritize joy in staff meetings, perhaps by starting with a round of gratitude or a funny anecdote. By leading in these areas, a principal demonstrates that joy is not just an occasional visitor but a valued resident in their school's culture.

💡 TEACHER TIPS

I realize work-social outings aren't possible for all people for a variety of reasons. If you can't make them work, don't worry. Please don't let this put extra stress on your shoulders. However, ask yourself what you could do to build connection and spread positivity in your team or grade level.

Chapter Summary

Joy is a profound contributor to a vibrant school culture, where students and staff alike benefit from the positive effects of a joy-infused environment. Despite the overwhelming challenges faced in recent years, joy in teaching is not only possible but essential. It is a powerful antidote to the stress and burnout that can otherwise cloud the educational experience.

You can rediscover and integrate joy into your personal life, recognizing it as an indispensable element of a fulfilling career in education.

Through celebrating academic achievements, nurturing relationships, and building a reservoir of positive experiences you can combat negativity bias and pave the way for a more optimistic and connected school community, where joy is a constant companion in the journey of education.

Call to Action

- **Savor the good:** Look for good moments to savor. Value the journey as much as the destination.

- **Be aware of negativity bias:** By learning about how our brains are meant to function and perceive stress, you can push back against it and choose joy in our modern context.

- **Prioritize community:** Look for ways to attend or organize staff outings outside of work.

Second Key Reflection Questions
Being Aware of the Adult Impact

Question	Answer
In what ways are you practicing self-care?	
Do you feel a sense of community care at your school? Why or why not?	
Do you feel a sense of systemic care in your district? Why or why not?	
In what ways does stress impact your personal life?	
In what ways does stress impact your professional life?	
How do you seek joy each day?	
How does negativity bias impact your life?	

For resources from the book, go to
www.unlockingsel.com/blueprint

The 3rd Key:
Come into the Classroom

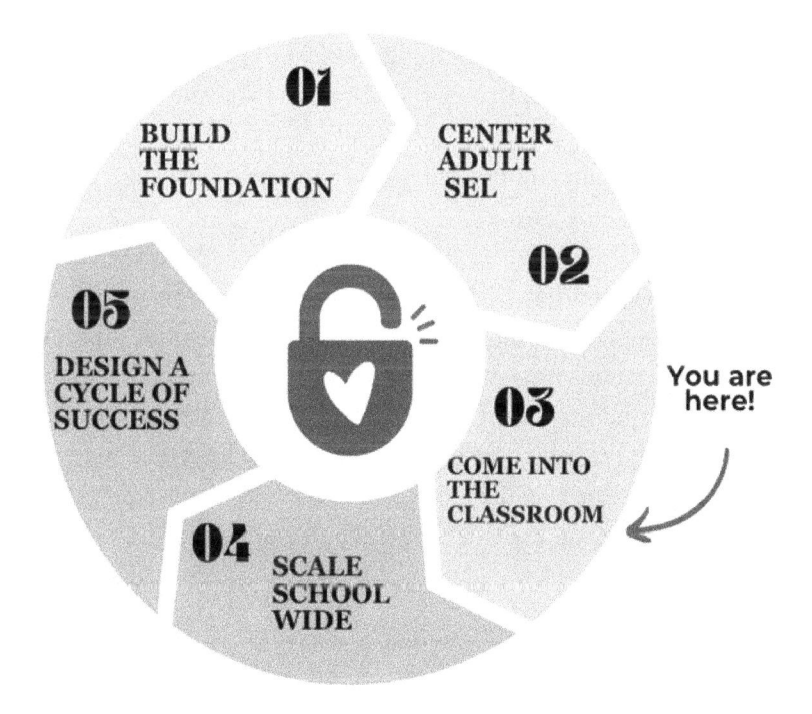

The Story of Nannie's Seeds

My grandmother, Nannie, was a very talented gardener who loved flowers. Her garden looked like something out of a magazine with layers of petunias in the front and tall sunflowers anchoring the background. On the other hand, I didn't love gardening. My interests lie in other areas. But I did love my grandmother.

Some years ago, when I visited her in Tennessee, she gave me some sunflower seeds from her beloved garden.

"I want to give you these so you can grow some sunflowers of your own," she said. "When you look at them, remember how much I love you." My eyes welled with tears as she placed the seeds in my hand.

I took those seeds back to Oregon with me and looked forward to seeing them grow into tall beautiful yellow flowers. After happily scraping the hard dirt in my backyard, I put the seeds into the ground. But then, I proceeded to forget about them. I'm not sure why. Perhaps I trusted they would just magically do their thing.

After a month or so, Nannie called me and asked me how my sunflowers were doing.

"Oh, I think they're doing great," I answered honestly. After all, why wouldn't they be growing?

As soon as we hung up the phone, I ran outside to check on them. I looked all around but all I saw was tiny greenish-brown growth. They were *not* doing great, in fact, they were barely alive at all. They never amounted to sunflowers. It wasn't their fault. They needed something from me to reach their potential. They needed ME to meet their needs with the right soil and the right amount of water, but I did not tend to them at all. I simply put the seeds in the ground and expected they would grow without realizing something essential: what they would become depended on the soil in which they grew and the water they needed to thrive.

Consider the SEL curriculum as a seed. In many cases, schools either overlook the necessity of these seeds altogether or focus solely on the seeds themselves–that is, selecting the appropriate SEL curriculum for their students. However, they frequently fail to consider the broader environment necessary for these seeds to thrive. This includes fostering conditions akin to nurturing soil and providing adequate sunlight, which are both essential for the seeds' growth. In other words, while choosing the right SEL curriculum is important, it's equally crucial to cultivate an environment conducive to the effective implementation and flourishing of the program.

The essence of the Third Key lies in **cultivating the ideal conditions for effective SEL implementation**. Let's delve deeper into advancing our SEL initiative by examining eight pivotal strategies designed to foster the optimal environment for student SEL.

Dubbed **'THE BIG EIGHT**,' these strategies are not just vital but also interdependent, each one reinforcing the others to construct the type of schools and classrooms we aspire to have. Together, they form the cornerstone of a positive school climate, one where every individual can flourish.

The Big 8: Classroom SEL Strategies

- 1 PRIORITIZE RELATIONSHIPS
- 2 MODEL MINDFULNESS
- 3 TEND TO SPACE
- 4 BEGIN WITH A SOFT START
- 5 DO A DAILY MINDFUL MOMENT
- 6 USE A TRAUMA INFORMED LENS
- 7 TEACH EXPLICIT SEL LESSONS
- 8 CREATE A PEACE CORNER

For a PDF of The Big 8 go to
www.unlockingsel.com/blueprint

Chpt. 10: Prioritizing Relationships

*"No significant learning occurs without
a significant relationship."*
–James Comer

Revising the Mantra

Early in my principalship, we had a mantra that we went by: Rigor, Respect, Relationships—the three R's. We had it posted in nearly every classroom and office in the school. Not a day went by that we didn't talk about the mantra, primarily focusing on the first word—Rigor. I was proud of our common language and felt it was a step toward changing our school climate in a positive manner. After all, the main focus of schooling is raising test scores. Right? **Wrong**.

One day, I was walking around after school checking in with various teachers. Our state test scores had just come out and I wanted the staff to know that no matter what the outcomes were, I was proud of them. I walked into Ms. Smith's room and quickly noticed her eyes were red. She looked like she'd been crying. Ms. Smith was one of our best teachers, but she wasn't the overly emotional type. For her to be crying, I knew it must be something serious.

"Oh my gosh," I said. "Are you okay? What's wrong?"

She looked at me, tears in her eyes, and said, "I feel like such a failure."

"What are you talking about?" I asked.

She told me that many of her students did not pass the state test and she felt like it was all her fault. It was clear she felt an overwhelming sense of sadness that her students had not performed as well as she had hoped. It was as if the weight of the world was resting on her shoulders.

I was taken aback by her statement of feeling like a failure. In my eyes, she was anything but; in fact, to me, she was a massive success. Ms. Smith was a dedicated teacher and had invested countless hours preparing her students to do their best and pass the test. Despite her best efforts, some of them had fallen short. And for her, this felt personal, as if she personally had failed them and had failed the school. I tried my best to comfort her and let her know I thought she was amazing.

As I left her room, I immediately began to wonder if I was part of the problem. And if one of our top teachers was feeling this way, how must the rest of the staff feel? Did our relentless pursuit of rigor put too much pressure on our teachers and take away from the wonderful job they had done that year?

Later that evening, I couldn't shake the feeling of seeing Ms. Smith so devastated. As I continually reflected on this, I was reminded once again of our mantra–Rigor, Respect, Relationships. And then it hit me.

We had the order of the words wrong. It was backward. The correct mantra of our school needed to be: **Relationships,** Respect, Rigor—in that exact order.

The next morning, I went back to see Ms. Smith. It was clear by her body language that her feeling of disappointment was still lingering. I told her about my new idea–**Relationships First**! I also told her I was sorry for any pressure I put on her. We hugged it out and I promised to do better.

Don't misinterpret my stance. I firmly believe in the importance of academics and our moral obligation to assist students in reaching their full academic potential. However, I also hold a strong conviction that academics, significant as they are, should come **after** the foundation of solid relationships. The primary focus, therefore, should be on establishing and nurturing these relationships. Because it is within the context of strong, supportive connections that academic success truly flourishes anyway.

Relationships Over Rigor

In the world of education, we face a significant challenge with prioritization. The prevalent trend in many schools and classrooms is to place academics at the forefront, resulting in a flawed formula. A primary focus on academics coupled with managing dysregulated behavior often leads to subpar outcomes.

My proposition is to rethink and reframe this approach. **A more effective equation would be prioritizing relationships + emphasizing and frontloading emotional regulation + focusing on academics + adult SEL = a healthy and thriving school.** This formula tends to yield fewer behavioral issues, stronger academic results, and a more positive classroom atmosphere.

The power of strong relationships between teachers and students cannot be overstated in creating an environment conducive to student success. These relationships foster trust, respect, and a sense of belonging. When students feel valued and supported, their engagement with learning naturally increases, paving the way for a more fruitful and harmonious educational experience.

What Does the Research Say?

Building relationships with students is THE most important component of healthy classrooms and schools. As humans, we have an inherent need to feel connected to others and seek belonging to certain groups and people. Relationships between students and staff make the classroom a safe space for learning and engagement. When students feel their teachers care about them and that they matter in the classroom, they are more likely to participate in learning instead of simply checking out.

According to researchers,

> Middle School students who reported high levels of developmental relationships with their teachers were eight times more likely to stick with challenging tasks, enjoy working hard, and know it is okay to make mistakes when learning, compared to students with low levels of student-teacher relationships (Roehlkepartain et al., 2017).

Eight times more likely! The research proves it. Students who have stronger relationships with teachers are more academically engaged, more connected to their peers and have more positive behavior.

Sadly, not all students have this experience. In fact, a survey of 25,400 sixth to twelfth graders in a large diverse district found that less than a third of middle schoolers had a strong relationship with their teachers. That number dropped to 16% by the time the students reached twelfth grade (Roehlkepartain e. al., 2017).

Students from low-income backgrounds report even fewer strong relationships with teachers (Scales, 2022). According to Roehlkepartain et al. 2017, "each relationship can be an important source of strength, but young people do even better when they have a strong web of many developmental relationships."

This was one of the biggest issues when it came to schools closing due to COVID-19. Many people discussed the learning gap, but what was most apparent was a relationship gap. Many students faced food and housing insecurity, lack of internet access, anxiety, and in some severe cases, trauma. And they faced all that danger without the safe foundational relationships and sense of belonging of schools.

Prioritizing relationships is like laying a strong foundation before building a house. Just as a house needs a sturdy foundation to support its structure, withstand various conditions, and maintain its integrity over time, students need strong, supportive relationships to underpin their academic growth and personal development. Without a solid foundation, a house is vulnerable to collapse under stress, just as without nurturing relationships, a student's academic performance and emotional well-being can falter under pressure. Relationships provide the essential support, stability, and resilience that students need to thrive academically and personally, just as a well-laid foundation ensures the durability and safety of a house.

In this analogy, academics can be seen as the structure built upon the foundation – important and visible, but reliant on the underlying support of strong relationships to truly flourish.

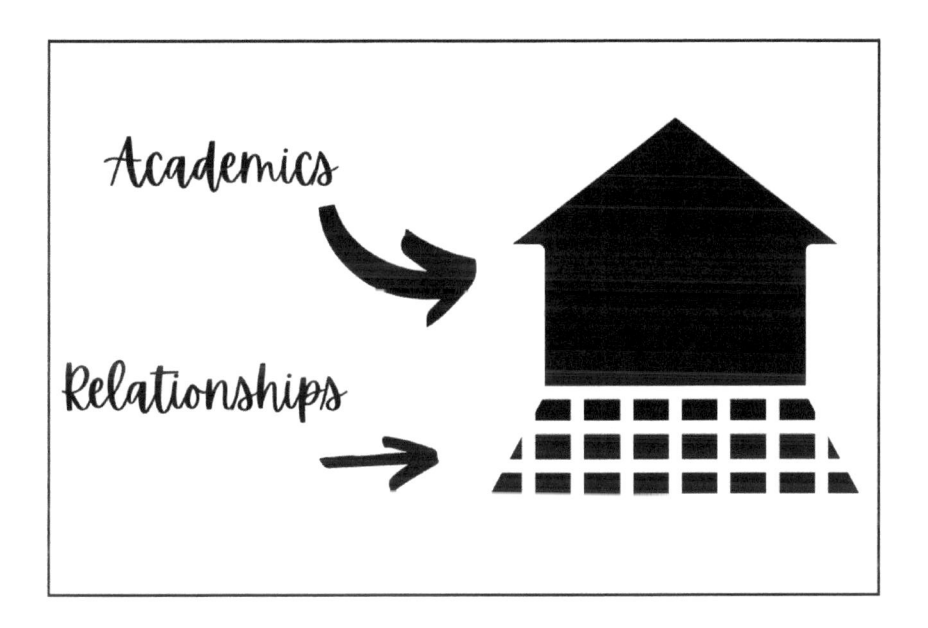

Build Relationships With Intention

Now that we know building relationships is the priority and is essential to create a positive environment, let's move to some ways to do just that. Here are seven strategies that can support building relationships with intention:

Unlocking SEL's 7 Strategies for Intentional Relationship Building

Action Item	Details
Create a safe environment	*When we are trying to create a container for learning, we must start with a sense of safety. Only then can a students' nervous system calm down, regulate, and prepare to learn.*
Create an inclusive environment	*Ensure the classroom space reflects the student's identity and interests which helps students feel connected to their classroom.*
Create a welcoming environment	*Create a welcoming environment that fosters a sense of belonging and safety among students. Greet each student by name when they first arrive. This personal recognition serves to help the student feel seen and known by the teacher.*
Get curious	*Get curious through interest surveys and informal conversations about their interests outside of the classroom. Knowing a students' hobbies, likes and dislikes can help to build a strong relationship that is not based on their academic performance alone.*
Have fun with the students	*Laugh, tell jokes, and smile. We must always keep in mind at the end of the day, students are just children, whether they are in kindergarten or seniors in high school. Play and fun are key components of childhood development.*
Do extracurricular activities	*One of my favorite things was shooting hoops with the students during recess. I felt like it exponentially grew my relationships with students, especially some of the ones that were most disconnected from school.*
Incorporate mindfulness in the classroom	*From modeling mindfulness to Mindful Moments, we are trying to create a culture of kindness in our community.*

For a PDF of this chart, go to
www.unlockingsel.com/book/blueprint

🎯 PRINCIPAL POINTS

Recess became my unexpected yet perfect venue for forging some of the strongest relationships with my students. There's something magical about joining the little ones in a lively game of Duck, Duck, Goose, or playfully challenging the middle schoolers to a game of basketball—yes, sometimes even outscoring them! These breaks from the structured classroom setting opened gateways to authentic, caring connections. In these unguarded moments, the simple joy of play dissolved the barriers between teacher and student, allowing for genuine interaction and the creation of shared memories that last far beyond the playground.

💡 TEACHER TIPS

Over the years, I've seen teachers build amazing relationships in their classrooms. One of the best ways is through infusing play into the fabric of our classroom interactions. It is a delightful and effective way to strengthen the bonds we share with our students.

For instance, you might start a class with a quick, impromptu game that involves teamwork, like a fun trivia challenge related to your lesson, or even a short storytelling round where each student adds a sentence. These moments of shared laughter and creativity not only break down barriers but also build a sense of unity and trust.

Chapter Summary

"Relationships Before Rigor," is a poignant reminder that the cornerstone of effective education is the bond between educators and students. Fostering deep, meaningful relationships within the school community is indispensable. Before educators can expect high academic achievement, we must first establish a rapport built on trust, understanding, and mutual respect. Such connections not only enhance student engagement and well-being but also create a classroom atmosphere conducive to learning and growth.

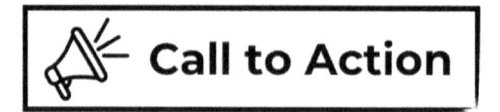

Call to Action

- **Focus first on relationships:** Ensure that you are prioritizing relationships each day.

- **Build with intention:** Build relationships with intention through connection, curiosity, play, and compassion.

- **Smile**: One of the things I remember most about one of my favorite teachers was the way he would smile every day when we came into his classroom. It made me feel he loved his job and wanted us to be there. It made me want to be there, too.

Chpt. 11: Modeling Mindfulness

"Be a thermostat, not a thermometer."
– Anon.

Sandra's Entrance

It was 8:50 am. The second-grade class was already quiet, having just finished their morning breathwork. There was a loud bang on the door as 7-year-old Sandra came in late for the third time that week. Her body was moving all over the place as she shouted in her loudest outdoor voice, "Hi, Ms. Penley."

As the teacher, I was feeling irritated. Sandra was disrupting the vibe that I had so carefully curated. My heart raced as I felt my blood pressure go up, and my breathing became shallower. I thought to myself, "How could she be late again????"

The situation hung in the balance, poised on the precipice of resolution or further escalation. As the teacher, I was faced with a critical decision, knowing that my response would shape not only this moment but also the classroom dynamic moving forward.

The number one way to teach mindfulness is to model mindfulness. Emotions are contagious. When we, the adults, are modeling mindfulness, we can have a calm presence, regulate our emotions, and maintain a positive presence through our tone, body language, facial expressions, and overall demeanor. If students see this on an ongoing basis, they will tend to behave this way. As we cultivate our own mindful skills, and build up our own regulation muscles, we are more able to be present in the classroom, handle situations with calm, and promote positive classroom environments.

> *The number one way to teach mindfulness is to model mindfulness.*

Adults Serve as the Thermostat

A thermostat regulates the environment, helping to maintain the desired temperature. On the other hand, a thermometer simply reacts to everything going on around it, going up and down, reacting to every change it detects. When we model mindfulness and embody the characteristics of calm, it is like our own behavior becomes an intervention for students in itself. We co-regulate our classrooms and schools just like a thermostat.

Now, let's go back and review the story at the beginning. Once again, I had my classroom quiet after just finishing their morning breathwork. Then, Sandra barged into the room, late again, dysregulated, speaking loudly, and disrupting the vibe. Instead of being a thermostat, I became a thermometer matching Sandra's dysregulation with my own. My tone, body language, and my facial expressions let it clearly be known that I'm irritated with her.

Perhaps I even said to her tersely, "Sandra, you are late again. It's the third time this week. Hurry up and go to your seat."

Sandra proceeded to go loudly to her seat and then disrupted everyone at her table. Soon the whole vibe of the classroom shifted toward the negative, as had my mood. I noticed and paused.

Fortunately, I remembered mindfulness. Taking some deep breaths, I became aware of any sensations I felt. Sure enough, my heart was beating faster, and my chest felt tight. Through slow breathing, I could be in the moment, and turn toward compassion.

Also, I remembered that it was probably not her fault she was late. She was in second grade, after all, and didn't drive herself to school or get herself out of bed in an untimely fashion.

"Be a thermostat," I reminded myself. **I remembered it was my responsibility to model the behavior I wanted from Sandra, not to reflect her dysregulation.** Slowly, I allowed my regulation to regulate her.

I softened my body and approached Sandra calmly.

"Good morning," I said slowly. "I'm glad you're here." Smiling, I tried to actually *feel* happy she was there. I may have even placed my hand on her shoulder as a way to anchor her in the room.

We practiced a few breaths together. (Perhaps it was the first time she felt in control of her body since she woke up.) Over time, with consistent modeling, Sandra became regulated and ready to learn.

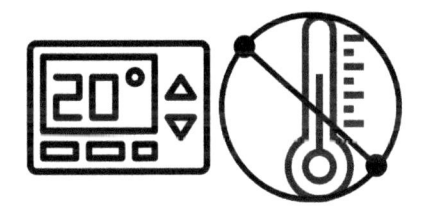

In the first scenario, what started as something small began to grow bigger and more problematic merely by the way I handled this situation. Though this scenario may seem rote, these situations happen over and over multiple times a day. Each time, there are decisions to be made and behaviors to be chosen.

It's like humans are mirrors, reflecting to each other how we are feeling. "The brain is a social organ, co-constructed with others," says Gerard Costa, PhD, the founding director of the Center for Autism and Early Childhood Mental Health at Montclair State University in New Jersey. "Most of what we become as individuals, and most of the unique wiring of our brains are experience-dependent."

In other words, we become what we are surrounded by. This is especially true when students are experiencing emotional upset.

A Bit About the Brain

It is helpful to know a bit about the brain as this emotional upset takes place in a part of your brain called the Amygdala. It is the emotional center of the brain and serves as a sort of guard dog, eagerly waiting to protect its owner. When the guard dog feels threatened, it can go into an **amygdala hijack.**

Daniel Goleman first coined the term amygdala hijack in his 1995 book titled *Emotional Intelligence: Why It Can Matter More Than IQ*. Goleman's term recognizes that we have an ancient structure, the amygdala, and it is designed to respond swiftly to a threat, whether the threat is real to survival or not. When it's triggered, we release stress hormones that prepare the body to fight, flight, or freeze to survive.

The problem is that we cannot always trust our brains. It can see something that is not a real threat yet react as if our life is in danger. **We are biologically hardwired to overreact to situations as a form of protection, i.e. survival.** So, it's just doing its job, but we must monitor it and decide how to respond.

When we develop an understanding of an amygdala hijack, what it is, and how it works, we can develop a better understanding of our students' responses. We can also better understand our personal triggers and provide support through our own modeling of mindfulness. It's on us to help manage and mitigate our students' emotional responses.

When learning about the brain at school, we often refer to Psychiatrist Dan Seigel's Hand Model of the Brain. This model serves as a simple, yet meaningful, teaching tool to demonstrate the major parts of the brain and give a visual as to what happens when we flip our lids. Let me explain.

If you put your thumb in the middle of your palm and then curl your fingers over the top, you'll have a pretty handy (get it? 😊) model of the brain. The face of the person is in front of the knuckles, the back of the head toward the back of your hand. Your wrist represents the spinal cord, rising from your backbone, upon which the brain sits. If you lift your fingers and raise your thumb, you'll see the inner brainstem represented in your palm. Place your thumb back down, and you'll see the approximate location of the limbic area/amygdala. Now curl your fingers back over the top, and your cortex is in place.

When situations arise that make us upset, we can "flip our lids." Our fingers pop up and our amygdala is exposed. This is an amygdala hijack. One thing that can help us prevent an amygdala hijack is the PAUSE.

Practice the Pause

What I didn't know at the time, when I was irritated with my student, was that I simply needed to pause. When I learned to practice the pause, it changed everything. This is one of the most powerful mindfulness practices for me. After learning about the power of the pause and trying to implement it, I was amazed at how it could shift a situation to a more positive outcome.

Respond, **DON'T REACT.**

In its simplest form, the pause is simply taking a moment to break a routine–a sort of time-out of the current energy flow. We have long known pausing is powerful as an instructional technique. In other words, when you teach, you give a lesson on a topic, ask a question, and then give time to let your students process the information. Though that is powerful, it is not what I am referring to.

I am speaking to those situations when a stimulus happens, and instead of immediately going into a reactive state, we pause, take a breath, and allow time for our brain to process. This space gives us time to **RESPOND, not REACT.** When we react, we can get swept away by high emotions. However, when we respond, we are more often coming from a place of compassion, kindness, and connection.

Let's say for the hundredth time Jimmy comes into the classroom without a pencil. Raise your hand if you have had this happen. You immediately want to literally jump down his throat. You're like, "I'm not asking for that much. I'm not even asking if your homework is done. I'm just simply asking if you could come to the classroom with a pencil!"

If you practice the pause, then when Jimmy comes in without a pencil, you pause and notice how you feel in your body. Maybe you feel a rise of anger. Your blood pressure goes up. Your heart rate accelerates. So, you pause again and breathe. That's when you realize that in reality, this is just a small thing, and you show Jimmy where the jar full of pencils lives. You keep it moving. This pause allowed you to **respond, not react.**

Envision a school where the pervasive atmosphere is one of stress, hyperarousal, and sheer exhaustion with individuals teetering on the brink of burnout amidst a constant barrage of stimuli. This was the aftermath of the fire–an entire community engulfed in what felt like a collective amygdala hijack. We were all desperate for a reprieve, a moment to breathe, pause, and reconnect.

Now, reimagine that same school but with a transformative shift: adults who are trained in mindfulness. Imagine them weaving it seamlessly into their personal and professional lives, speaking of the power of the pause, employing it as a habitual tool to navigate challenges. Each day begins with mindful breathing, as they become attuned to the sensations within their bodies.

The impact of mindfulness on our schools defies description on paper—it's more akin to a palpable sensation, a pervasive energy, a movement, rather than a mere mandate or curriculum requirement. **It's the organic cultivation of a culture of care, fostering well-being for all within the school's embrace.**

🎯 PRINCIPAL POINTS

Practicing the pause holds immense potential for principals in navigating the complex and often demanding landscape of school leadership. It is like hitting the reset button on a busy day. It's about taking a breather amidst the chaos, giving us a chance to gather our thoughts and approach challenges with a clear mind. When we pause, we're not just reacting–we're responding thoughtfully. Plus, by showing our staff how to do it, we're setting an example of self-care and mindfulness that can ripple through the whole school, making it a calmer and more supportive place for everyone. So the next time someone asks you about something you aren't sure about, PAUSE, check in with yourself, and say, "Hmmm, let me get back to you on that."

💡 TEACHER TIPS

A word of caution here: though we are shooting for emotional regulation *and modeling mindfulness, we must not hold ourselves to a perfect standard. It is impossible for us adults to get it right every time. This is especially true when we are not getting enough sleep and are chronically stressed or overworked. **(This is another reason Adult SEL is critical for healthy schools!)** I had to realize my mistake with my student coming in late. I had to choose to admit it so that I could pivot and do something new, and so can you.*

Chapter Summary

There is a transformative potential of mindfulness in educational settings, particularly when we focus on practicing the pause. By modeling mindfulness, educators can create a calm, supportive environment that promotes positive behavior and emotional regulation among students.

Likewise, it's important for us to model mindfulness to regulate the emotional climate of the classroom. When we manage our own emotions, we can support students in navigating their own challenging situations. Ultimately, we can create a school culture where mindfulness is integrated into daily practice when we foster a sense of well-being and connection for all members of the school community.

📣 Call to Action

- **Model mindfulness:** Remember, be the thermostat, not the thermometer.

- **Practice the pause:** Look for opportunities to practice pausing throughout your day. Notice the difference it makes.

- **Watch the video of Dan Siegel's The Hand Model**: https://bit.ly/4fH8asl

Chpt. 12: Tending to Classroom Space

"I changed my office space to be more mindful. I softened the lighting, added plants, reduced clutter, and played soft music. From the moment the students entered, the behavior shifted. My attention to the physical space of my office has made a huge positive difference."
– *Assistant Principal, Oregon*

Jose's Calm Classroom

In the heart of the bustling school, nestled away from the clamor of the hallways was a sanctuary of serenity–a classroom adorned with soft hues, gentle lighting, organized spaces, soft music, variety of seating, and the soothing presence of nature.

It was the beginning of the school day. Jose, a typically restless student, walked hurriedly toward his 5th grade room. His teacher, Ms. Clark, was positioned strategically at the door. She smiled warmly and welcomed him.

"Hello, Jose. Good to see you."

"Good morning Ms. Clark," Jose replied as he bounded into the room.

Instantly, the calm classroom environment embraced him and a subtle, yet remarkable transformation took place. His shoulders relaxed, his breathing steadied, and it was as if a sense of calm had washed over him.

He belonged in this calm community. Jose unpacked his backpack, greeted his classmates, and took a seat as he got ready to start his day.

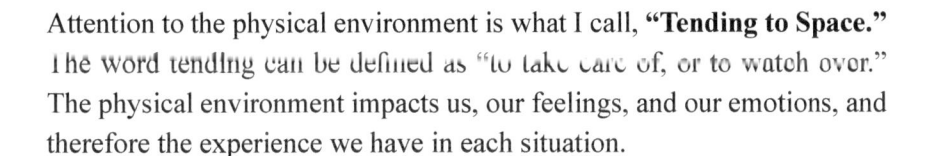

Attention to the physical environment is what I call, **"Tending to Space."** The word tending can be defined as "to take care of, or to watch over." The physical environment impacts us, our feelings, and our emotions, and therefore the experience we have in each situation.

The importance of such a space extends far beyond mere aesthetics. It serves as a refuge for students and teachers alike, offering a place where minds can wander freely, creativity can flourish, and connections can deepen. In classrooms such as this, seeds of curiosity are planted. With each passing day, the impact of this calm, beautiful space reverberates throughout the school, fostering a culture of mindfulness, empathy, and resilience that transcends the individual classroom walls.

Think of when you walk into that special coffee shop or perfectly lit restaurant, and how your mood changes for the better just by entering the space. If we know this to be true, then we must wonder why many of the spaces of our educational environment look the way they do.

We want inspiring spaces not just because they are pleasing to the eye. Research tells us that classroom design can impact student learning. In the meta-analysis of The Impact of Classroom Design on Pupils' Learning: Final Results of a Holistic, Multi-level Analysis (Barrett et al, 2015), the research showed classroom design can have a 16% positive impact on student learning with both environmental and non-environmental factors analyzed. Though further study is needed, it seems obvious.

Our space plays a role in our ability to learn, connect with others, and feel a sense of safety. Furthermore, research findings suggest that classroom design creates a community of learners, helps students work at their optimal levels of challenge, and encourages students to learn holistically.

The classroom is where the students spend most of their time. It is like their home away from home. We want to teach students the importance of caring for their space and that we have a shared responsibility to protect it and keep it looking good.

Have a Tidy and Organized Classroom

Tending to space starts with a tidy and organized classroom. This is crucial for creating an optimal learning environment. When a classroom is well organized and free from clutter, it helps students feel calm, focused, and ready to learn. Without distractions from scattered materials or cluttered spaces, students can better concentrate on the lesson at hand, leading to improved academic performance. Additionally, an organized classroom facilitates efficient teaching by enabling educators to quickly locate resources and materials, which maximizes instructional time.

Beyond academic benefits, a tidy classroom fosters a sense of pride and responsibility among students, teaching them valuable life skills such as organization and time management. By maintaining an organized environment, students learn the importance of taking care of their surroundings and respecting shared spaces. In addition, a tidy classroom promotes a positive classroom culture, where students and teachers can collaborate effectively and feel comfortable expressing themselves. It sets the stage for a positive and productive learning experience for both students and teachers alike, paving the way for academic success and personal growth.

Perhaps you find yourself wanting an organized classroom space, but at the end of the day, it looks like a tornado has torn through your classroom. Know that you're not alone. This happens to many of us.

As you prepare to close your classroom for the day, I'd like to share an approach I call, "**The Restaurant Closing.**" I am sure that you, either through personal experience or observation, are familiar with the closing rituals of a restaurant. Regardless of the day's hustle and bustle, with customers coming and going, dishes being prepared, and occasional spills and messes, the restaurant is always restored to its original state at night's end with cleaned spaces, cleared tables, and organized utensils.

End the day with a Restaurant Closing.

This principle of returning to a 'set point' is what we aim to replicate in our classrooms. Imagine your classroom like a restaurant at closing time: no matter the activities or the level of engagement throughout the day, by the end, everything should be organized and tidied up.

This practice ensures that the classroom is a welcoming, orderly space, primed for a fresh start and optimal learning as students walk in the next day. Adopting this "Restaurant Closing" strategy in your classroom underscores the importance of a well-maintained learning environment. In short, it sets the tone for continuous educational success.

Ensure the Classroom is Aesthetically Pleasing

Take a moment to think of your favorite classroom you ever attended as a student. What did it look like? What can you remember?

I remember my Kindergarten classroom the wonderful Ms. Kilgore created for us. It was a welcoming space with soft seating and beautiful decorations. That classroom felt like home.

The reason is simple. An aesthetically pleasing classroom enhances the overall learning environment. Such a classroom creates an inviting, comfortable atmosphere. It encourages student engagement and sparks their interest and curiosity. These are both key elements for effective learning environments.

The visual appeal of the classroom, characterized by calming colors, natural light, and pops of brightness, can serve to uplift moods and increase motivation because it's an enjoyable space for students.

However, this doesn't just apply to students. Educators need great spaces too. A well-designed calming environment can reduce our stress and anxiety allowing us to focus more on the teaching at hand. Plus, it just makes us happier. And who doesn't want to be happier? I know I do!

What does it look like to have a classroom that is both organized and aesthetically pleasing? I'm glad you asked!

Tending to Space Examples

Below are some examples of what Tending to Space looks like from the classroom perspective: (Barrett, 2015):

- **Comfortable, non-institutional classroom environments**
  This can be defined as naturalness (light, sounds, temperature, air quality, links to nature). Offer soft lighting, play gentle music, or bring in nature with plants and animals. Make sure you have low noise levels, and that your classroom is properly ventilated.

- **Individualization: Ownership, flexibility, connection**
  This could look like thoughtful displays of student work, relevant learning materials, personalized signage, and flexible seating which allows students to find seating that best fits their learning.

- **Stimulation: Color and complexity**
  Color refers to how color affects the room and complexity is how the different elements combine to create a visually coherent and structured environment. This would look like a room or school that is not overloaded with clutter, is organized and clean, and has calm or muted colors mixed with pops of vibrancy.

As you can see, creating a warm, inviting, vibrant class environment takes both organization and mindful beautification. With the right tools in hand, you can make your classroom whatever works best for your students. What small step or change could you make in your classroom environment today?

🎯 PRINCIPAL POINTS

As leaders, we must remember that the appearance of our principal's office matters. It can set the tone for the entire educational community. A well-organized office not only reflects the professionalism and efficiency of the school's leadership but also sends a message about the importance of organization and structure.

In visiting schools around the country, I have seen it all. From offices so beautiful they look like they came right out of Restoration Hardware catalog, to offices that look like they should be condemned, like you might see a rat going by at any moment. 🐭

As people enter the office, we want them to be greeted with an environment that exudes professionalism and warmth. Let's recall our quote at the beginning of this chapter, "I changed my office space to be more mindful. I softened the lighting, added plants, reduced clutter, and played soft music. From the moment the students entered, the behavior shifted. My attention to the physical space of my office has made a huge positive difference."

💡 TEACHER TIPS

Though the deeper cleaning of classroom space may fall to the custodian, we want to ensure that students are caring for their classroom space. This instills a sense of responsibility, ownership, and a deeper appreciation and respect for their surroundings.

I have seen some wonderful classroom job charts where students take turns doing cleanliness tasks for their classrooms. I have also heard a wonderful classroom cleanup song used in elementary schools to help tidy things up at the end of the day. Check out this one–5 Minute Clean up Song. *https://bit.ly/3B1ZSLJ*

Chapter Summary

In the educational setting, creating a mindful, organized environment is powerful. Creating inviting spaces makes school a place students want to pay attention, a place they enjoy being. Cultivating this ambiance enhances the learning environment and fosters a sense of pride, responsibility, and community among students.

Through attention to detail and the adoption of practices like the "Restaurant Closing," educators can prioritize organization and aesthetics, creating spaces that inspire curiosity, engagement, and well-being for all.

Call to Action

- **Examine your classroom space with fresh eyes:** What looks visually pleasing and welcoming? Where can things be tidied up?

- **Add a Restaurant Closing:** Add an end-of-the-day clean-up ritual to your classroom. Ensure that everyone is responsible for the upkeep of the space.

Chpt. 13 Beginning With a Soft Start

"How we start our day matters most."
– Lana

Melinda's Lesson to Me

In the beginning of my principalship, I was adamant that our school should plunge into academics from the moment students entered our front door. Driven by the urgency to catch up those lagging behind, I championed the notion that instruction should begin immediately, leaving no room for wasted time.

When the bell rang, I would be out in the hallways, barking orders in my best principal voice.

"Hurry up, you're going to be late to class," I used to say with the tone of a drill sergeant as students scurried to class.

In those early days, I was all about efficiency and academic rigor–until Melinda, a bright student with weary eyes, changed my perspective. One particularly rushed morning, Melinda was trailing behind, and my insistence on punctuality was met with an unexpected response. She looked up at me with a mix of defiance and vulnerability, explaining that her tardiness wasn't a simple act of rebellion; it was a consequence of a challenging home life where her mother struggled to get out of bed each morning.

It struck me at that moment how my fixation on academics could overshadow the complex lives students lead outside the school walls. It was a moment of reckoning that shifted my focus toward creating a school environment that prioritized not only intellectual growth but also emotional support, acknowledging the diverse challenges our students face every day.

My early approach to the beginning of the day overlooked a fundamental need of our students upon their arrival–a need to feel welcomed and valued. My critical misstep was not recognizing that before their minds could open to knowledge, their hearts needed the affirmation that they mattered and that their presence was significant.

The way we start our day is pivotal as it sets the tone and atmosphere for the entire day. As humans, we need to start something new in a slow way. I call this **the Soft Start.** A soft start in schools isn't just a gentle beginning to a day or a term; it's a purposeful strategy aimed at fostering a positive and supportive learning environment right from the get-go.

Imagine walking into a space where the initial moments are dedicated to easing you into the day's activities, providing a buffer to transition from the external hustle of home and getting comfortable in the focused, learning mindset required in the classroom. Now, juxtapose this against the start I mentioned at the beginning of this chapter. Which start would you want your child to partake in? I know what I would choose.

A soft start is akin to a warm, gentle embrace that acknowledges students varied emotional and cognitive starting points each day. It's a time when students can engage in quiet activities, such as reading, drawing, or journaling, all while acclimating to the school environment. This thoughtful approach allows educators to meet students where they are, providing individual attention, gauging emotional states, and gently guiding them into the day's structured activities.

Welcome Students in a Warm and Caring Way

As the principal, I considered it my top duty to cultivate a sense of belonging among everyone who walked through our front doors. I envisioned our school not just as some sort of stark institution, but as a warm and inviting home where people felt like honored guests. To embody this philosophy, I aimed to be one of the first faces they saw, greeting them at the front steps each morning.

Accompanying me was Quincy, my canine companion, who served as our cherished therapy dog. Twice a week, his gentle presence would provide comfort and joy, softening the edges of academic rigor with the unconditional love that only a pet can provide. Quincy's wagging tail coupled with his sloppy kisses were as much a part of our welcome as the school itself assuring students that there they would be seen and deeply valued.

Our teachers shared the same heartfelt philosophy. The classrooms were extensions of the welcoming space that I tried to create on the front steps. Like me, they recognized that academic achievement took a back seat to emotional well-being.

Teachers greeted their students with smiles, asked about their evenings, and listened, truly listened, to the stories and concerns of their students. This connection forged bonds, built trust, and created a sense of safety, right from the start.

Our morning rituals, the staff on the front steps, the presence of Quincy, and our teachers in front of their doors greeting their students with an authentic smile, were all emblematic of our collective approach: education with the soul, lessons taught not just through books but through empathy understanding and the gentle pat of a dog's head. Together, we stood united in the belief that before we could fill their minds with knowledge, we needed to fill their hearts with love. That is what the Soft Start is all about.

Let's unpack the Soft Start for more details. In general, the Soft Start lasts about 15 minutes from the opening bell and is all about community building. It is the key time for building and nurturing positive relationships for students with peers and teachers, forming the backbone of a collaborative and supportive classroom culture. This time allows teachers to connect with their students, check on their well-being, assess their readiness, and provide an opportunity for immediate feedback. It also allows for adjustments or for tending to their needs.

This time caters to the student's social and emotional well-being, but it also significantly impacts their ability to absorb, engage, and retain learning throughout the day. In essence, a soft start serves as a bridge as it facilitates a smooth transition from home to school and paves the way for a day of effective learning.

Emphasize Community Building Activities

During the initial 15 minutes of 'soft start' time, students engage in a meticulously structured entry routine. Upon arrival, students neatly store their backpacks and settle into their seats. The activities that follow are tailored to suit different educational stages. For instance, kindergarten students might spend this time enjoying their breakfast and browsing through books. In contrast, third graders may engage in journaling exercises while middle and high school students could be involved in conversation prompts centered around community topics. This period is governed by what I refer to as the '4C's of the Classroom Soft Start', a framework designed to ease students into the learning environment in a calm and organized manner.

Unlocking SEL's
The 4C's of the Classroom Soft Start

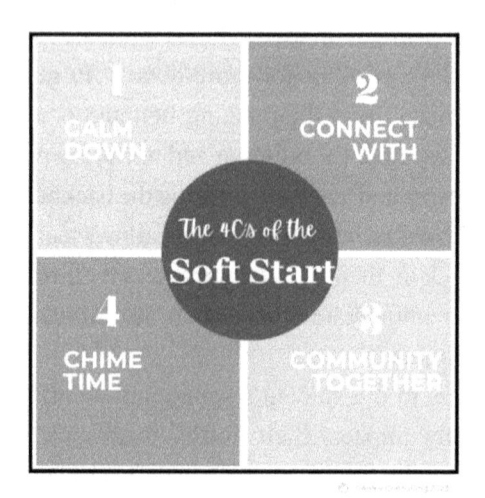

For a PDF of the 4 C's, go to
www.unlockingsel.com/blueprint

1. **Calm down**: We want to make sure that students are entering a calming space—a place where their brains can get ready to learn and their bodies can regulate. This can look like soft lighting, soft music, and a teacher with a calm yet friendly demeanor.

2. **Connect with**: Next is connections. This is when we want to make sure the teacher is connecting and forming relationships with students. Some examples could be teachers asking everyone by name how their morning is going or walking around and giving a positive comment on what the students are working on. Teachers could ask open-ended questions such as how the baseball game went last night or even telling a quiet joke or two. This connection allows students to be in a place of openness where learning can occur.

3. **Community together**: After we have connected one-on-one, it's time to connect in a larger sense with the community. This is a great time to do community circles, sharing prompts that can help classrooms work through issues, build bonds, and celebrate wins. For many rooms, it looks like students in a circle being asked a question such as, "What makes a kind classroom?" Students can pass a baton and be invited to share their answers. Meanwhile, other students practice mindfully listening to their classmates.

4. **Chime time:** This last part is the time for the chime. It is a morning breathing practice, our Mindful Moment, which we will cover in our next chapter.

🎯 PRINCIPAL POINTS

As a school leader, especially at an underperforming school, you may feel the same urge I did in the story—to skip a soft start and dive into academics. ***Resist it.*** *Focus on what matters most first: connection and relationships. Remember, relationships come before rigor. When we prioritize that order, everything improves.*

💡 TEACHER TIPS

If you aren't used to doing a soft start, it may feel a bit challenging at the beginning. You may be worried that students can't handle it, or that you will lose valuable instruction time. Perhaps you're wondering what you'll talk about for fifteen minutes. But trust me. I have seen it work in classroom after classroom. It is a great time to build up community with inclusive practices such as community circles and restorative practices. Once you get it going, you will be gearing up for our next practice.

Chapter Summary

A soft start, your 15-minute period dedicated to building community, can change everything. Armed with the 4C's of the Classroom Soft Start, which includes calming the environment, connecting with students, fostering community, and a ritual chime time for collective focus, you'll be able to put it into practice. Your soft start will offer your class the best chance for a successful day. From starting the day with a warm welcome to adding connection activities, you have the power to help your students have their best day possible.

📣 Call to Action

- **Review the start of your day:** How do you welcome your students with warmth and care?

- **Add connection activities:** Morning is the perfect time to do community building activities such as community circles and classroom discussions.

- **Wait for rigor:** Remember, relationships first, then rigor.

Chpt. 14 Doing Daily Mindful Moments

*"Perhaps the most important thing we can teach students
is the power of their breath."*
– Lana

Tiny Teachers

The day was Monday, the first day of the new quarter. I walked the halls greeting everyone, doling out hugs, and smiles. As I made my way down to the kindergarten wing, I peeked in the doorway of Ms. Harris's room, observing a scene brimming with potential: a mosaic of little ones shedding their coats with the morning's restlessness. Their giggles and jostles for space gradually gave way to a calmer stance as they engaged in gentle welcoming activities and eased into the rhythm of the day.

It was during these initial moments that I witnessed the start of a subtle shift from frenetic energy to focused harmony. The room, filled with story books, breakfast items, and the hushed tones of morning greetings, felt alive and full of possibility.

About 15 minutes after the first bell rang, Ms. Harris said in the happiest voice possible, "Good morning class."

"Good morning Ms. Harris," they responded.

"Please join me at the carpet," Ms. Harris called invitingly.

The students made their way to the colored squares at the front of the room, knowing exactly where to sit. There was no fighting or arguing, just twenty or so five-year-olds doing a routine they had done countless times before.

"It is time for our Mindful Moment, a time to give our brains a break and focus on our breathing," Ms. Harris said. Then, as if by some unseen signal, the room fell silent, save for the resonant sound of the chime that marked the beginning of their morning breathing exercise.

These kindergartners, mere minutes ago a whirlwind of motion, suddenly sat as still as ancient statues, their busy bodies anchored by a newfound stillness. Tiny chests rose and fell with each mindful inhale and exhale. For up to two minutes, an eternity in the realm of five-year-olds, they engaged in the mere act of stillness.

"In this space, they are not just learners," I thought. "They are tiny teachers, reminding us all of the power of breath."

Ever so quietly, Ms. Harris rang the chime again. The students quietly opened their eyes. She concluded with one last question: "How did the Mindful Moment make you feel?"

About ten little arms went up in the air. Ms. Harris called on Sophia, a shy, curly-haired girl sitting at the back of the carpet. In the cutest voice you have ever heard, Sophia said, "It makes me calm, happy, and ready to learn."

As we turn the page from exploring the 4Cs of the Soft Start, we arrive at a pivotal component: Chime Time, aka The Mindful Moment. This is the moment when the daily work of classroom life pauses for a collective breath—a mindful moment designed to bring young minds to a place of focus and calm.

The Mindful Moment is a strategy that, I believe, **holds the greatest potential for transformative impact on a student's well-being**. Its power lies not in a single day's practice but in the cumulative effect of day-in, day-out consistency.

Reflecting on the profound simplicity of this practice, I often wonder how different my own emotional landscape might be had I been introduced to such a practice at the tender age of five. The notion that a few minutes of intentional breathing could vastly improve one's emotional management and awareness is a revelation that captures the essence of why the Mindful Moment holds such a revered place at the beginning of our day.

The Why of a Mindful Moment

In the dynamic and often distracting environment of a classroom, the ability to center oneself through focused breathing is a key tool. It significantly enhances a student's engagement with, and absorption of, educational content.

Compelling research, including studies by Carsley et al. in 2018, underscores the substantial positive impact of mindfulness interventions on students. Furthermore, these breathing practices serve as an empowering tool, teaching students to recognize and regulate their emotions and bodily responses.

The ability for **self-regulation, defined as the ability to understand and manage your own behavior and reactions,** is a cornerstone in the development of a student's educational and personal growth. It is the foundation upon which all other learning constructs are built. Without the ability to manage their emotions, impulses, and behaviors, students may find it challenging to focus, engage with their peers productively, and fully embrace the learning process.

Self-regulation is not just about discipline; it's about understanding and harmonizing one's inner world with the external demands of the classroom environment. It empowers students to navigate the complexity of their thoughts and feelings and to make choices that are conducive to learning and social interaction. For educators, fostering this skill is as critical as teaching math or literacy, for it underpins a student's capacity to learn effectively and to cultivate relationships that are vital for a collaborative classroom.

Mindful moments are instrumental in cultivating this vital skill of self-regulation. Through mindfulness, students are guided to attune to the present, bringing awareness to their breath and body sensations. This practice equips them with the ability to pause and respond to situations with intention rather than react out of habit or impulse. Over time, as students regularly engage in mindful moments, they build a reservoir of calm they can draw upon when faced with stress or distraction. This reservoir becomes a wellspring of patience and poise, allowing them to approach their academic and social challenges with a steadier hand and a clearer mind.

By integrating these practices into the daily routine, educators provide students with a gift that extends far beyond the classroom walls. It is a skill set that lays the groundwork for emotional intelligence and lifelong resilience.

> *By integrating these practices into the daily routine, educators provide students with a gift that extends far beyond the classroom walls—a skill set that lays the groundwork for emotional intelligence and lifelong resilience.*

Teach Students Brain Science

As we teach students about their ability to control their breathing and use it as a tool to manage stress and anxiety, and focus on learning, we don't want to stop there. We want to let them in on the secrets of their brain. Teaching students basic brain science equips them with a deeper understanding of themselves as they gain valuable insights into emotional regulation, memory, and learning processes.

These changes such as calm and focus are not momentary, as regular practice over time can cause the brain to change through something called **neuroplasticity.** Neuroplasticity underpins the very essence of learning, allowing us to adapt, acquire new skills, and overcome challenges. The brain's capacity to reorganize through building new neural connections means that experiences, including the practice of mindfulness, can lead to lasting changes in how we think, feel, and respond to the world around us.

This knowledge empowers them with self-awareness. As they learn about the impact of stress on the brain and discover techniques to manage their responses, it becomes invaluable for emotional and behavioral control. Understanding the brain is not merely an academic exercise; it's a foundational aspect of fostering well-rounded, empathetic, and resilient individuals.

When you teach your students about brain science, it all starts with their brains' twin powers. I'm talking about the amygdala and the prefrontal cortex. We call these the **Twin Powers**, because when your students sync these up, they'll be unstoppable.

Of course, we want to simplify the understanding of the brain and teach it age-appropriately, but even students as young as kindergarten can understand these basic two components of the amygdala and the prefrontal cortex. As stated earlier, the amygdala plays a key role in processing our emotions, especially fear and anger. As students understand its function, they can better comprehend their emotional responses and learn strategies to best manage them.

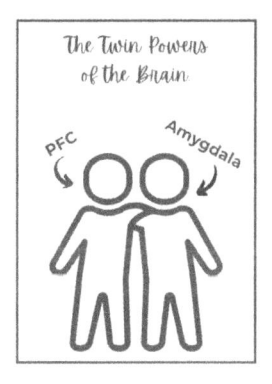

The prefrontal cortex (PFC), on the other hand, is involved in executive functions such as decision-making, problem-solving, and impulse control. This is where learning takes place. Knowledge about the PFC can help students understand the importance of thoughtful decision-making and the consequences of impulsive actions.

When students understand how to synchronize these twin powers, they unlock a remarkable capacity for focus and resilience. The amygdala's heightened alertness can be tempered by the prefrontal cortex's reasoning, allowing emotions to inform but not overpower the thought process. This interplay enables students to approach situations with a balanced perspective, responding thoughtfully rather than reactively. A student with well-integrated brain functions can navigate academic challenges with strategic thinking, manage emotional impulses to maintain concentration, and harness the energy of their emotions to fuel positive actions. Essentially, when these two regions work cohesively, students are not just more focused; they embody a powerful synergy that enhances their entire learning experience, allowing them to be present, engaged, and ready to tap into their full potential.

Practice Daily

Just as muscles require regular exercise to grow stronger, the brain needs consistent practice to master the art of self-regulation. By dedicating time each day for students to engage in mindfulness, we provide them with repeated opportunities to develop focus, calmness, and an awareness of their emotional states. This consistent practice equips students with the tools to notice and manage their emotions, which can lead to improved concentration, better stress management, and more thoughtful responses to challenging situations. Over time, these daily Mindful Moments can significantly enhance students' ability to navigate their emotional landscapes with skill and confidence.

When stress surfaces during the school day, such as the nerves before a big test or the aftermath of a playground disagreement, the Mindful Moment becomes a powerful tool for students. This practice of deep breathing acts as a reset button, allowing students to momentarily step away from the stressor, concentrate on their breath, and regain equilibrium. This intentional break fosters a mental clarity and tranquility that helps students navigate stressful situations with greater ease and effectiveness, thanks to the emotional regulation skills they've been cultivating through their routine mindfulness practice.

Consider the children in Ms. Harris's kindergarten class, who are learning to integrate deep breathing into their daily rituals. This practice plants the seeds of emotional wellness that can grow with them, providing a resource not just for their kindergarten challenges but as a lifelong strategy for well-being. The regularity of these mindful exercises promises a cumulative benefit, potentially enriching their lives far beyond the walls of any classroom.

🎯 PRINCIPAL POINTS

The transformative power of beginning each day with a Soft Start and seamlessly transitioning into a Mindful Moment is immeasurable in cultivating a school atmosphere steeped in calm, regulation, and joy. These practices synergize to create an ideal foundation for a day filled with focused, contented learning.

Implementing this initiative is a thoughtful process that unfolds gradually. When I teach schools these practices, I ensure a cohesive approach by simultaneously providing comprehensive training to the entire staff, equipping them not only with the necessary materials but also instilling the confidence required to embark on this journey. This unified effort is pivotal in embedding these practices into the fabric of the school's daily routine, setting the stage for a consistently positive and productive educational environment.

TEACHER TIPS

Teaching a mindful moment in your classroom is a bit of a long game, more like a marathon and not a sprint. Some students will get it right away; they're ready to go and are immediately impacted. Others who are experiencing more dysregulation will need more time. One of the key points is that you want to get on a winning streak. What I mean by that is to start small. Perhaps you're just trying to be quiet and still for 10 seconds, then maybe 30 seconds, then 45 seconds, graduating all the way to the goal of two solid minutes.

Chapter Summary

As you can see, there are profound benefits of integrating a daily Mindful Moment into your classroom routine. It aids in self-regulation, engagement, and emotional intelligence. Through consistent practice, students can experience a transformational shift from chaos to focus, learn to manage their responses, and harness their breath to achieve calm.

Likewise, it's important to teach students about brain science, including the concepts of neuroplasticity and the functions of the amygdala and prefrontal cortex. This knowledge equips students with a deeper understanding of their emotional and cognitive processes, empowering them to synchronize these "Twin Powers" for enhanced focus and resilience in their educational journey.

Call to Action

- **Do a morning mindful minute:** Taking the time to teach students the practice of mindful breathing can help them build lifelong skills.

- **Teach students about brain science:** Teach lessons on the basics of the amygdala and the PFC to help them understand their brain and behavior better.

Chpt. 15 Using a Trauma-Informed Lens

"After trauma, the world is experienced with a different nervous system, every new encounter or event is contaminated by the past."
-Bessel Van Der Kolk

Marcus's Dad

Marcus's bright smile had the power to illuminate any room, yet his challenging behaviors posed significant obstacles to learning, not only for himself but also for his peers. His actions, ranging from the use of profanity to inappropriate sexual behaviors, created turmoil in the classroom. It distracted not only him but also the rest of the students.

Reflecting on this now, I realize he was what neuroscientist Bruce Perry would describe as "dysregulated" or out of balance (Perry, 2023). My encounter with Marcus came early in my tenure as an administrator, a time when my understanding of trauma-informed care was still nascent.

One day, Marcus got in trouble for using bad language toward a teacher. He was sent to my office. I called his dad and asked him to come in so we could meet and discuss the situation.

When his dad arrived, he marched into my office, clearly upset. As I began to tell him what had happened, much to my surprise, the dad began to yell at ME! He was screaming about how the teacher must have been picking on Marcus or his son wouldn't have called her those names.

"Tone it down," I told him before reminding him that we spoke "with respect in this office." The situation continued to escalate before finally, after what seemed like an eternity, things began to calm down. I told the dad that Marcus needed to apologize to the teacher, and we could move forward but with a behavior plan to help support Marcus in his educational journey at his new school.

This idea of a behavior plan set the dad off again, stating that he did not want his kid **labeled**.

"Labeled?" I asked. "This plan is only to support him, not to send him down any particular educational path," I said. His father sighed in relief as his body language softened. He slowly began to share with me about his own distressing experiences in school. Tears filled his eyes as he detailed how the stigma of being labeled a 'problem child' left deep, enduring marks on his life, patterns he did not want to be repeated for Marcus.

Watching Marcus's dad recount his painful school days, my perspective shifted. Compassion replaced frustration, and I saw the situation through a new lens—one that didn't just focus on the disruptions but on the underlying struggles and the cyclical nature of trauma. It was a profound reminder that our actions as educators can either perpetuate cycles of distress or foster paths to healing. In that moment, our shared goal crystallized: to create a supportive plan for Marcus that avoided labels and instead offered guidance, with the hope of charting a new, positive course for his future.

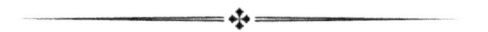

The profound impact of trauma on individuals is undeniably significant, especially in the context of schools. Schools are not just centers of learning but are also pivotal in the lives of students, where they spend much of their time. Trauma has a profound effect on how students interact with the world and perceive their surroundings. The 2018 National Survey of Children's Health revealed that one in three children under 18 had experienced some form of trauma. Considering the widespread effects of the COVID-19 pandemic, it's reasonable to assume that the prevalence of trauma among children has increased. This underlines the urgency for schools to adopt a trauma-informed approach.

Incorporating a trauma-informed lens in educational settings is crucial for recognizing and effectively responding to the needs of students who have experienced trauma. It means understanding the pervasive nature of trauma and its potential impact on learning, behavior, and relationships within the school environment. By adopting such an approach, schools can become more supportive and nurturing spaces that acknowledge and address the complex challenges faced by traumatized students.

Though we didn't call it that at the time, following the fire we leaned into a trauma-informed approach. We realized there had been a trauma and it impacted everything. We proceeded with caution and looked for ways to go slow and focus on relationships. We thought of the school as a place of healing first and then academics. We put energies into regulation, community, and belonging. Little did we know these are all trauma-informed practices.

The need to address trauma is becoming increasingly evident for schools to be able to teach effectively, support behavior management, and create positive school climates. To understand the varied impact of traumatic events on individuals, it's crucial to consider the following insight:

> Although many people who experience a traumatic event will go on with their lives without lasting negative effects, others will have more difficulty, and experience traumatic stress reactions. Emerging research has documented the relationships among exposure to traumatic events, impaired neurodevelopmental and immune systems responses and subsequent health risk behaviors resulting in chronic physical or behavioral health disorders (SAMHSA, 2014).

The 4R's of Trauma

With hindsight and new learnings into trauma, now I'm able to see the pattern with Marcus. It seems likely that the trauma endured by Marcus's father had repercussions on Marcus's life, perpetuating a cycle of distress. Marcus's extreme behaviors were likely manifestations of his and perhaps the family's own traumatic experiences. The approach to understanding Marcus, I now realize, should have been to start with relationships, lead with compassion, and inquire about his experiences—what he had been through—rather than what was wrong with him. This shift in perspective might have led to a deeper understanding and more effective support for Marcus, and I often find myself wondering about his journey since then.

As educators, we are increasingly being asked to support students like Marcus who have experienced trauma. To be prepared, I recommend learning about SAMHA's 4 R's of trauma-informed care (2014) as a framework for understanding a trauma-informed approach.

- **Realize:** We want to realize the widespread impact of trauma and the potential path to recovery. We want to understand that trauma changes student's nervous systems, and how they view the world.

- **Recognize:** We want to recognize signs and symptoms of trauma such as lack of impulse control, hyperactivity, increased hypervigilance, lacking trust, and difficulty processing.

- **Respond:** We want to respond using the principles of a trauma-informed approach. We want students to feel safe, connected, and regulated.

- **Resist:** The final R is that we, through applying our knowledge about the impact of trauma, resist re-traumatization.

We adopt these assumptions because they are fundamental to creating a supportive and effective learning environment for all students, especially those affected by trauma. By **realizing** trauma's impact, we acknowledge the profound effects it can have on a student's behavior, learning, and relationships. This understanding prompts us to look beyond surface behaviors and to consider the underlying experiences that may drive them.

Recognizing the signs and symptoms of trauma allows us to identify students who need support and avoid mistaking trauma responses for mere disobedience or disinterest. This recognition is critical in intervening appropriately and preventing further harm. **Responding** with a trauma-informed approach means that we actively apply this understanding to our interactions with students, aiming to provide stability, support, and safety, which are crucial for their ability to learn and grow.

Lastly, by **resisting** re-traumatization, we prevent our educational practices from inadvertently triggering past trauma, which can further harm a student's emotional and academic well-being. Instead, we strive to be a consistent force of healing and empowerment in their lives. These assumptions guide us in modifying our educational practices to be more empathetic, patient, and constructive, ultimately fostering a nurturing school culture that recognizes and supports the varied needs of all students.

Mindful-Based, Trauma-Informed Practices

Trauma-informed care and mindfulness are deeply intertwined in educational settings because both approaches prioritize understanding and responding to the emotional needs of students; one brings the lens of recognizing and accommodating the effects of trauma on behavior and learning, while the other cultivates a practice of presence and emotional regulation to help heal these effects. **There is a synergy between the two methods and a collective aim to foster emotional well-being in students.**

Mindfulness techniques, such as focused breathing and meditation, can provide practical tools for students to manage stress and anxiety, which often stem from traumatic experiences. Meanwhile, trauma-informed care offers a compassionate framework for educators to recognize and sensitively address the impacts of trauma, which creates a safer, more supportive learning environment. **It is not an either-or situation but rather a both and.**

For example, a trauma-informed teacher will work to ensure the room is a safe and supportive environment while taking into consideration certain things that may trigger a student. They may recommend that students close their eyes while doing morning breathwork. However, this doesn't have to be the case. We always make it an option saying, "You may close your eyes if you'd like or just gaze down; or you may participate or not, but you may not disrupt others."

Unlocking SEL is designed to be a book richly laden with practical, actionable strategies. Let's explore seven specific mindful-based trauma approaches, each meticulously developed to enhance your understanding and implementation.

Trauma Informed Care and Mindfulness

Two pieces of the SEL puzzle.

Unlocking SEL's
7 Mindful-Based Trauma Approaches

✯ **MODEL MINDFULNESS:** Students who are trauma-impacted witness fragmented families and highly intense emotions. We must model the difference for them. They need us to show them and help them regulate.

✯ **PAUSE AND REFRAME:** When faced with challenging situations, take a deep breath, and look at our frame of reference instead of asking, "Could this be a trauma response?"

✯ **BE THE KEY ADULT:** We know it takes just one person who really cares about you, gets you, will be there for you, and supports you to make all the difference. This is the Key Adult. Be that person.

✯ **FOCUS ON RELATIONSHIPS:** Relationships play a crucial role in the healing and development of students who have experienced trauma. When trauma occurs, it can disrupt a child's sense of security and trust in the world. We can help build that back.

✯ **TEACH STUDENTS ABOUT THEIR BODIES:** By teaching students about their brains and stress response system, we can empower them to both know and care for themselves.

✯ **BE AWARE OF INTERSECTIONALITY:** To promote the healing power of safety, we need to attempt to understand the many reasons that can promote a lack of safety for students: racism, sexism, classism, ageism, ableism, etc. If we are teaching students who are different from us, we could run the risk of saying things that could be offensive.

✯ **TEACH SELF-REGULATION:** This is an essential component of trauma-informed care, concentrating on effectively managing dysregulation often linked to the aftermath of trauma. Incorporating Daily Mindful Moments aids students in developing and enhancing their regulation abilities

🎯 PRINCIPAL POINTS

Being a trauma-informed principal means leading with empathy and an awareness of the complex backgrounds and needs of your school community. It's about recognizing the signs of trauma in students' behavior and guiding teachers to respond with more understanding rather than harsh punishment. You can foster a nurturing environment where students feel safe to express themselves and learn. If your leadership reflects a commitment to professional development in trauma awareness for your staff, you can ensure that the entire school adopts practices supportive of healing and resilience. By setting policies and a school culture that prioritizes emotional well-being, you have the power to champion an educational atmosphere where all children have the opportunity to succeed, regardless of the challenges they face outside the classroom.

💡 TEACHER TIPS

In the realm of trauma-informed teaching, it's vital for educators to cultivate self-awareness about their emotional triggers and recognize signs of personal dysregulation. Understanding the nuances that can lead to emotional upheaval allows us as educators to maintain a composed, regulated state. By doing so, we can effectively guide students in managing their emotions, aiding them in soothing their limbic system and engaging their prefrontal cortex. As educators, our stability and calm can become the regulatory interventions of the classroom.

Chapter Summary

As we discussed, there's a critical need for trauma-informed practices in education. The 4Rs—Realize, Recognize, Respond, Resist—help us understand and implement a trauma-informed approach.

It's crucial that we create an environment that is aware and responsive to the signs and symptoms of trauma. Through the 7 Mindful-Based Trauma Approaches, we can weave mindfulness into the fabric of trauma-informed care and advocate for strategies that acknowledge the impact of trauma while also equipping students with the skills to navigate and regulate their emotional responses.

Call to Action

- **Internalize the 4 Rs of trauma:** Realize, Recognize, Respond, and Resist.

- **Incorporate mindful-based trauma-informed practices:** Look for practices that intertwine mindfulness with being trauma-informed.

Chpt. 16: Teaching Explicit SEL Lessons

"The research is clear: emotions determine whether academic content will be processed deeply and remembered."
– Mark Brackett

SEL in a Science Lesson

In addition to teaching science, 8th grade instructor Mr. Rodriquez taught his students explicit SEL lessons on a weekly basis. These lessons were compiled using a research-based student SEL curriculum. In addition to the explicit SEL lessons, Mr. Rodriguez also built his students' SEL skills by doing daily mindful moments, modeling mindfulness, and integrating all these skills into his content area of science.

One day, he introduced a group project on energy where each cooperative group had to research a form of renewable energy, create a model, and present their findings to the class. Along with the science targets he also added SEL targets: how to calm your nervous system through deep breathing, reviewing what good teamwork looks like, how to listen to different perspectives, assign roles, and then coming to a consensus all while supporting each other.

One of these students, Alex, struggled with public speaking and another Anna, had good ideas but would sometimes have difficulty listening to others. Mr. Rodriguez gave Alex the role of group leader, which encouraged him to step out of his comfort zone. Anna was assigned the role of note-taker so she could practice active listening.

Mr. Rodriguez felt incredibly proud as the group came together with a cohesive and engaging presentation. Alex spoke clearly and confidently while Anna and the rest of the team supported each other, each demonstrating a deep understanding of both of renewable energy and the importance of crucial SEL skills.

The success of Mr. Rodriguez's students, like Alex and Anna, demonstrates the tangible benefits of integrating SEL into daily lessons. This microcosm of SEL's impact within a single classroom mirrors the positive outcomes that research has consistently documented on a much broader scale. Though doing projects like this would only be a small part of a student's academic journey, you could see where the SEL skills develop and could play a significant role in their personal growth. This is where teaching explicit SEL lessons would come into play.

While the methodical teaching of SEL may be a departure from the more incidental character education of the past, it is a critical evolution that addresses the complex emotional and social needs of today's students. We can't just expect students to know or learn these SEL skills. On the contrary, we must teach them.

Let's travel back in time for a moment to your own experience as a child in school. Did you have any social and emotional learning? Probably not. Sure, many of us had the good fortune to be in classrooms where teachers fostered a sense of community or sporadically touched upon character development. However, it's a safe bet that few of us experienced structured, intentional lessons focused squarely on nurturing our social and emotional skills. I know I did not.

Oh, how times have changed—and for good reason. Today's students confront an array of challenges and traumatic experiences. From escalating levels of anxiety to a concerning rise in suicidal thoughts, the stakes have never been higher. But there is good news. **Direct, step-by-step instruction in SEL can make a world of difference in combating these issues.**

Explicit Weekly SEL Lessons

How do we teach SEL lessons? We must teach them **explicitly** during a dedicated weekly block where the focus is spotlighted specifically on a particular SEL skills or strategy.

Explicitly teaching SEL means incorporating intentional, structured lessons and practices into the curriculum that are designed to develop the competencies of self-awareness, self-management, social awareness, relationship skills, and responsible decision-making. It involves clearly defined learning objectives and outcomes that relate to these social and emotional skills, just as with any academic subject.

In practice, this could look like dedicated time each week for SEL activities and integration into existing subjects through discussions and projects. These teaching methods employ various strategies including role-playing, group discussions, reflective exercises, and personal goal setting.

By deliberately making SEL a part of the educational experience, students are provided with regular opportunities to practice and apply these new skills in a safe and supportive learning environment. Ultimately, of course, it will prepare them to navigate the complexities of their inner lives and social interactions both within and outside of school.

By embedding dedicated lessons for SEL and then weaving them into the content area, we underline its importance in holistic student development. Just as we wouldn't compromise on foundational subjects like math or science, we must prioritize SEL with the same rigor and commitment. Such proactive approaches not only fortify students' emotional intelligence but also enhance their capacity to navigate life's complexities with resilience and empathy. In the broader context of education, this is not just about curriculum enhancement—it's about preparing students for real-world challenges, both inside and outside the classroom.

On the surface, teaching SEL seems like a no-brainer. But in recognizing the crucial role of SEL, we must turn to the data to guide our implementation strategies and confirm the value of these lessons in shaping the holistic development of our students.

> ***By embedding dedicated lessons for SEL, we underline its importance in holistic student development. Just as we wouldn't compromise on foundational subjects like math or science, we must prioritize SEL with the same rigor and commitment.***

What Does the Data Say About SEL Lessons?

In the post-pandemic era, SEL is crucial as it equips students to build pro-social skills, the strategies of emotional regulation, and the resiliency needed to navigate the challenges of a rapidly changing world. The pandemic amplified stressors like isolation and lack of routines. Fortunately, SEL can help students process their emotions as well as foster empathy and develop coping strategies. All of these are vital for mental health and well-being. Additionally, SEL supports the building of a healthy school and classroom community by strengthening relationships among students, teachers, and families. In the wake of global disruption, this is now essential.

An increasing number of studies have focused on SEL, and the data emerging from these investigations highlight its significant positive impacts on students' academic performance and overall well-being.

Firstly, research has consistently shown that SEL programs can lead to improvement in students' social and emotional skills, attitudes, relationships, academic performance, and perceptions of classroom and school climate. According to the Collaborative for Academic, Social, and Emotional Learning (CASEL), students participating in SEL programs showed an 11 percentile-point gain in academic achievement. This is compared to students who did not participate in such programs.

Furthermore, SEL not only benefits academic outcomes but also plays a crucial role in mitigating problems such as bullying, aggression, and substance abuse. A meta-analysis of 213 studies involving more than 270,000 students found that SEL participants demonstrated significantly improved social and emotional skills, behavior, and attitude toward self and others. They also showed a reduction in emotional distress and conduct problems.

Long-term data also support the sustained positive impact of SEL. A follow-up study by CASEL found that the effects of SEL programs lasted for months and even years after the programs had ended, indicating the long-term benefits of these interventions. This is significant because it shows that SEL helps build a foundation for positive adjustment and success far beyond the school years.

In terms of economic impact, SEL programs are shown to be cost-effective. For every dollar invested in SEL programming, there is a return of eleven dollars, according to a study conducted by Columbia University. This return on investment comes from lower costs of public health, criminal justice, and social services, as individuals with better social and emotional competencies are less likely to need such services.

Lastly, the promotion of SEL in schools has been linked with more inclusive and safe learning environments. SEL helps to create schools where students feel heard, supported, and engaged, which are key components of a successful learning environment that encourages all students to thrive.

In sum, the data on SEL underscores its vast potential to positively transform students' lives academically, socially, and emotionally, both in the short term and for years to come. It makes a compelling case for integrating SEL into educational policies and practices at every level.

And teachers know this already. 93% of teachers believe SEL is just as important as academic learning. When implemented, SEL can increase academics and prosocial behavior while decreasing behavior problems, emotional distress, and risky behavior (CASEL, 2023). With this compelling evidence at hand, it becomes clear that as educators, we have a responsibility to prioritize SEL with the same commitment we give to core academic subjects.

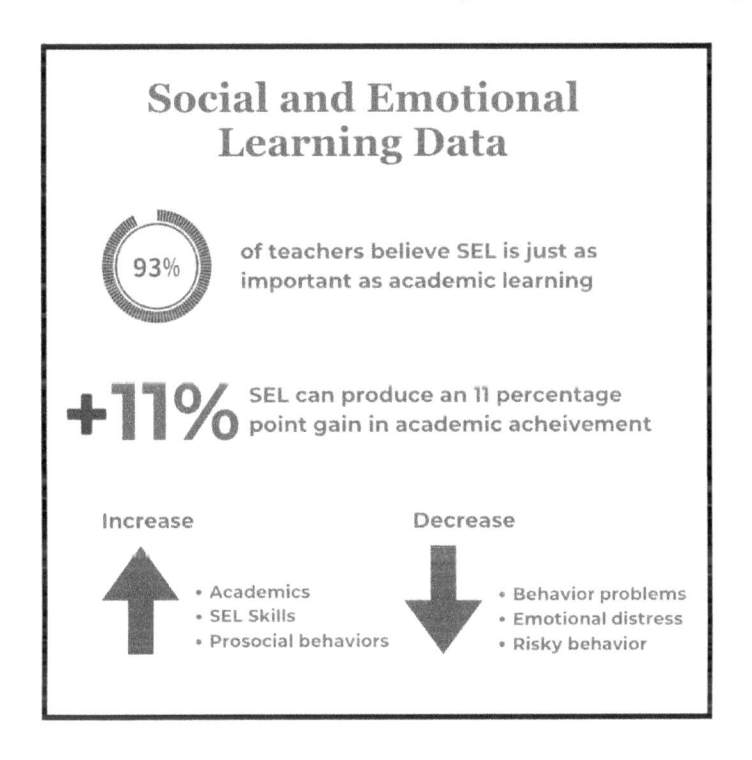

Social and Emotional Learning Data

93% of teachers believe SEL is just as important as academic learning

+11% SEL can produce an 11 percentage point gain in academic acheivement

Increase
- Academics
- SEL Skills
- Prosocial behaviors

Decrease
- Behavior problems
- Emotional distress
- Risky behavior

SEL Braided Into Content

We don't want the SEL lesson to just live within the walls of the explicit lesson. We want it to spread into the natural part of the everyday school experience. Braiding social and emotional learning into classroom content requires a strategic approach that recognizes the interconnectedness of academic learning and social and emotional development. When SEL is woven into the curriculum, it enhances the learning experience, making it more engaging and relevant to students. SEL skills are more effectively learned and retained when they are taught in context. Integrating SEL into academic content helps students see these skills' practical applications in different subjects and scenarios, thus reinforcing their learning.

SEL can be seamlessly braided into various content areas, including literacy, by using children's literature that highlights SEL themes. For instance, the book *Charlotte's Web* by E.B. White offers a profound opportunity to explore the theme of kindness. In this classic story, kindness is embodied in the actions of the spider Charlotte as she goes to great lengths to save her friend Wilbur, the pig from being slaughtered. Charlotte's selfless acts, from spinning words into her web to praising Wilbur's qualities, provide tangible examples of what kindness looks like and how it can deeply affect the lives of others.

While engaging with this text, educators can prompt discussions about how Charlotte's kindness helped Wilbur feel valued and loved and how the other characters responded to her gestures. Students can be encouraged to share personal experiences of kindness in their lives or brainstorm ways to show kindness in their school and community. Such discussions and

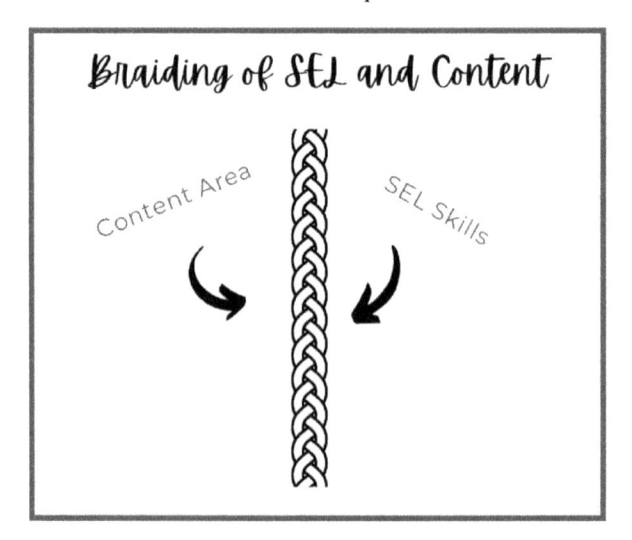

Braiding of SEL and Content

Content Area

SEL Skills

activities not only enhance comprehension of the text but also allow students to internalize the importance of kindness and reflect on how they can exhibit this trait in their own lives. Through this integration, SEL is not taught in isolation but as an intrinsic part of the academic content, making the learning experience richer and more relevant.

🎯 PRINCIPAL POINTS

In our schools, we must afford SEL the same structured attention and rigor as subjects like math or reading. The reason is simple. SEL isn't just an enhancement to the academic curriculum; it's a vital part of the foundation that supports all learning. Explicitly teaching SEL through a consistent and dedicated curriculum ensures these crucial skills are not left to chance with sporadic lessons. When SEL is embedded systematically, students receive repeated opportunities to practice and internalize skills such as empathy, self-regulation, and collaboration, much like they would with multiplication tables or grammar rules. This consistent exposure is crucial; it allows for the reinforcement and gradual building of competencies that are critical for students' academic and personal growth.

Moreover, structured SEL lessons can significantly contribute to a safer and more inclusive school culture, reducing behavioral problems and improving academic outcomes. It's about giving every student the tools to navigate not only the challenges of the curriculum but also those of their emotional and social worlds, ensuring no child's development is left to a 'hit or miss' approach.

💡 TEACHER TIPS

As you craft your lesson plans and explore your content areas, look for natural intersections where SEL can enrich and deepen the educational experience. Whether it's a character's resilience in a story that mirrors the persistence needed for problem-solving in math or the cooperation among historical figures that highlights relationship skills, SEL concepts are ripe for integration. Dive into literature that showcases empathy, highlight historical events that necessitate self-awareness and ethical decision-making, and employ scientific group inquiries that demand teamwork and effective communication.

These are but a few examples of how SEL can come alive within your curriculum. Keep in mind that SEL is not an addition to your workload but rather a lever that makes everything else easier.

Chapter Summary

When deliberately taught with the same dedication as traditional academic subjects, SEL integration is powerful. SEL's positive ripple effects on students' academic performance, emotional well-being, and social interactions make it an absolute necessity in today's classroom. We must embrace and prioritize SEL, not as a supplementary initiative but as a core pillar of education. You have the power to do this, and you can do it through organic SEL integration.

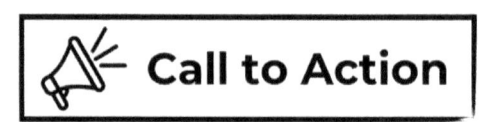

📣 **Call to Action**

- **Teach weekly SEL lessons:** To help students grow emotionally and socially, teach weekly lessons. Make these important skills a regular part of the routine.

- **Braid SEL into the content area:** Look for ways to seamlessly integrate SEL skills into subject areas. This will help students see how these skills are relevant and useful in real-time.

Chpt. 17: Creating a Peace Corner

"Peace begins with a smile."
– Mother Theresa

Angel and the Peace Corner

Angel, an eighth-grade student, was known for her vibrant energy and creative spirit. Though this combination served her well with her peers, this energy, at times, translated into disruptive behavior in the classroom. She frequently found herself in trouble, struggling to sit still during lessons, inadvertently interrupting her classmates, and disrupting the flow of the lesson. Her teachers noticed that Angel seemed restless and often overwhelmed, but they were unsure how to help her channel her energy positively.

The classroom became a bit of a tug-o-war. Angel was pushing for less restriction and more space, while the teachers were pushing for an orderly learning environment for all. Recognizing the need for balance, Angel's teachers sought to find a middle ground that could both harness her enthusiasm and maintain the classroom's learning atmosphere. They introduced structured breaks for movement and moments for mindfulness throughout the day, providing outlets for her dynamic energy. But it wasn't enough. They needed an innovative strategy to support Angel. They found it in the Peace Corner.

This was a space carved out in the room where Angel could self-select to go to gain a moment of peace and reset her nervous system.

Stories like Angel's are not unique. They happen in schools across the country every day. Students are restless and have the need to move more, have more space, and have more room to breathe. This is where the Peace Corner comes into play.

Envision a Peace Corner as a self-selected little oasis within the lively world of a classroom. Tucked away in a corner nook, this special spot is strategically placed at a comfortable distance from the classroom's energetic pulse. It's often furnished with inviting, soft seating options—perhaps a plush bean bag or a cushioned chair—that beckon students to a quieter space.

It's there, amidst the buzz of learning and activity, that the Peace Corner offers a retreat where students can still engage with class material but are afforded a gentle reprieve from the collective energy. In other words, it allows for moments of calm and self-regulation.

Let's put it in an adult context. Imagine feeling cramped on a five-hour plane ride. There is little time to get up and move, and little space to stretch out. Perhaps you feel anxiety rising in your body with each passing hour causing you to feel a sense of irritability or a lack of focus. When you feel like you MUST move, you realize the fasten seatbelt sign is on. Getting up isn't an option. The stress is really starting to get to you as your seatmate takes the armrest the moment you move your arm away reaching for a snack. You begin to watch the clock, as the minutes slowly pass like a parade of turtles.

"This is miserable," you think, promising never to be back in this situation again.

For some of our students, the airplane analogy is what it feels like to navigate the daily hustle and bustle of a busy classroom. Just as being in a tight airplane seat for hours can leave you feeling stressed, overwhelmed, and in need of a stretch, a classroom filled with activities, interactions, and constant stimuli can make some students feel similarly cramped and overwhelmed.

Now imagine that same scenario, but you CAN get up, stretch your legs, and have a bit of space to yourself. Oh, the feeling of relief.

A Peace Corner in the classroom acts much like the small luxury of an airplane's aisle where you can stand, stretch, and take a moment to breathe. It offers a brief but crucial escape from the confined space and the busyness around you. Just as a walk down the airplane aisle helps you regain your composure and feel refreshed, a visit to the peace corner allows students to step away from the confines of the classroom. It's where they can calm their minds, process their emotions, and eventually return to their seats refreshed and ready to learn.

Benefits of a Peace Corner

In practice, the Peace Corner is more than just a quiet area; it's a stepping stone to cultivating self-awareness and emotional intelligence.

Here, students are encouraged to identify their emotions, practice deep breathing, or engage with calming strategies, fostering a sense of autonomy over their feelings and actions. When a student feels overwhelmed, instead of an escalation leading to a potential classroom disruption, they have the option to retreat to a safe space and recalibrate their emotions. Over time, they can learn to recognize their signs of emotional distress and **proactively** seek out the space to support them in coming back to baseline.

Let's explore the four cornerstone benefits that the Peace Corner offers to both individuals and the classroom community as a whole.

- **Fostering Emotional Regulation:** The Peace Corner provides students with a space to practice self-regulation techniques in a non-disruptive way. By using the corner, students can take the time they need to identify their emotions, utilize coping strategies, and return to learning activities with a renewed focus and calmer disposition.

- **Reducing Classroom Disruptions:** When students have a designated area to address their emotional needs independently, it naturally leads to fewer interruptions. This dedicated space can help prevent minor issues from escalating into larger classroom management challenges, thereby maintaining a conducive learning environment for all.

- **Empowering Student Autonomy**: Utilizing the Peace Corner allows students to take personal responsibility for their emotional well-being. This empowerment is critical in helping them understand that they have control over their actions and responses. The ability to self-soothe and self-regulate without adult intervention is a valuable life skill that contributes to a student's overall personal development.

- **Supporting an Inclusive Learning Environment:** The Peace Corner supports inclusivity by acknowledging and respecting the diverse emotional needs of all students. For example, let's say a student is a quiet student, that doesn't necessarily mean that the student may not have some sort of anxiety or stress. The Peace Corner accounts for that by providing another learning option.

Peace Corner Protocol

As we know, the implementation of new things can be challenging in classrooms. The peace corner is no different. As with any routine, it's important to explain the purpose at the beginning and model how to best use it.

Unlocking SEL's Peace Corner Protocol, a thoughtfully crafted six-step guide, can empower young learners to recognize the swell of overwhelming feelings and seek solace in a safe space. Let's take a closer look at the recommended steps. Feel free to tweak the protocol as needed to tailor it to your school or classroom.

Unlocking SEL's Peace Corner Protocol

1. **Teach the tool:** Think of the Peace Corner as a tool that students can use when learning has stopped. Like any tool, students must be taught the proper way to use it before they need it.

2. **Recognize the need:** Educate students on the signs of emotional distress or overstimulation and how to recognize when they might benefit from using the Peace Corner. This step is crucial for self-awareness and ensuring that the Peace Corner is used effectively.

3. **Request permission:** Establish a non-disruptive signal or procedure that allows students to request the use of the Peace Corner. This ensures that the teacher is aware of the student's needs while maintaining the flow of the classroom activities. This is the reason I prefer the name of Peace Corner as opposed to Calming Corner. Students can make a peace sign as a quiet request to use the space.

4. **Start the timer:** Use a liquid 3-to-5-minute timer that lives in the Peace Corner. Have the student turn the timer over when they arrive. When the timer ends, the student will rejoin the class.

5. **Choose an activity**: Have a small selection of calming activities available in the Peace Corner. Encourage students to select an activity that helps them self regulate, such as deep breathing exercises, guided imagery, or a journal inviting them to reflect on their emotions and the effectiveness of the self-regulation strategies they used.

6. **Rejoin the class:** Once the student feels more regulated and the set time has elapsed, they should quietly rejoin the class activities. Ideally, the teacher will acknowledge their return with a discreet nod or gesture, affirming the student's decision to take charge of their emotional needs.

Let's revisit Angel's story. A massive turning point came in her journey when we decided to implement this Peace Corner in each classroom. Though this quiet, comfortable space was equipped with calming tools and soothing visuals, mainly, it was just a place she could go to be removed from others' energy.

Angel was initially skeptical about the Peace Corner, but, on one particularly challenging day, feeling the familiar surge of restlessness, she decided to give it a try. In the Peace Corner, Angel found a place where she could take a few minutes to breathe deeply and gather her thoughts. To her surprise, Angel felt her body relax and her mind clear.

Gradually, the Peace Corner became an essential part of Angel's routine. Whenever she felt her energy bubbling up in a way that might disrupt the class, she would quietly move to the peace corner. The short breaks there helped her to refocus and rejoin the class with a calmer demeanor.

As the principal, I noticed a significant change in her behavior. Angel was not only getting into less trouble, but she was also participating more constructively in class discussions and group activities. The Peace Corner didn't just help Angel regulate her emotions; it also gave her the tools to understand and manage her energy better. This small change in the classroom environment had a profound impact on her, turning her school experience from a series of reprimands into a journey of self-discovery and growth.

How do I know this? Angel told me. I remember that day like it was yesterday. As I went into her room, just doing my daily rounds, I looked over and saw her in the peace corner. It made sense to check in and see how she was doing. We had a very pleasant conversation, and then I left. At the time, I didn't think much of it.

Later, I saw Angel in the hallway. She said, "You know Ms. Penley, if you would have implemented the Peace Corner years ago, I wouldn't have gotten in so much trouble." I smiled, turned, and looked at her.

"Oh really, why is that?" I asked.

"It really helps me," she said before turning to walk away.

I stood there just amazed. "Wow!" I thought. "How insightful of her to say that." And kudos to her teacher for implementing something that supported Angel's well-being.

🎯 PRINCIPAL POINTS

*A mistake we made when first implementing the peace corner was providing too many tools. What was meant to support student regulation in fact became a distraction as we added fidgets, mirrors, stress balls, and more. When we reduced the number of tools to no more than three, the distraction faded, and the idea of the Peace Corner took off. The three tools I highly recommend are **a timer, a journal, and a book.** That's it.*

💡 TEACHER TIPS

A Peace Corner is not meant to be a timeout or a place of punishment. It is a place to go when learning has stopped. Peace Corners are also private, self-selected, and structured but can include choice. Some teachers like to keep documentation.

For example, a student would sign in when they go and when they leave. Other teachers find it easier to be a little less formal. Just figure out what best works for you and your classroom.

Chapter Summary

Creating a Peace Corner presents an innovative solution to the challenges of emotional dysregulation in the classroom. A strategically implemented Peace Corner can provide students with a designated area to practice self-regulation and manage overwhelming emotions. The Peace Corner not only reduces classroom disruptions but also fosters student autonomy and supports inclusivity.

The six-step protocol can guide teachers to introduce and students to effectively utilize the Peace Corner. It will offer significant help to students like Angel who, with this support, can gain valuable skills in emotional management. This has the power to create a more harmonious and productive learning experience for the entire class.

Call to Action

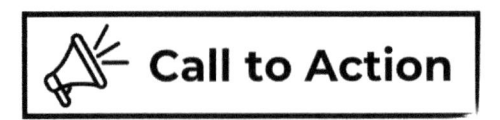

- **Explain the benefits of the Peace Corner:** Explaining the rationale behind it will help students understand the benefits of using it.

- **Teach the Peace Corner Protocol:** Go over the routines and expectations of using the Peace Corner.

This section comes with an important caveat: it's not an exhaustive list of every possible student SEL strategy, nor does it offer an in-depth analysis of each strategy discussed.

Instead, it serves as a curated collection of strategies that I've personally seen yield positive results in my own experience and observed being very effective in other schools across the country. Though due to length restraints, some very important strategies are not included, this list, when implemented can have an enormous impact on a classroom's success.

Third Key Reflection Questions
Come Into the Classroom

Question	Answer
What strategies do you use to build relationships in your classroom or school?	
When do you best model mindfulness? When do you not?	
Describe the first 15 minutes of the school day.	
How do you think a Mindful Moment would impact your classroom/school?	
What are the 4 R's of Trauma Informed Care?	
Why are explicit SEL lessons important?	
How could a Peace Corner support student well-being?	

For resources from the book, go to
www.unlockingsel.com/blueprint

The 4th Key: Scale Schoolwide

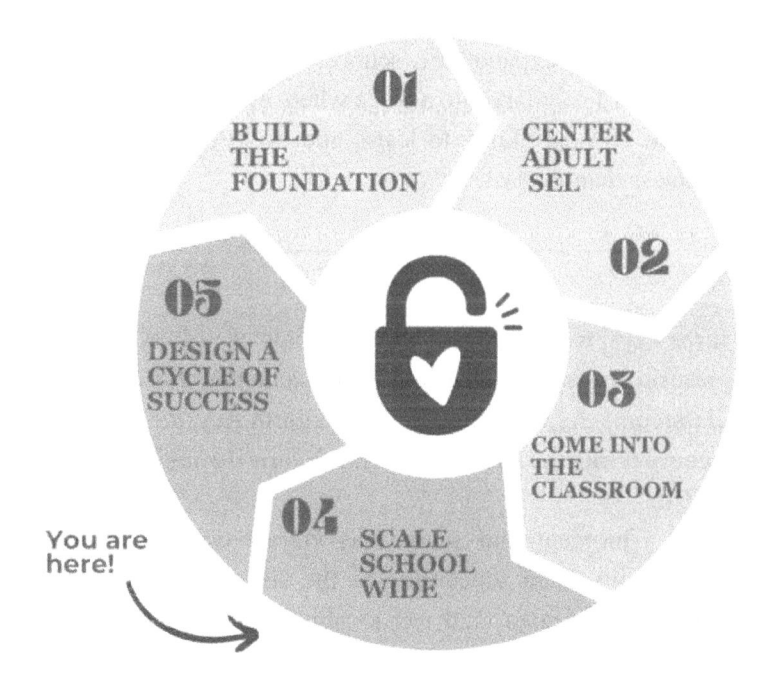

01 BUILD THE FOUNDATION
02 CENTER ADULT SEL
03 COME INTO THE CLASSROOM
04 SCALE SCHOOL WIDE
05 DESIGN A CYCLE OF SUCCESS

You are here!

Willow Elementary

At Willow Elementary, a gentle revolution began to unfold. The school, known for its cheerful murals but frenzied atmosphere, had stumbled upon the transformative power of SEL. Initially skeptical, the staff watched in disbelief as, over time, their schoolwide program turned once tumultuous classrooms into spaces of kindness and calm.

It was Ms. Bennett, a veteran first-grade teacher with an infectious smile, who first championed SEL in her classroom. Through learning about emotions, her room became a place where small voices discussed big feelings and tiny hands learned the language of kindness. The change was palpable: hallway squabbles gave way to peacemaking, and the morning rush softened to a composed Soft Start.

Seeing this, Principal Evans, whose tenacity for excellence was only matched by her love for her students, recognized the need for this serenity to spill over into every corner of Willow Elementary. She envisioned a school not as a backdrop for academic endeavor alone but as a community where emotional wisdom was as prized as the A's on report cards.

Once the initiative to expand SEL schoolwide was set in motion, it transformed Willow Elementary into a place where every voice was heard, every conflict was an opportunity to learn, and every day ended with a little more kindness than the last.

In the first three keys, we delved into the essentials of SEL by laying the foundation, prioritizing adult well-being, and channeling this energy into SEL in the classrooms. As we venture into the Fourth Key, the perspective broadens, **encompassing the entire school landscape through SCALING SCHOOLWIDE.**

Imagine, for a moment, our schools as vibrant ecosystems. Many aspects of school life, from scheduling to the steady pulse of student movement, curriculum design, and relationship-building, are intricately woven together.

It reminds me of snorkeling. I don't often have the chance to go, but when I do, I find myself submerged in an underwater realm where fish, turtles, and octopi coexist in a vibrant multicolored reef. There's a rhythm to marine life—the constant yet varied interactions with each other and with the environment. A school is much like this. If we were to draw parallels, the school and classrooms would be this intricate reef, a home where everyone, like the diverse marine animals, finds a niche to thrive.

The very structure of the school itself, like the coral formations, should offer a safe haven for our students. Every element—from the resources and support structures to the collaborative ethos—must work in unison. That is what we are working on with our Fourth Key: **The school, working together as a healthy ecosystem to create one harmonious environment.**

Why does a Schoolwide Approach Matter in SEL?

A common challenge faced in educational systems is the solitude of operations. It's easy, almost instinctive, for educators to immerse themselves deeply into their own spaces, focusing intently on their immediate environment. In these pages to come, we will dive into taking what we have learned about SEL, elevate our perspective, and engage with the school as a holistic entity. This is what we need to do to scale SEL schoolwide.

By broadening SEL beyond the confines of individual classrooms, we invite perspectives and strategies that enrich the learning environment. A schoolwide approach knits a consistent fabric of emotional and social support, ensuring that every student benefits from a culture that values empathy, self-awareness, and interpersonal skills. It is within this collective embrace that children learn to navigate the complexities of their inner world as well as their social surroundings, not in isolation, but as part of a concerted, community-driven effort.

> *It is within this collective embrace that children learn to navigate the complexities of their inner world as well as their social surroundings, not in isolation, but as part of a concerted, community-driven effort.*

Let's start with the school physical space itself.

Chpt. 18: Tending to Schoolwide Space

"This school looks like a well-cared for space. From the clean hallways to the freshly cut grounds, it's evident that we all take immense pride in this space. Our collective effort ensures a warm and welcoming environment where everyone can thrive."
– *Middle School Principal*

A Tale of Two Schools: The Power of Environment

On a recent trip, I pulled into School A. The grass was knee-high, litter from fast food restaurants was strewn about on the steps to the front door, and graffiti was rampant with multiple walls tagged. As I walked inside, the lights were dim, trash was all over the floor, and posters were falling off the wall. There was no signage as to where to go. As I waited in the main office, no one ever even said hello to me. Though I am sure it was not true, the message was that the school was not cared for.

On the other end of the spectrum was School B. I pulled into clearly marked parking spaces, the grounds were tidy with freshly cut grass, and groomed bushes and flowers were blooming. There was freshly painted signage with a welcoming and inclusive message stating that, "All are Welcome Here." As I walked inside, I noticed the walls were crisply painted, the school was bright and airy, and the hallway floors looked so clean you could see your reflection. The vibe was enhanced even further with soft music playing in the background. When I walked into the office, I was quickly greeted by a friendly face as the secretary said, "Hello there. Welcome to our school. How may I help you?" I paused, and thought to myself, "Wow, this school has it going on!"

Both schools were in the same district but with vastly different environmental impacts. Even though the assumptions made are generalizations, **we must ask ourselves which school would we want our child to attend.**

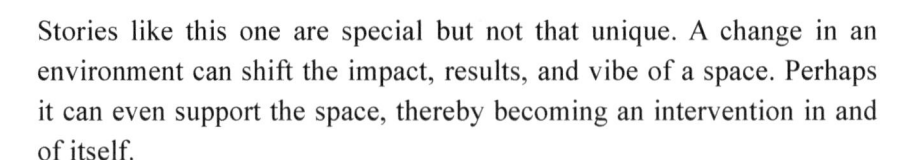

Stories like this one are special but not that unique. A change in an environment can shift the impact, results, and vibe of a space. Perhaps it can even support the space, thereby becoming an intervention in and of itself.

In working with schools, I've been fortunate enough to travel to many programs across the country, and I know firsthand just how vast the differences in school environments are! I've seen schools that are aesthetically beautiful and inviting, with clean and colorful hallways, fresh flowers, and wonderful attention to detail. I have also seen schools that are drab, gray, and monotone, with unkempt grounds, graffiti, and trash splayed about the grimy floors.

Sadly, this often correlates with the school's zip code. Repeatedly, I have seen schools in higher-income neighborhoods have better facilities than lower-income neighborhoods. **Our students, regardless of where they live, and our teachers, regardless of where they work, deserve beautiful, calming, inspiring, and engaging educational environments.**

> *Our students, regardless of where they live, and our teachers, regardless of where they work, deserve beautiful, calming, inspiring, and engaging educational environments.*

It is this understanding that brings us to consider the physical aspect of our schools as more than mere buildings—it is about creating an atmosphere that resonates with the values of education itself. Let's explore a bit more.

A Tidy and Organized School

School environments extend beyond the classroom and serve as integral parts of the learning experience. When these schoolwide spaces are tidy and organized, it means they are kept in order, clean, and free from graffiti. I am referring to the building, the playground, and common spaces such as the cafeteria, office, library, and gym. We envision these spaces as places of tranquility, order, and purpose. A well-kept school not only leaves a positive imprint on the community, but it can also elevate morale and cultivate pride, which fosters a harmonious feel for all.

A tidy and organized setting goes beyond aesthetics—it can instill an entirely new 'rhythm' of upkeep and orderliness. When people encounter a meticulously maintained school, they inherently value and uphold their standards. They *want* to keep it looking beautiful.

This extends beyond hallways and common areas—the school grounds play a pivotal role. Far from mere patches of ground surrounding our schools, these grounds can influence the holistic growth of our students. By cherishing and investing in these spaces, we enhance the quality of the educational experience.

Research conducted in Northwestern Mexico highlights the significant influence of the school environment. The school environment functions not just as a backdrop but as a dynamic element that interacts with students' learning experiences and well-being (Tapia-Film, 2020).

Unlocking SEL's 6 Ways to Tend to Space Schoolwide

1. **ROUTINE CLEANING RITUALS:** Implement daily or weekly rituals that encourage students and staff to participate in maintaining a clean school environment. This could involve classroom routines where students help tidy up at the end of the day or a rotating schedule for older students to assist with common areas.

2. **WELCOMING ENTRYWAY AND COMMON AREAS**: Ensure that entryways and common areas are not only clean but also welcoming. This can be achieved by having a well-maintained reception area with plants, comfortable seating, and displays that showcase school achievements and SEL initiatives. Regular maintenance and decluttering of these spaces are key to making a positive impression on anyone who enters the school.

3. *ADOPT A SPOT*: Engage students and staff in the care of their environment through programs that encourage responsibility and pride in the school. Initiatives like 'Adopt a Spot' where students take charge of maintaining a specific area can make a large project suddenly more manageable. You can also have different groups that focus on specific initiatives rather than spaces. For instance, 'Green Teams' focus on sustainability efforts, which fosters a culture of stewardship and collective ownership over the school's space.

4. *BEAUTIFICATION PROJECTS*: Schools can undertake beautification projects that not only improve the aesthetic appeal but also enhance the functionality of the space. This might include planting gardens, painting murals, updating furniture, or redesigning common areas to be more collaborative and student-friendly. Such enhancements can boost morale and inspire creativity.

5. **REGULAR MAINTENANCE AND UPKEEP:** Schools can implement a consistent and comprehensive maintenance routine that includes regular cleaning, repairs, and updates to the physical environment. This could involve daily cleaning schedules, seasonal maintenance checks, and timely refurbishments.

6. *LEAVE NO TRACE LESSON*: Each year, we taught a schoolwide lesson of 'Leave No Trace.' We discussed how when we enter a space, we want to leave it exactly like we found it. We connected the lesson to hiking and how we want to care for nature and not leave any trash. Reframing and renaming the concept of cleanliness went a long way in supporting our clean, organized environment.

For a PDF of our 6 *Ways to Tend to Space Schoolwide* go to the Fourth Key at www.unlockingsel.com/blueprint

Walls Reflect the School Ethos

The walls of a school, frequently unnoticed, can be the school's silent narrators. They celebrate student achievements through display boards filled with academic and extracurricular triumphs. They showcase intricate works of art, expressions of the myriad students who walk the halls. These walls are also educational pillars, plastered with pivotal content that enriches and complements the learning environment. In their quiet but profound way, these walls underscore the school's values and crystallize its identity, offering a mosaic of what education—and life within a school's halls—truly represents.

This idea really hit home with me with the visit of my new boss, Jessica. Several years ago, I eagerly anticipated Jessica's inaugural visit. Though I had many supervisors over my decade-long tenure as a principal, I had heard Jessica was a shining star, a positive light in educational leadership. I was stationed in my office, expecting her arrival through the main entrance. My heart raced as the clock's hands inched closer to the time of her arrival. I expected her to make a grand entry.

To my surprise, she chose a more discreet route, entering from the back and embarking on an impromptu tour through the school, keenly observing our walls. She navigated the corridors like someone tracing their roots, absorbing every detail—the vivid artwork created by students and the meticulously crafted posters endorsing our core values of mindfulness, equity, and SEL.

When she finally made her way to my office, she smiled warmly and extended her hand. "It's a pleasure to meet you," she said. **"I already have a sense of what this school stands for,"** she added, **her voice imbued with admiration. "It's written all over your walls."** Our school's wall space was a chapter in our story, and she read it thoroughly.

Those words made me stop in my tracks. In that moment, I felt seen—truly seen—in a way I hadn't before. And I knew that we were on the threshold of something extraordinary.

"The ride is going to be different with this supervisor." I thought. "And it is going to be good."

Fueled by that inaugural compliment, she and I began our shared journey, destined to add new chapters to those walls, stories waiting to be read by every person who entered our humble school. It was more than a good start: It was a promise.

But the impact of space is more than just physical, we also need to have a vibe of joy.

Joyful School Space

The impact of our surroundings on our emotions is undeniable. We all feel something special when entering beautiful spaces, from the coziness of the dark walls of our favorite steak restaurant to the comfortable feelings of familiarity when entering our beloved go-to coffee shop. A space's unique ability to make us feel emotions has significant implications for educational settings, which often go unnoticed.

Would it surprise you that the Global Youth Survey (Lister, 2018) revealed that 61% of students felt uninspired and unmotivated by their school environments? Probably not. In education, we don't typically factor in the 'user experience' too highly. But what if we raised the bar and held the belief that our school spaces could inspire joy? By purposefully curating school spaces emphasizing joy, we can greatly enhance the educational experience for all stakeholders.

At its core, joy is the profound experience of positive emotion. It manifests in laughter, engaging conversations, smiles, and an overall uplifting demeanor. Beyond just feeling good, joy offers many benefits, such as improved physical health, stress reduction, enhanced creativity, and a heightened sense of happiness. Given its importance, why isn't joy central to our discussions about the future of education?

Well, some forward-thinkers are trying to change that. In Ingrid Fetell Lee's illuminating TED Talk (Lee, 2018), *Where Joy Hides and How to Find It*, Lee speaks to the importance of finding joy in our everyday lives and how joy isn't some superfluous extra; it's directly connected to our fundamental drive towards a bountiful life. Lee adds that tangible things, like schools, can make us feel intangible things like joy.

Ms. Lee also highlights the commendable efforts of the non-profit Publiccolor. By painting school buildings in vibrant hues, Publiccolor hoped to foster a more jubilant atmosphere for learners. The results? As Lee shares, graffiti in schools nearly vanished, and students reported feeling much safer. She suggests that our affinity for color might be evolutionary; vibrant colors signify life and abundance, crucial for survival. Further research corroborates the positive effects of color, as individuals working in colorful offices tend to be more alert, confident, and amiable compared to those in drab spaces.

In essence, a joyful environment does more than just uplift spirits—it transforms the educational experience. From fostering participation and nurturing a positive school culture to optimizing learning and retaining top-notch staff—a joyful setting is instrumental. Joy isn't merely a transient emotion; it's a cornerstone of the educational journey. It deepens, enriches, and transforms schools from mere institutions into thriving hubs of happiness and personal growth.

> *Joy isn't merely a transient emotion; it's a cornerstone of the educational journey. It deepens, enriches, and transforms schools from mere institutions into thriving hubs of happiness and personal growth.*

I want to end this chapter by sharing a story of what can happen when a school embraces the idea of tending to space and it becomes a schoolwide norm.

As I was walking down the hallway one day, I turned the corner to see two students walking side by side about 20 feet or so ahead of me. I saw the student on the right drop a baseball-sized, wadded-up piece of paper. And before I could even say anything, the student on the left, who was walking with him said, "Hey, remember Leave no Trace." Without missing a beat, the other student picked up the paper and kept it moving. It was just two kids going about their day caring for our school, but its effect on me was profound.

I did not say a word. I just stood there not believing my eyes. Sometimes students can do way more than we think they can if we just set them up for success.

'Tending to Space' is not just the responsibility of adults but everyone within the walls of the school. We all deserve to learn and work in beautiful and inspiring spaces.

🎯 PRINCIPAL POINTS

As a principal, it was very important for me to uphold the standard of a beautiful building and grounds, but the truth is, it was never an easy task. It took a lot of energy and resources, but in the end, it was always worth it. I wanted people to FEEL like they were in a special place the second they walked into the building. And that can only happen in a place that looks and feels cared for.

P.S. Make sure the staff lounge is calming, organized, and peaceful and reflects this same type of ethos.

💡 TEACHER TIPS

After tidying and organizing, see if you can add some splashes of vibrant color to your classroom. You don't need too much, just enough to spark some inspiration. You could even have the students vote on what color they would like to add.

A note of caution: in some districts it is okay to paint some walls in your classrooms but in other places it is against policy. Although, I must admit that I always found a way to paint my walls and office. Shhhhh!

Chapter Summary

The stark contrasts between School A's neglect and School B's nurturing environment underscore how the physical space of a school can profoundly affect both perception and reality. Tending to the physical space is not merely about aesthetics; it's about broadcasting a message of care, respect, and community values. The tale of two schools serves as a compelling call to action, challenging us to look beyond the surface to the heart of what our educational spaces could and should be—a place where every student and teacher feels valued and inspired. We can reimagine our schools not just as buildings, but as canvases of possibility. What do the walls of our schools reflect? Do they showcase our aspirations and shared values?

📢 Call to Action

- **Examine your school space with fresh eyes:** What looks visually pleasing and welcoming? Where can things be tidied up?

- **Watch Ingrid Fetell Lee's illuminating TED Talk:** *Where Joy Hides and How to Find It.*

- **Ask yourself, does your space inspire joy?** If so, what about it makes you feel joyful? If not, what could you add to bring more joy?

Chpt. 19: Implementing an Anchor Curriculum

"If we want students to be grateful, kind, and compassionate, we must teach gratitude, kindness, and compassion."
– Lana

The Story of Mariposa Elementary

Mariposa Elementary, set against the bustling backdrop of a large West Coast city, once found itself in a season of struggle. Test scores were a perennial concern, student engagement was waning, and teachers felt the weight of challenges too complex for traditional methodologies to address. In the classrooms, a mosaic of backgrounds and stories unfolded each day, but the school lacked the tools and resources to harness this into academic and community strengths. There was a palpable desire for change, a yearning to turn the tide and uplift every student not just in grades but in life skills and emotional resilience.

The school decided to integrate a full SEL implementation framework including delivering their chosen student SEL curriculum. With it in place, Mariposa Elementary became a hive of concerted effort. Teachers trained eagerly, staff aligned their roles with SEL objectives, and weekly SEL lessons were taught to all students. The school's leadership rallied the community around this shared vision of social and emotional learning.

Systemwide implementation was not without its challenges, but with the added strategy of a student SEL curriculum, shifts began to happen. As the lessons began to layer, new transformations strengthened with each passing week. The school shifted, and everyone could feel it. The hallways were beginning to echo, not of high tension and dysregulation but with a common language of feelings and friendship, conflict resolution, and self-management.

Anchor Curriculum

Imagine a school as a boat navigating the choppy waters of education. The SEL direct instruction curriculum is its anchor, grounding the school with the principles of SEL. Just as an anchor keeps a ship steady against the current, the anchor student SEL curriculum provides a stable foundation amidst the ebb and flow of educational trends and challenges. It is the steadfast base from which all SEL activities extend and ensures that even when new approaches or programs ripple through the school, it remains securely rooted in its core mission of SEL.

Over the years, I've had the chance to work with or see in action a variety of SEL curriculums: Tool Box, Mind UP, PBIS, 7 Mindsets, and Character Strong to name a few. Each curriculum has brought its strengths to the forefront, offering insights crucial for navigating the waters of SEL. Yet, setting sail with the right SEL curriculum can feel overwhelming as the sea of options widens.

It's like choosing the right anchor: too light, and you drift aimlessly; too heavy, and you might resist pulling it up to move forward. The key is finding that balance–selecting an SEL curriculum that holds your school firmly in place without hindering your journey towards progress. Remember, while the anchor is essential and it is important to make an informed decision on the SEL curriculum, progress is much more important than perfection.

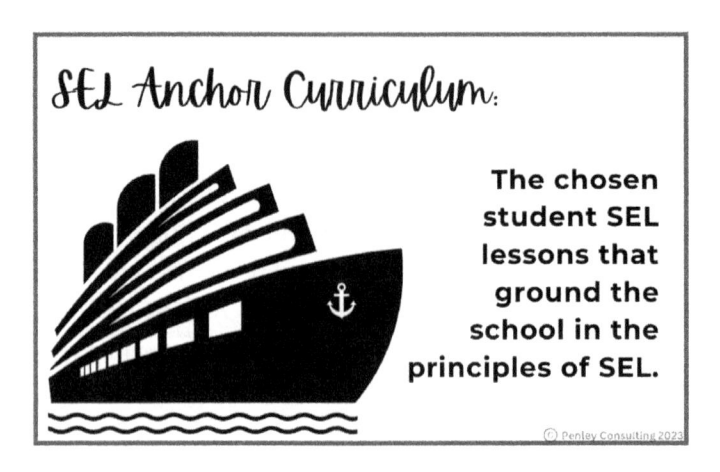

SEL Anchor Curriculum: The chosen student SEL lessons that ground the school in the principles of SEL.

Let's look at four reasons schools need an anchor curriculum:

- **Supporting teachers**: It eliminates the burden on teachers who might otherwise struggle to find or create their own resources, ensuring that educators can focus more on effective teaching rather than curriculum development.

- **Providing structure:** It provides an organized approach that lays out clear outcomes, specifying which social and emotional skills students should acquire and demonstrate.

- **Building unity**: It serves to create a unified vision and a standard set of goals across all classrooms and grade levels.

- **Developing skills**: It allows for sequential skill development, wherein each skill builds upon the last. This not only creates a logical progression but also offers age-appropriate activities tailored to facilitate each stage of skill development.

As we anchor our educational journey with a well-chosen SEL curriculum, ensuring that every student and teacher has the support and structure to thrive, we must now navigate into the crucial waters of equity.

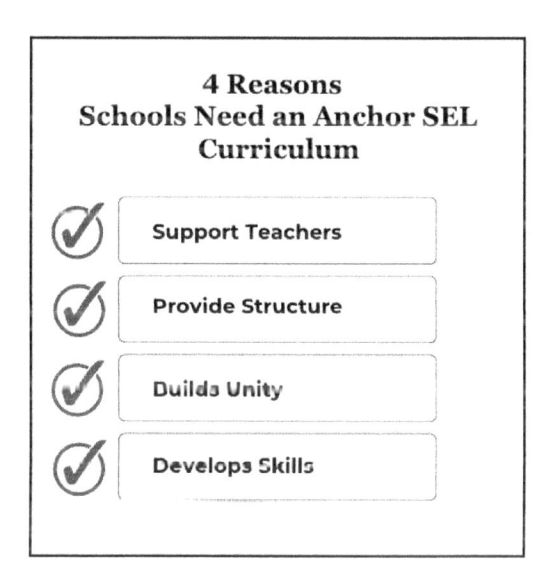

4 Reasons Schools Need an Anchor SEL Curriculum

- ✓ Support Teachers
- ✓ Provide Structure
- ✓ Builds Unity
- ✓ Develops Skills

Use an Equity Lens

Our chosen anchor curriculum must not only hold our schools in place during the shifting tides of education but also promote fair and inclusive practices that are as critical to the journey as the anchor itself. Through SEL, we want to cultivate school communities in which all students can flourish and benefit from an education that nurtures their overall development. Sadly, this isn't a reality for all students. We all know that there are significant disparities in both the experiences and outcomes of different students. This can be influenced by factors such as race, language, socioeconomic status, disability, sexual orientation, and identity. Therefore, in any anchor curriculum we choose, we want to ensure it has an equity lens.

To support this more inclusive stance, CASEL has created what it calls "Transformative SEL, "which is described as a form of SEL implementation, built on strong, respectful, and lasting relationships. It offers a critical examination of individual and contextual factors that contribute to inequities offering collaborative solutions that lead to personal, community, and societal well-being. We are aiming for a learning environment that is caring and just focuses on:

- **Identity:** How adults and students see themselves as individual beings and members of a large world.
- **Agency:** The feeling of being in control and capable of making your own choices that lead to positive change.
- **Belonging:** Feeling accepted, respected, and included within a community or group.
- **Collaborative problem-solving:** Capacity to create mutual understanding and collectively work towards a solution by merging different perspectives.
- **Curiosity:** Being open to new ideas and different perspectives.

We must remember that inclusive SEL instruction involves making connections with our students' lived experiences, identities, and cultures. This requires allowing for opportunities where students can use their voices.

SEL must support equity to create an inclusive and fair educational environment where every student can develop the critical emotional and social skills needed to thrive. Without an equitable lens, SEL is incomplete at best. At worst, it risks perpetuating systemic inequality, failing to address the diverse needs and experiences of all students to ensure lifelong success and well-being.

The Story of Jose

Let's look at a particular student to see how this could play out. Jose, a bright-eyed third grader at Mariposa Elementary who loved to draw, often found himself lost in translation. His mind was full of the rich threads of his native language, but English, with its strange twists and unfamiliar sounds, was a maze he struggled to navigate. The school, a mosaic of cultures, buzzed with chatter, yet Jose sometimes felt like a silent observer, and he yearned to find his voice.

As the school embraced SEL, lessons on belonging and identity began to bridge the divide. An SEL activity that involved sharing stories about their favorite things made Jose feel important and connected to his new community; his classmates listened attentively as he recounted stories from his culture, stories of football and fun. His words painted pictures in the air.

His teacher, Ms. Alvarez, recognized the power of these SEL lessons that could not only teach empathy and understanding but could also empower students like Jose. In each lesson, she skillfully wove in principles of equity, ensuring that every child, no matter their language or background, had their moment to shine. Group activities were crafted to foster unity through diversity, allowing Jose to take the lead through his gift for art. As each day unfolded, Jose's sense of isolation was replaced by a feeling of community, his newfound confidence a testament to the inclusive spirit nurtured through SEL.

This approach enabled Jose and his peers to discover common ground, sparking curiosity and promoting the exchange of diverse perspectives in a collage of collaborative learning.

As Jose's story illustrates, there is a profound impact when we embrace individuality and foster a sense of belonging. It's clear that selecting the right SEL anchor curriculum is pivotal.

Here are six steps to guide you in making an informed and effective choice for your SEL program:

Unlocking SEL's 6 Steps to Choosing a SEL Anchor Curriculum

1. **Review evidence-based programs:** Check out the program guide on CASEL's website for a detailed list (https://bit.ly/3TrobZS)

2. **Ask questions:** What is the evidence of effectiveness? What training and support is offered? Which level does it focus on: elementary, middle school, or high school? How does it support educational equity? Does it include an adult SEL piece?

3. **Speak to others for user experience:** Speak to other schools and educators who use SEL programs to get their take on it.

4. **Bring in various perspectives**: Speak to staff, students, families, and community members to gain input.

5. **Decide**: Too often we don't move to act, because we want every decision to be perfect. Don't suffer from analysis paralysis. Make a choice and stick with it

6. **Implement a plan**: Create a multi-year implementation plan and get going.

6 Steps to Choose a SEL Anchor Curriculum

1. Review evidence-based programs
2. Ask questions
3. Speak to others for user experience
4. Bring in various perspectives
5. Make a Decision
6. Make a Plan

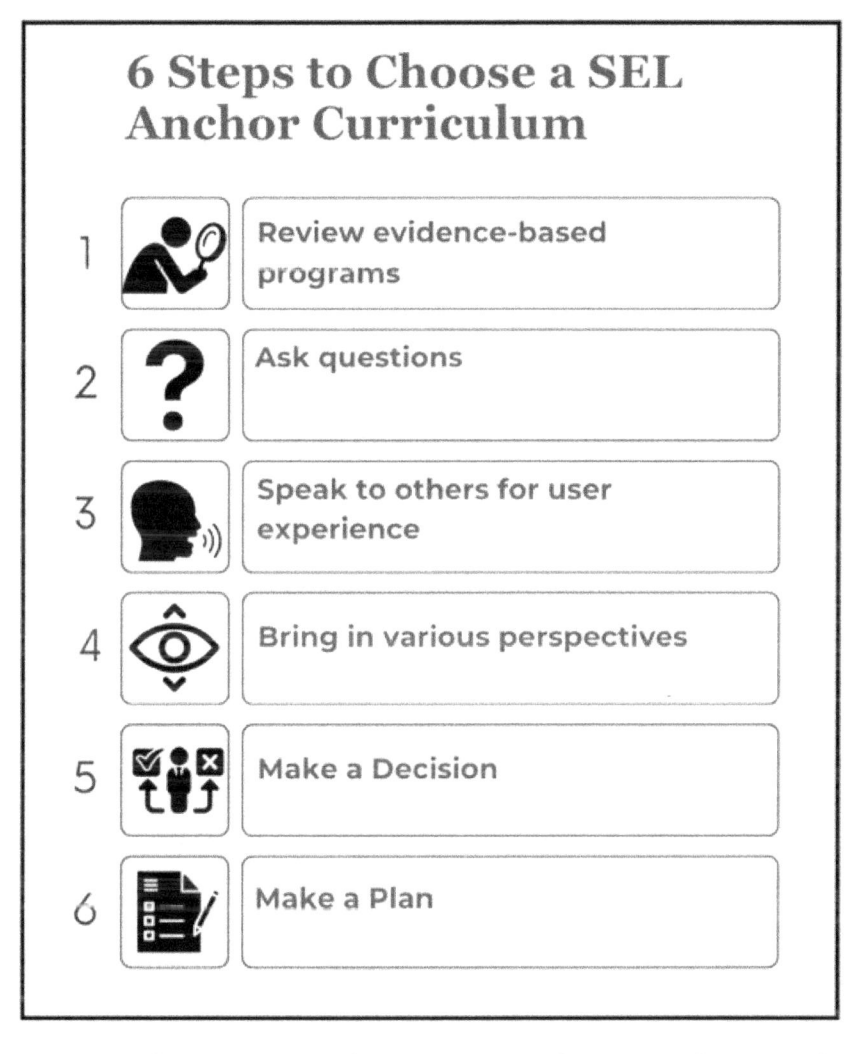

For a PDF of our 6 *Steps to Choose an SEL Anchor Curriculum,* go to the Fourth Key www.unlockingsel.com/blueprint

Intentional Rollout

Once you have decided on an anchor curriculum, it is time to be intentional with the rollout. Too many times I have seen poorly rolled-out school initiatives. This is too important. It's crucial to put in the time and effort to get the rollout right. When thinking about the rollout, there are three main areas of focus:

ALL STAFF: Training the entire staff in SEL is essential for a unified and effective approach to schoolwide implementation. When everyone from teachers to administrative staff understand and apply SEL principles, consistency can be ensured across all student interactions. This integrated approach helps embed SEL as a core part of the school culture, not just a segment of the curriculum. It helps to foster a supportive and empathetic learning environment.

ADULT MODELING: Practice adult modeling, which is one of the key components of SEL. Students learn by observing the behaviors of adults around them. Thus, when the staff members are practicing the same SEL principles, like gratitude, empathy, and emotional regulation, it sets a powerful example. Though most adults know these traits, it can be helpful to unpack them a little deeper with professional development.

ONGOING TRAINING: Make the training ongoing. There is no one-and-done around here. After the initial training is complete, it's crucial to actively oversee the rollout to make sure the training is continuous.

We have all been to the exciting staff meeting where everyone left feeling motivated and inspired, believing they could collectively change the world. But life seems to take over eventually, and the training doesn't stick. We need to have a process for ongoing learning that keeps the work right in front of us. A way to ensure ongoing learning is to dedicate at least one staff meeting each month exclusively to the SEL rollout. During these meetings, staff can share feedback, discuss challenges, and celebrate success stories. Regular check-ins allow for fine-tuning your approach and keep the momentum moving upward!

🎯 PRINCIPAL POINTS

In my experience, the best practice is to do a whole staff SEL training at the beginning of the year, and by all staff, I mean everyone. If it is a whole school initiative, we want the whole staff there. Following this kickoff, monthly staff meetings should be scheduled to maintain momentum, review progress, and address any emerging challenges.

If organizing whole-staff training or monthly meetings proves to be logistically challenging due to scheduling conflicts, budget constraints, or other issues, alternative methods should be considered. Online training modules can serve as a flexible yet effective substitute, allowing staff to engage with material at their own pace while still covering essential topics. Similarly, utilizing Professional Learning Communities (PLC) time for targeted training sessions can be another viable option. PLCs provide a collaborative space for educators to discuss, analyze, and improve their teaching practices. Integrating training into such meetings can be an efficient way to ensure staff are continually learning and growing.

💡 TEACHER TIPS

What should you do if your school lacks an SEL curriculum? My suggestion would be to take advantage of one of the no-cost online resources, such as Choose Love, and start integrating it into your classroom activities. Follow the guidelines provided as if you're running a small, independent school within your classroom. With any luck, the success you experience could serve as the catalyst for introducing a schoolwide SEL curriculum.

Chapter Summary

The SEL curriculum that each school implements serves as the keystone for fostering an environment where academic growth and social and emotional development are interwoven. The selection of an SEL curriculum acts as an anchor, offering stability and direction amidst the shifting tides of educational demands and societal changes.

The right anchor curriculum can support teachers, provide structure, and build across various educational levels, facilitating sequential skill development. We also must progress with intention rather than striving for elusive perfection, paving the way for a discussion on the crucial role of equity in SEL and how an inclusive approach is essential for a truly comprehensive education.

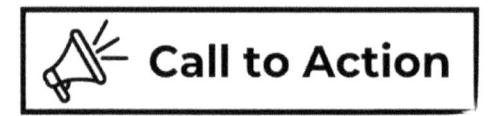

Call to Action

- **Explore evidence-based SEL programs:** Look up the CASEL website and begin to gather information. Narrow the decision down to two or three.

- **Engage your community:** Ask for input on the chosen ones.

- **Commit to the choice:** Make an informed decision and get going.

- **Schedule ongoing trainings:** Calendar out ongoing PD to keep the momentum going.

Chpt. 20: Building a Schoolwide SEL Block

"There is no power for change greater than a community discovering what it cares about."
– Margaret J. Wheatley

The Power of the Weekly SEL Block

In the heart of a bustling district, the Middle School had been striving to navigate the complex journey of school transformation through SEL. Teachers were passionate, and resources were available, yet something was amiss. The attempt to infuse SEL into the school day was sporadic, with each classroom adrift on its own course. Lessons were conducted at the discretion of each teacher. It resulted in a fragmentation of well-meaning efforts that seldom intersected. Students received uneven exposure, and the staff grew frustrated at the lack of results.

The turning point came when the SEL leadership team, after much reflection and consultation, instituted a clearly defined weekly SEL block. It was decided that SEL would no longer be left to chance or crammed into the margins of the school day. Instead, every Monday morning, the entire school would drop anchor and engage in SEL.

This decisive action created a ripple effect that brought about a cultural shift within the school community. A collective focus during this dedicated time meant that every student and teacher were now connected, with shared experiences and common language. It was in these synchronized moments of learning and reflection that the school began to truly transform.

Choosing the right anchor curriculum for SEL is pivotal; equally crucial is pinpointing *the ideal time for all to teach it*. This common time for SEL implementation is called a SEL block. Building a common SEL block—time earmarked solely for focused SEL instruction—can be transformative.

I've seen firsthand, while assisting and mentoring schools in their own SEL implementation, that this aspect is often overlooked. When that happens, it's always to the program's detriment.

An example of a common SEL block could be each Monday from 9:00-9:45 am when the entire school teaches a SEL lesson. That means no specials and no small group instruction, just a schoolwide focus on SEL. Imagine the synergistic impact of an entire school focused on a singular lesson at once.

Let's draw a parallel with how we teach science as an example. We don't leave the instruction of scientific concepts to chance by simply saying, "Make sure you teach some science." Rather, educators are given specific time blocks allocated for that purpose and often directed that: "This is your designated science block; these are the hours dedicated solely to science instruction." SEL deserves the same level of planning and specificity. But **why** do we need a schoolwide common SEL block?

First, a SEL block allows for a **systemic approach**. When we set aside designated time to discuss SEL, we ensure it receives the attention it deserves. You don't have to worry about it being taught in classrooms, because you know it is being taught within the dedicated time frame. This method takes the pressure off teachers struggling to decide where and when they'll teach SEL; time built in and set aside makes this simple.

In addition, a SEL block creates **consistency and continuity.** When teachers and administrators decide on a dedicated SEL block, instruction becomes more consistent and continuous throughout the year. It helps administration, counselors, and others outside of the classroom know what is being taught.

Finally, a SEL block is a **proactive measure.** Implementing it is proactive in building a positive school climate, fostering a sense of community, and improving academic performance. With regular practice and reinforcement to help build their skills, students can internalize and apply them in different situations throughout their lives—both at home and in the classroom.

3 Reasons
Schools Need a Common SEL Block

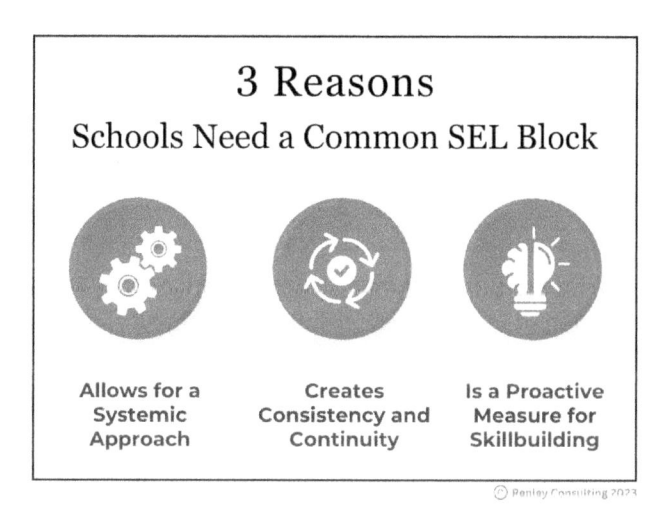

| Allows for a Systemic Approach | Creates Consistency and Continuity | Is a Proactive Measure for Skillbuilding |

© Penley Consulting 2023

When I discuss implementing a schoolwide SEL block, various obstacles may come to mind. Let's explore some of these challenges.

Obstacle #1: There is no time in the schedule.
Solution: One of the first things I hear when talking about this strategy is that we don't have time. Integrating a dedicated block into the day can be challenging, especially in schools where curriculum time is already stretched thin. Some ways to address this could be utilizing health minutes for these lessons as the lessons are about well-being or shortening the other subjects by five minutes on the day you have the SEL block.

One thing to keep in mind is that when we spend time on the front end, supporting and building students' social skills and emotional regulation, classroom disruption goes down and relationships strengthen. This, in turn, creates a positive classroom environment. In other words, you get the time back in spades.

Obstacle #2: There is a lack of staff training and buy-in.
Solution: Effective SEL implementation requires well-trained staff who are committed to it; however, ensuring that everyone is trained and on board can be a significant challenge. Some staff may feel resistant, skeptical, or simply unprepared. Some ways to address this could be: ensuring staff have a voice in the process, providing time for staff to prepare for lessons, and ensuring everybody has been trained.

Obstacle #3: Pay attention to the diverse needs and ensure inclusivity.

Solution: Many of our schools have a very diverse student population. Addressing these diverse emotional and social needs with a single SEL program can be complex. There is a risk that this one-size-fits-all approach may not adequately cater to the unique experiences and backgrounds of all students, such as those from different cultural backgrounds or with varying emotional and learning needs.

One way to address that is to ensure that the SEL curriculum you choose is inclusive and adaptable—you could add a lesson if you see one is needed but not offered. For example, we realized our students needed a lesson on how to apologize. We noticed the curriculum we used did not have a lesson on apologies, so we just created that lesson, and because we had a space reserved, we were able to push it out to all students.

Allocate a Weekly Designated Block

Allocating a specific weekly slot for your SEL block isn't just a matter of scheduling; it's a cornerstone practice that can significantly influence the success of the program. This decision is far from trivial, as I've observed in my consultations with various schools committed to providing SEL support. The common challenge schools face is finding a common goal among the competing demands of the school day. It's a complex dance of balancing academic priorities, staff availability, and the diverse needs of students, which often leaves SEL struggling to find its place.

Yet, I cannot stress enough the vital importance of this commitment. Securing a regular, uninterrupted time for SEL lays a robust foundation for consistent, impactful learning experiences. Establishing this common SEL block does more than just add structure; it signals to students and educators alike that their emotional and social development is as valued as their academic growth. This dedicated time often becomes a powerful tool, transforming the sporadic nature of SEL into a deliberate, meaningful practice that nurtures resilience and emotional intelligence schoolwide.

Protect and Name the SEL Block

Once you've pinpointed your schoolwide designated SEL block—for instance, let's say it's every Monday from 8:00 to 8:45 am—the next vital step is to protect this time. By 'protected,' **I mean the block should be exclusively reserved for SEL direct instruction**. No pull-outs for specialized programs, no 'specials' like art or music, and no field trips should interrupt this period. It's critical to protect this time for all students. This is one reason I advocate placing the SEL block early in the day.

Why is this time block so crucial? Fundamentally, it's an issue of equity. When we make sure the SEL block is always respected and kept free from interruptions, we ensure that all students, without exception, benefit from these important lessons.

I've seen the pitfalls of deviating from this approach in real time. In one of my classroom observations of an SEL lesson, an English Language (EL) teacher entered the room at the start of the lesson and called her EL students to leave the room with her. This both disrupted the classroom teaching and learning flow and had the inadvertent effect of segregating these students, cutting them off from a crucial opportunity to bond with their classmates and partake in essential SEL skill-building.

The teacher meant nothing of it. She and I chatted later, and we made the change to have her pull the students following the SEL lesson. In fact, the EL teacher was happy to pop in to support the classroom.

I recognize that the complex nature of school schedules, especially in the upper grades, can make this a challenging task. However, maintaining these boundaries around your SEL block is not simply possible—it's essential. It's a defining factor that elevates a school from being merely *good* to *truly great*.

Respecting the boundaries of the SEL block ensures that social and emotional learning is not a privilege afforded to some but a right accessible to all. It sends a message loud and clear: Emotional and social competence are as important to us as any academic subject. Moreover, it's deserving of dedicated time and universal participation.

After zeroing in on the time for your SEL block and setting protective boundaries around it, the next step is to give it a name. In our case, we chose "Wellness Wednesday," and the impact was immediate. Suddenly, this wasn't just an anonymous slot in a crowded schedule; it became an event—a dedicated time everyone knew was earmarked for vital SEL instruction.

> *Maintaining boundaries around your SEL block is not just possible—it's essential. It's a defining factor that can elevate a school from being merely good to truly great.*

Naming something lends it power, especially in educational settings. It does more than just label an activity; it solidifies it with significance and clarity. By naming your SEL block, you're not just allocating time for social and emotional learning—you're elevating it to the status of a community-wide priority. This creates a cultural touchpoint that students, teachers, and even parents can identify with and rally around.

Whether it's a name with a positive intention like "Mindfulness Monday," "Thoughtful Thursday," or your own unique moniker, a well-chosen name serves as both a rallying cry and a constant reminder of social and emotional learning's importance. It turns your SEL block from an abstract concept into a concrete, identifiable part of your school's educational fabric.

Here is an example of a SEL block with time, day, name, and topic.

SEL Block Example

SEL Block Time: 8:00-8:45
Day: Each Wednesday
Name: Wellness Wednesday
Today's Topic: Self-Regulation

The time dedicated to our block will be different depending on the grade level.

For example:
Grades K-2nd   9:00-9:25- a 25 minute lesson
Grades 3rd-8th   9:00-9:40- a 40 minute lesson
Grades 9th-12th   9:00-9:50- a 45 minutes lesson

🎯 PRINCIPAL POINTS

If specialized teachers don't have their own classes to teach during this period, they can serve as invaluable resources to reinforce SEL efforts across the school. They can co-teach or assist in classrooms with a substitute, ensuring that the SEL instruction remains consistent and effective. Their expertise could also be particularly useful in classrooms where students may need extra guidance or individualized attention during SEL activities.

In essence, special teachers can serve as roving mentors, going to classrooms to build rapport and help create a more enriched, focused, and supported SEL experience. This not only maximizes the use of your staff but also elevates the quality of the SEL instruction.

💡 TEACHER TIPS

When planning your SEL block, consider the different needs of each grade level, as one size does not fit all. Younger students in grades K-2 may find that a 25-30-minute lesson is just right for their attention spans and developmental stage. For those in grades 3 through 8, extending the block to 40 minutes can provide the additional time needed for deeper engagement and reflection. Meanwhile, high school students in grades 9 through 12 may benefit from a 45-minute session, allowing for a more comprehensive exploration of SEL topics appropriate for their level of maturity and the complexity of the issues they face. This tiered approach ensures that each SEL block is tailored to the developmental nuances and educational needs of the students. Because when we maximize the effectiveness of this time, it helps cultivate their social and emotional skills.

Chapter Summary

It's critical that schools have designated SEL time woven into the schedule. This intentional time acts as the cornerstone of social and emotional development within the educational process.

Schools encounter many pitfalls when SEL is left to chance without a structured timetable. Often, it leads to sporadic, unequal delivery and a diminished impact on student growth. But with a clear, schoolwide SEL block in place, SEL instruction can be synchronized across all classrooms. By cementing a set period each week for SEL, educators ensure consistency, equity, and a shared commitment to the holistic development of every student. Ultimately, this fosters an environment where social and emotional learning is given the same priority and meticulous planning as core academic subjects.

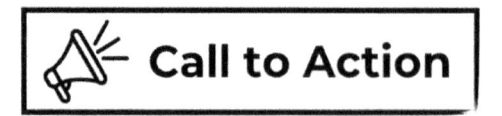

Call to Action

- **Set a designated weekly time for SEL:** After looking at the school schedule, decide what makes the most sense and ensure the whole staff is teaching the lesson.

- **Protect the SEL block from disruptions:** We must watch for disruptions given how precious time is in school. It's easy to let things take away from the SEL time, so it's important to guard it.

- **Name and celebrate the SEL block:** Decide as a staff how you want to name this block. Make sure to stick to the name and then celebrate when students make the right choice.

Chpt. 21: Following an SEL Scope and Sequence

"Kindness is a universal language"
– RAKtivist

The Roadmap: A Unified SEL Journey

As the principal, I watched with a mixture of pride and concern as our SEL curriculum initially took root. Our staff embraced the new framework with genuine enthusiasm, eager to nurture our students' social and emotional capabilities alongside academic achievement.

But something wasn't quite right. Despite our best efforts, the approach felt disjointed. Without a common thread tying the lessons together, our school's SEL journey resembled a well-intentioned patchwork rather than the cohesive unit we aspired to weave. Each classroom was a bit of an island, with its unique interpretation of what should be taught in our SEL anchor curriculum.

The breakthrough came when we introduced a scope and sequence to serve as our roadmap for SEL. It guided not just what we taught, but when and how we moved forward together. This roadmap provided direction and continuity, ensuring that every step taken was part of a deliberate path towards our goal.

The unity that scope and sequence brought to our school was nothing short of remarkable. For example, when the SEL focus was kindness, we adopted a "Marysville Gives Back" program during which each class, from the vibrant kindergarteners to the sophisticated eighth graders, dove into lessons to design a service project to support those who supported our school. In second grade, the children grew their own flowers, and then when the time came, made a neighborhood field trip to deliver the goods. It was the cutest site to see the parade of students, staff, and parents bring their flowers in a little red wagon, knock on the neighbor's door, and leave a carefully grown flower. And it wasn't just the littles. The eighth graders had their own special project designing and building a lemonade stand. When they were done making it, we held a field trip to the district office and they handed out free lemonade to tired, thirsty employees.

This simultaneous focus created a buzz, a wave of positive energy that you could feel in the air. The synergy was tangible; doors opened to discussions about kindness in the lunchroom, playground, and even spilled over to the community. It was as if our entire school building had synchronized to the rhythm of kindness. It transformed our space into a living lesson of empathy and connection.

No matter where you are going, you need a map to get you there. That is exactly what the yearlong SEL scope and sequence was for us. It was a strategic roadmap guiding everyone through a structured journey toward emotional intelligence and well-being. This structured framework outlines not just what skills and competencies will be covered but also when they will be taught, ensuring a developmentally appropriate approach.

But let's dig a bit deeper. Why do we need a SEL scope and sequence?

- **It provides for targeted skill development:** An SEL scope and sequence allows educators to target specific skills at appropriate times, ensuring that lessons are developmentally suitable and that students acquire and build upon SEL skills in a structured manner, much like they would in academic subjects.

- **It promotes consistency:** A scope and sequence ensures consistency between SEL lessons. For example, let's say the SEL practice is gratitude, and you plan to teach it on September 7. On September 8, everyone will know that all students have had the lesson on gratitude.

- **It builds community**: Establishing a schoolwide SEL scope and sequence fosters community as the whole school knows what everyone else is doing. The direction teachers and students are traveling is clear. It also creates a common language that unites the community even further.

- **It supports measurable progress and outcomes:** With a clear scope and sequence, schools can set specific goals, track progress, and measure outcomes more effectively. This helps assess the impact of the SEL program, identify areas for improvement, and demonstrate accountability to stakeholders from parents to the entire community.

I've seen schools attempt to implement SEL without a schoolwide scope and sequence, and the result can be a series of obstacles. These range from inconsistent delivery of SEL across classrooms to logistical hurdles like scheduling conflicts. Teachers may even struggle to integrate SEL lessons into an already packed day. This can lead to a scattered approach to social and emotional learning, where efforts are sporadic and uncoordinated between classes and grade levels. Educators may struggle to build upon previous lessons or skills, leading to gaps in students' SEL development and missed opportunities for deeper understanding.

Ultimately, this can result in a school environment where the full potential of SEL is not realized, and the impact on students' growth and school culture falls short of expectations.

To pivot from these challenges to a solution, it's imperative to establish a scope and sequence. By charting out a clear path for SEL implementation through a yearlong scope and sequence, we can prioritize this vital component of education and ensure that it receives the attention it deserves across all educational touchpoints.

But simply knowing a scope and sequence is necessary isn't useful without understanding how to implement it. **Here are three critical steps to implementing the scope and sequence.**

Unlocking SEL's 3 Steps to Implementing a Scope and Sequence

👣 Step 1- The SEL Team convenes for strategic planning

Allocating focused, uninterrupted time for your SEL team to convene is the first step for planning to build an **SEL scope and sequence.** This could look like a meeting before the school year begins that sets the course for the year. Then, the team could meet each quarter to progress monitor.

During any dedicated session, equip the team with key resources such as state and district SEL standards, previously conducted surveys, and information gleaned from your schoolwide SEL curriculum. This comprehensive set of information standards, surveys, and curriculum will serve as the cornerstone for an informed discussion in the decision-making process.

Given the complexity and importance of SEL, the session should enable a deep dive into every aspect of your school's program. This meticulous planning ensures that your SEL strategy aligns with broader educational objectives while also being tailored to the specific needs and characteristics of your school community. In this way, you can forge a well-rounded and effective SEL program that maximizes both student well-being and academic achievement.

👣 Step 2- Set clear SEL goals

Ensure that your team has set clear SEL goals. When it comes to identifying your goals, there are three essential approaches to consider.

First, align your objectives with those of your state and district, taking note that 27 states have officially adopted K-12 SEL competencies, while all 50 states have endorsed pre-K SEL standards, according to the Collaborative for Academic, Social, and Emotional Learning (CASEL, 2022).

Second, review the SEL anchor curriculum you've selected to discern its specific goals. This will not only clarify what the curriculum intends to achieve but will also guide you in seamlessly integrating it into your broader educational framework.

Lastly, engage with your school stakeholders to gather information as to their aspirations for student development.

👣 Step 3- Create your yearlong SEL scope and sequence

Now it's time to create the actual document. For instance, let's say you've elected to incorporate a "Wellness Wednesday" morning block dedicated to SEL across the entire school. In executing this plan, first, obtain the academic calendar for the year. Then, carefully earmark each Wednesday, and strategically slot in SEL curricular lessons that align with your overarching SEL objectives.

This approach helps ensure that each "Wellness Wednesday" is not merely a placeholder but a meaningful educational opportunity. The sessions can become an integral part of your school's educational fabric, designed to advance specific competencies and objectives outlined in your carefully crafted scope and sequence. By doing this, you guarantee the SEL program is both systematic and delivered to all students, which maximizes its impact on student well-being and academic success.

Let's revisit the story at the top of this chapter. Part of the reason our service project was successful was that there was a clear roadmap with our scope and sequence. We planned out the dates of the service project to give teachers plenty of notice when it was coming so they could prepare appropriately and build momentum in their classrooms. Our SEL scope and sequence was then conveniently made available in our shared Google document. It was accessible to all teachers and staff, which promoted transparency and collaboration in our approach to SEL.

By synthesizing these three distinct but complementary perspectives, you can formulate holistic and targeted SEL goals that are both compliant with guidelines and responsive to local needs.

🎯 PRINCIPAL POINTS

Navigating the logistical complexities of scheduling time for your SEL team might be a formidable challenge. Schools often face constraints related to time, scheduling, and available resources. They may require innovative solutions to overcome barriers.

Some potential strategies for accommodating these crucial meetings could involve allocating paid time after school hours specifically for SEL planning, offering compensatory time for work carried out during the summer months, or providing class coverage to free up teachers so they could fully participate. We often used all three of these strategies to think outside of the box to ensure ample time for our team to meet.

As a reminder, make sure to incorporate a teacher's perspective in the creation of the scope and sequence for your SEL program: Teachers offer invaluable insights into classroom dynamics and student needs, enriching the planning process and ensuring that the resulting curriculum is both practical and effective. So, despite the logistical hurdles, focusing on facilitating teacher involvement in your SEL team's planning process is not just advisable but imperative for the success of the program.

💡 TEACHER TIPS

I assume that, as a teacher, you do not have space for anything else on your plate. And I get it. One way to get around this is to have the SEL lessons created for you and then sent your way. How about suggesting this to your school principal? Your school could have the counselor or teacher team create corresponding lessons on slide decks such as PowerPoint or Google Slides that are tied to the specific SEL lesson. For example, if the topic is Understanding Emotions, there could be a centrally created SEL lesson sent out to all staff.

At my school, we did this exact thing and our counselors created beautiful PowerPoints and sent them out on the Friday before the lessons. It was a win-win. We had schoolwide SEL lessons being taught, but the teachers did not have to create them. And not to forget our counselor's workload, we compensated our counselor with comp time for her creation of the lessons.

Chapter Summary

It's important to follow a strategic, yearlong plan for social and emotional learning. Schools can move from a fragmented to a structured approach when implementing SEL, ensuring that all classrooms are aligned in their efforts. This leads to a school culture where SEL is seamlessly integrated into its very fabric.

The benefits of this approach include targeted skill development, consistency in delivery, community building, and the ability to measure progress and outcomes. Therefore, an SEL approach is crucial for fostering a community where every student's social and emotional growth is nurtured with intention and precision.

📢 Call to Action

- **Understand the why of a scope and sequence:** Get clear on the reason for a scope and sequence so that you're able to answer questions as they arise.

- **Convene the SEL team:** Gather your SEL team together so they can identify the SEL goals, create the schoolwide scope and sequence, and share it with the staff.

- **Decide who will create the lessons:** Decide who will create the lessons that will be shared by the school.

For an example of an SEL Scope and Sequence, go to the Fourth Key at www.unlockingsel.com/blueprint

Chpt. 22: Creating a Common Language

"Education without common language is like a ship without a compass: full of potential but lacking direction."
- Anon

The Buzzer Beater

I've been an athlete for as long as I can remember, playing a variety of sports like basketball, softball, and soccer. While the thrill of competition was undoubtedly a driving force, what I cherished even more was the sense of community that came with being part of a team. The feeling of putting on the same jersey, sharing highs and lows, and striving for a common goal was nothing short of amazing.

Drawing on my experience as an athlete, I've come to appreciate the unspoken language of teamwork—the knowing glances and subtle signs that convey volumes on the court or field. In the thick of a game, a quick hand signal or a pointed look can orchestrate a play that we'd run countless times in practice.

I am reminded of this idea during one basketball game during my college years. The game was close, the score was neck and neck, and the seconds were ticking down. As the point guard dribbled the ball down the court, I was keenly aware of my teammate's presence at the top of the key.

With the pressure mounting, one of my teammates and I connected with just a look. It was a silent conversation we had perfected in practice. She faked a screen near me, drawing her defenders with her, and I received the cue. With rehearsed precision, she sprinted backdoor receiving her no-look bounce pass. Catching and shooting in one motion, the ball sailed through the air as the buzzer sounded.

This teammate communication is akin to the shared understanding that a school community develops when transforming their school through social and emotional learning. Teachers and staff become adept at reading each other's cues, moving fluidly to support one another, and anticipating the needs of the day. This intuitive synergy is what turns a group of individual educators into a cohesive unit. Each contributes to the collective goal of creating an ecosystem of care, both academically and emotionally.

Much of this connectivity depends on a common language. In the context of schools, a **common language refers to a set of terms, concepts, phrases, and frameworks that are uniformly understood and used by all members of the school community**. It serves as the glue that binds all stakeholders together, fostering a cohesive and harmonious learning environment.

Create Consistency

As we strive for transformation of our classrooms and schools, we need to build consistency. Common language is a high-leverage strategy to help us do just that. The power of speaking the same school language creates consistency across grades and subject matters. It provides a seamless academic experience as students transition from grade to grade or switch between subjects throughout the day. This continuity reduces confusion, making it easier for students to focus on learning rather than navigating different terminologies or the jarring effects of classroom changes.

Common language can also be used in a variety of other ways to propel school change. One example is from Harlem Academy, a school in NYC that supports underserved communities. They created a pivotal shift using common language for behavior expectations and character development, as was encapsulated in their school creed (Scanfield et al., 2018).

The school's creed outlines the four pillars of community the school aims to instill in its students: initiative, integrity, compassion, and determination. Before the creed was established, teachers had disparate systems of classroom management which led to a fractured approach in cultivating positive student behavior. With a common language in place, the school was able to foster a cohesive culture of high academic and behavioral expectations.

This common language didn't just standardize behavior expectations; it transformed the way they were perceived and internalized by students. By framing desired behaviors as habits aligned with higher ideals, the school transcended the limitations of a rule-based system. Rather than seeing themselves as rule-followers, students began to view themselves as individuals in the process of becoming someone embodying the four pillars of their community. The development of good habits became both meaningful and aspirational.

For us, the adoption of common language was instrumental in crystallizing our focus on SEL, particularly through the lens of mindfulness. It wasn't just about incorporating new terms; it was about embedding these concepts into the daily rhythm of school life. Our common language became a beacon that guided our interactions, our strategies, and our shared vision, weaving the principles of mindfulness into the very fabric of our school culture.

In echoing the success of Harlem Academy, we recognized the profound shift that a united language could bring. It helped our students see beyond the immediacy of rules. They embraced a broader vision of themselves as contributors to a community anchored in shared values.

There are five pivotal ways in which a consistent common language supports school transformation:

1. A consistent common language leverages **synergy** across the school by establishing a shared understanding of objectives and expectations among everyone involved. This shared language not only aligns efforts but also builds positive energy and momentum, driving the school community toward common goals.

2. This common language streamlines **communication**, cutting through potential confusion to enhance clarity and efficiency for teachers, students, and parents alike.

3. It acts as a **scaffold** for collaborative practices, enabling educators to synchronize their planning, instruction, and assessment with precision and unity.

4. Moreover, shared terminology is a cornerstone in **reinforcing the very culture of a school.** It resonates through the hallways, embodying the values, vision, and ethos that the community upholds.

5. Lastly, it **underpins inclusivity,** which is an accessible, universally understood language. It ensures every student finds their place within their school's narrative, irrespective of their unique background or learning needs. This contributes to a more cohesive educational environment.

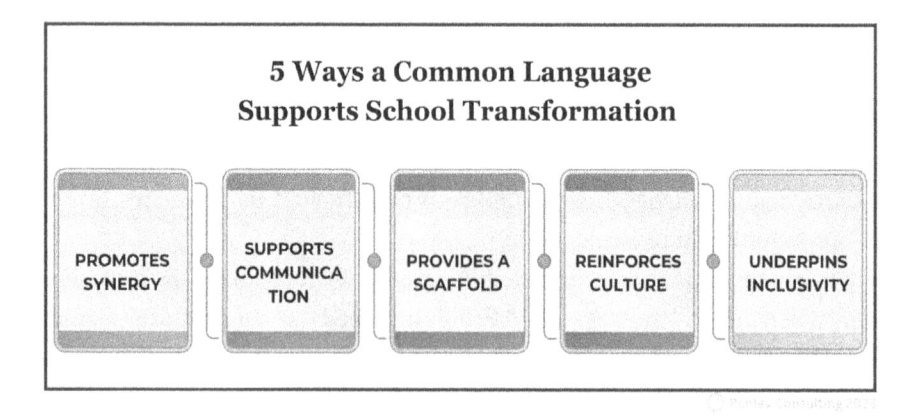

5 Ways a Common Language Supports School Transformation

| PROMOTES SYNERGY | SUPPORTS COMMUNICATION | PROVIDES A SCAFFOLD | REINFORCES CULTURE | UNDERPINS INCLUSIVITY |

Compile a Schoolwide Glossary

To further cement our shared language, take the pivotal step of compiling a schoolwide glossary. Envision the scene: a new cohort of 7th graders arrives, their backgrounds as diverse as their academic journeys. As they step into an environment peppered with terms like "regulation," "amygdala," "mindfulness," and "compassion," some will transition smoothly, especially those continuing from sixth grade. Yet new arrivals or those for whom English is a second language might find some concepts unfamiliar or even daunting.

A schoolwide glossary can be a transformative tool here. Accessible to every student, it bridges the gap between confusion and understanding, fostering an inclusive academic atmosphere.

When a topic like brain science expands into discussions on the amygdala's role in learning, students can confidently consult the glossary to refresh their understanding. Far from being a forgotten document, this glossary is envisioned as an evolving resource, dynamically integrated into the school's daily life.

Our counselors took on the ownership of this glossary, ensuring its relevance and responsiveness. They served as the guardians and communicators, keeping the glossary current, clear, and central to our endeavors. A schoolwide glossary doesn't just clarify; it connects, empowering every student to grasp and use the language that is so integral to the collective educational journey.

Let's look at the practical steps that will bring our vision to fruition with *7 Steps to Build a Schoolwide Glossary.* These steps are designed not just to create a glossary but to embed it into the fabric of the school culture.

7 Steps to Build a Schoolwide Glossary

1. Create a 30-minute meeting block during a staff meeting. Explain the what and the why of your schoolwide glossary.

2. Have each table group of staff identify key terms that would benefit from standardization. This is not limited to simply words; it can encompass a wide array of elements such as teaching strategies, policy frameworks, and subject specific jargon.

3. Gather all terms into a single Google document.

4. Next, take the list of terms to the SEL committee that can define each term.

5. Take a second 30-minute staff meeting period to review each term and answer any questions that arise.

6. Teach the glossary to your students.

7. Review and revise the glossary on a quarterly basis.

🎯 PRINCIPAL POINTS

As I mentioned earlier in Chapter Ten, one way we used a common language was through our mantra: Relationships, Respect, Rigor. We created posters and hung them in each schoolwide space. This created a common language and uniformity that helped amplify our key focus areas, shared purpose, and collective identity.

Our Mantra

MARYSVILLE
RESPECT · RIGOR
RELATIONSHIPS
MANTRA

💡 TEACHER TIPS

Even if a schoolwide glossary isn't part of your school's practice just yet, there's immense value in pioneering one within your own classroom. Carve out a space on your wall and start building your SEL vocabulary one term at a time. Begin with essential terms like 'regulation' to help students understand how to manage their emotions, 'belly breathing' for practicing calming techniques, or 'compassion' to foster empathy.

Each word you add becomes a building block in your students' understanding, a linguistic tool they can use to articulate their feelings and actions. Encourage your students to contribute to this word wall, making it a collaborative and living resource. As you weave these terms into daily lessons, discussions, and activities, they become more than just words; they become the language of your classroom culture, shaping the way students think, learn, and interact with one another. This proactive approach not only enhances the SEL experience in your classroom but also could set a precedent that could ripple out to inspire a schoolwide adoption.

Chapter Summary

A shared linguistic framework is pivotal in an educational setting. Unified vocabulary fosters collaboration and consistency in schools. Having a common language can shape both behavior and culture.

Using this comprehensive guide, you can establish a schoolwide glossary, ensuring inclusivity and aiding in comprehension for all students. By aligning communication through common terms and phrases, you can create a harmonious learning environment that empowers students and staff to work toward shared goals with clarity and purpose.

Call to Action

- **Develop an understanding of the importance of common language:** Gain clarity on the why of doing a schoolwide glossary.

- **Create a glossary:** Take staff meeting time to create a glossary to hold the school terms and their definitions

- **Appoint someone in charge of managing the glossary:** This person will be responsible for creating, managing and updating the glossary.

Chpt. 23: Building Belonging

"We may all be different fish, but at this school we swim together."
-@weareteachers

The Story of Vicky

One fall, we had a new addition to our school, an adorable little black-haired second grader named Vicky. She had recently moved to the country and was learning English as a second language. Understandably, Vicky arrived with a range of emotions, including anxiety, fear, and a tendency toward emotional dysregulation. Her emotional difficulties showed up in several ways, such as having trouble focusing, which disrupted the learning environment because she found it hard to follow school procedures.

While some might have viewed Vicky as a problem to be managed, our school chose to see her as an opportunity—she was someone to help. As educators, we considered Vicky's unique background, acknowledging the immense changes and uncertainties she'd experienced. Recognizing this, our first step was building a meaningful relationship with her. Our initial goal, before diving into academics, was to help Vicky feel a sense of connectedness within our school community.

What Vicky needed was belonging, and that started with relationships with her teacher, the school staff, and her peers.

One of the biggest issues facing education today is a lack of belonging. During my journeys assisting schools nationwide, I often hear a recurring question: How can we improve both the emotional well-being and academic engagement of our students? The answer tends to be multi-layered, often couched in terms like "it's complicated" or "it depends." This is because each educational context is unique. However, a universal constant exists that underpins most successful school environments: the principle of belonging.

This is not merely an uplifting idea: belonging is a critical element of school culture that profoundly influences students' emotional health and academic dedication. It has been identified as a fundamental human need. The urge to belong can forecast various outcomes in mental, physical, social, economic, and behavioral spheres. In fact, we all, regardless of age, seek connections, a sense of importance, and the assurance that we matter to others. Belonging plays a critical role in a student's successful school life (Koepershoek, et al. 2019).

As a child, and specifically through my K-8 experience, I felt belonging most of the time through my sports teams, clubs, and wonderful teachers. However, that changed as I moved on to high school. Our high school was a combination of various middle schools, meaning I did not know many of the students. I remember walking the halls, feeling lost, and struggling even to open my locker. As I went to my first class, I barely made it as the bell rang as soon as I entered the space. And then I didn't know where to sit. This story repeated itself multiple times a day as I went through various class changes.

The worst was lunch. "Where does a ninth grader go to sit?" I wondered as I looked at what seemed like a cafeteria as large as a concert arena.

And then I saw them: my friends from middle school. We smiled, hugged, and promised to sit together for lunch forever. From this small moment of belonging, my nervous system could calm down. Exhale. You see, I could not learn anything until I found somewhere where I mattered, somewhere I belonged.

We have all felt a sense of belonging in our lives. Furthermore, most of us can remember times when we didn't feel as if we belonged like we weren't part of a group or a team. We may have felt excluded. When we don't prioritize relationships as school leaders, belonging suffers, and we run the risk of students feeling excluded.

This is especially true in the equity work we do supporting our marginalized students. Students who are not in the majority, whether by race, gender, sexual orientation, socioeconomic status, or special needs, can feel a lack of a sense of belonging.

In the book, *Belonging Through a Culture of Dignity* (2019), authors

Floyd Cobb and John Krownapple propose that the keys to success in equity work are inclusion, belonging, and dignity. All of this is built by relationships. While academic rigor is undoubtedly crucial in shaping futures, it cannot overshadow the significance of healthy relationships we all need.

Let's dig deeper. What does 'belonging' mean? The most commonly used definition comes from researchers Carol Goodenow and Kathleen Grady who provided a widely accepted definition in 1993, describing school belonging as "the extent to which students feel individually welcomed, respected, included, and supported by others in the school social environment" (Goodenow & Grady, 1993).

Students who feel a sense of belonging in school are more likely to graduate and acquire skills essential for professional and social success. In contrast, students who feel alienated are at greater risk for negative behaviors, such as substance abuse and smoking, as well as mental health challenges like depression and anxiety (Dadds et al., 2006). A recent study by Qualtrics (2022) shows that only 49% of high school students feel they belong to their school community.

Social isolation has emerged as an alarming issue in many developed societies, exacerbated by factors like technological shifts, social mobility, fragmented family and community structures, and the accelerated pace of contemporary life (Baumeister & Robson, 2021). The COVID-19 pandemic has only amplified these pre-existing struggles as there was a large break of belonging when schools closed. When schools reopened, new connections had to form, relationships had to be mended. Frankly, many students struggled with being off their devices and plugging back into society.

Strong Staff and Student Relationships

The relationship between the educator and the student is the key to a student's sense of belonging (Allen, et al., 2021). Such relationships serve as the foundation for emotional safety, allowing students to feel secure enough to engage academically and show up as their true selves. Feeling emotionally safe at school can be particularly impactful for students who face instability or challenges in their home lives.

Additionally, when staff know their students well, they can offer personalized academic and emotional support, thereby increasing each student's chance of success. Teachers and staff who interact positively with students also serve as role models, teaching essential social skills such as empathy, active listening, and conflict resolution. This social modeling is critical for students' social development and contributes to a sense of belonging both inside and outside of school.

A positive relationship with even one staff member can significantly impact a student's perception of the entire school community, leading to a ripple effect that enhances comfort and engagement across various school settings.

Furthermore, strong relationships with staff equip students with increased resilience against school-related stressors. This is crucial as it

> *A positive relationship with even one staff member can significantly impact a student's perception of the entire school community, leading to a ripple effect that enhances comfort and engagement across various school settings.*

helps them build coping skills that will serve them well in life.

Let's revisit the story of Vicky and how her teacher went above and beyond to do the small things that positively impacted Vicky's journey through belonging.

Ms. Thomas, a thoughtful second-grade teacher, was happy about Vicky being in her class. She was a curious teacher who viewed each one of her students as someone special. She especially had compassion for Vicky as she could only imagine how hard it must be to move across the world away from one's friends, traditions, and culture. Ms. Thomas warmly greeted Vicky each morning, making sure Vicky could feel the universal language of feeling loved.

Several weeks in, Ms. Thomas noticed Vicky seemed isolated during group activities. Seeking to cultivate a sense of belonging for her, Ms. Thomas began incorporating topics into her lessons that resonated with Vicky's interests like space exploration and small puppies. She also paired Vicky with a classmate who had a similar interest which facilitated a connection. These small yet thoughtful gestures helped Vicky feel seen and valued, gradually boosting her confidence and engagement in class.

While there are fundamental beliefs about what belonging entails that are common across diverse groups, it's important to recognize that this concept can vary significantly for individual students, as it's influenced by factors such as race, gender, sexual orientation, and socioeconomic background. This nuanced understanding acknowledges that a student's specific context plays a crucial role in shaping their personal definition of belonging.

For instance, let's say you have a young girl who likes to play sports rather than play with dolls; belonging may not look 'typical' for her. If time is allowed during recess for all girls to spend time playing with a dollhouse, she may want to shoot hoops instead.

The point is, we need to look at each INDIVIDUAL student for signs of their context of belonging along with the broader strokes of belonging in general. While healthy relationships with staff can help foster this in individual students, it's only a piece of the puzzle because students also need positive peer relationships.

Positive Peer Relationships

The relationship between peers plays a pivotal role in whether a student's experience in school is a positive or negative one. I'm sure we can all remember that friend who was there for us, the one who made school fun and made us feel happy even just being around them. We can also probably remember a peer who made things difficult for us and made us feel less than, shamed, or picked on.

Children's peer relationships have longitudinal effects on mental health and adjustment. Children who had qualitative peer-relation problems were more likely to exhibit internalizing problems as adolescents (Shin et al., 2016).

There are several effective strategies schools and classrooms can employ to cultivate positive peer relationships among students. Encouraging students to conduct interviews with each other is a great start; this not only gives them a chance to share their stories but also to practice active listening and show support for their peers. Collaborative learning projects can also play a significant role. They provide an environment where quieter students can comfortably engage with others, contributing to group goals and forming connections in a natural, low-pressure setting. Additionally, incorporating fun, group-based activities into the curriculum can break down barriers, allowing students to connect through shared laughter and joy, further cementing the bonds of friendship and collaboration in the classroom. These approaches help weave a social fabric in the classroom that's inclusive and conducive to mutual respect and camaraderie.

Harm is Repaired

Despite the best proactive measures, schools are microcosms of broader society, and as such, they are not immune to challenging or negative situations that inevitably arise, especially given that a student's brain is still forming. These situations can manifest in various forms, including behavioral issues, conflicts between students, bullying, or even difficulties between staff members. External factors, such as family stressors or community events, can also seep into the school environment, creating additional layers of complexity.

Such circumstances not only disrupt the immediate educational process but can also have long-term effects on the social and emotional well-being of all involved. They can create a climate of tension and uncertainty, which can hinder the ability of students to engage fully in the learning process. It may also impact teacher morale and effectiveness. Therefore, while proactive work is essential for minimizing these issues, schools must also be well-equipped to handle these inevitable setbacks in a thoughtful and constructive manner.

When these challenges happen, we want to be mindful of how we respond. If we're looking to create a positive school community and classroom, which is what social and emotional learning's goal is, then we must respond in a way that protects this goal and employ practices that develop community by repairing harm and building relationships.

Let's go back to Vicky one last time. You see, she struggled at times with certain students. Her default way to handle mild irritations was to go right at the other person. There was no stepping down for her as her nervous system was in fight or flight.

In one particular incident, another classmate, Clyde, with a busy body had bumped her during recess accidentally, but it knocked her off her feet. Instead of apologizing, he rudely told her to get out of the way. Vicky had some choice new English words for him. The classmate took offense at the words, and the two kids went chest to chest. A teacher quickly intervened, separating them. Vicky would not talk to the staff member and went into shutdown mode as she often did, refusing to come in from recess or reenter the class she shared with her recess nemesis.

Ms. Stallings, a talented staff member and behavior coach was notified of the scuffle. She found Vicky in the recess yard, sitting under the slide, arms crossed and body stiff as a statue. But Ms. Stalling was skilled, and she knew repair needed to happen. If not, it would only be a matter of time before things bubbled up again. She approached carefully, low, and slow. Both Vicky and Clyde willingly came with her as she had an established relationship with them. She walked the long way back to her office with the kids, allowing for their amygdalas to calm down and their prefrontal cortexes to come back online.

When they arrived, the children sat down in her comfortable office space. As Ms. Stallings began the restorative process to repair harm, she started with some ground rules about speaking calmly and allowing each other to speak. Next, she asked some key questions:

- What happened?
- How did it make you feel?
- What was your brain saying?
- How do you make this better?

One at a time, Vicky and Clyde spoke, listened, and processed the situation. After about 15 minutes, Ms. Stallings had worked her magic. As she walked them back to class, she led an informal conversation about their favorite animals, as they all walked side by side. Once they arrived at their classroom, they quietly knocked. Ms. Thomas answered and welcomed them back with her warm smile. It was another successful intervention thanks to healthy connections and a sense of belonging.

🎯 PRINCIPAL POINTS

A few months ago, I received a text from a former principal friend, Amy, who was serving as a substitute principal. She texted, "You are not going to believe who I have in my office. Did you have a former student named Vicky?" She went on to say, "I am substituting here at the high school, and I met Vicky. She told me she went to Marysville in elementary school. I asked her if she knew Ms. Penley, and she said, 'Yes!' And that you were an incredible human being who made a huge difference in her life. She wanted to tell you hi." My heart melted. I loved that girl so much. And to know that I mattered to her is the greatest gift. I would like to think the 'seeds' of belonging were planted for her many years ago and were now blooming in her high school experience.

💡 TEACHER TIPS

According to PBIS (Epperson, 2021), the praise-to-criticism ratio is at least 4:1. This means at least four positive comments are given to one redirection. This positive reinforcement can serve as a powerful tool in shaping belonging. It can uplift self-image and create connections that can motivate students to participate in the classroom more actively. This positive ratio approach safeguards the emotional well-being of students, preventing the detrimental effects of compounding critiques. A positive feedback ratio isn't about overlooking bad behaviors, but about nurturing a resilient, confident, and proactive learner-one who feels they belong.

Chapter Summary

The concept of belonging is crucial in the educational context. This positions it as a vital component of school culture that has far-reaching implications for students' emotional and academic lives. The reason is simple. Belonging is a fundamental human need, critical to a student's success and well-being. Fostering strong relationships within the school community can create this necessary sense of connectedness.

The role of an educator is pivotal to building this belonging. Through cultivating positive peer interactions and helping repair harm to ensure a cohesive, supportive environment.

Call to Action

- **Engage in active listening:** Take the time to really listen to your students. Encourage them to share their thoughts, feelings, and experiences.

- **Incorporate students' interests into lessons:** Personalize your teaching by integrating topics and activities that resonate with your students' interests. This will make learning feel more relevant and engaging for them.

- **Foster peer-to-peer connections:** Create opportunities for students to collaborate and interact in positive ways. Activities such as group projects, peer mentoring, or team building can strengthen peer relationships and enhance the sense of community in your school and classroom.

Fourth Key Reflection Questions
Build the Foundation

Question	Answer
What does the aesthetic of your educational space say about your school community?	
Do you currently use an Anchor curriculum? If so, how is it going? If not, would now be the right time to onboard one?	
How could you adjust your schedule schoolwide to allow for a common SEL block?	
Why would an SEL scope and sequence support SEL goals?	
What are the common words used in your school currently?	
In what ways does your school build belonging?	

For resources from the book, go to
www.unlockingsel.com/blueprint

The 5th Key:
Design a Cycle of Success

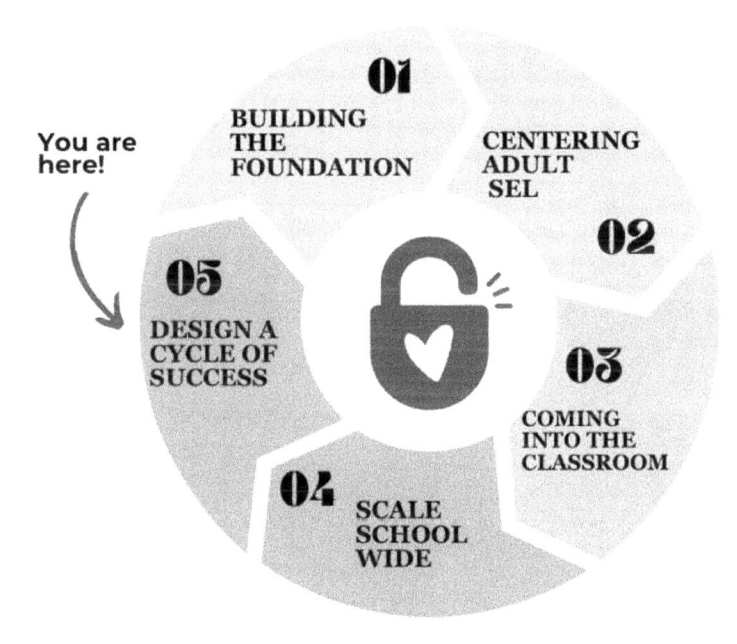

You are here!

- 01 BUILDING THE FOUNDATION
- 02 CENTERING ADULT SEL
- 03 COMING INTO THE CLASSROOM
- 04 SCALE SCHOOL WIDE
- 05 DESIGN A CYCLE OF SUCCESS

Think of SEL as a journey, not a destination—a cycle of success that's constantly evolving. This dynamic process of continuous improvement, adapting to changes and challenges in the educational landscape. Whether responding to changing societal norms or emerging technologies like social media and AI, this cycle ensures our approaches remain relevant and effective. The cycle shows how to evaluate our strategies, celebrate our successes, and make necessary adjustments. In essence, it's about creating a continuously improving educational experience for all.

It's all about the cycle of growth. By checking how we're doing and reflecting on our results, we can discern where to do better, where to give ourselves a pat on the back, and where to celebrate our major wins.

Chpt. 24: Aligning Resources

"Alignment: The key to success nobody ever taught you."
-Shane Parrish

The Power of the Lever

In my garden, a hefty rock stood in the path of the sprinklers, casting a long shadow over the vibrant flowers that struggled for every drop of sunlight and water. This rock seemed immovable as I tried my best to lift it out of the way. Perplexed at how to solve this problem, I thought about the lever, a simple yet profound tool that has moved the world since the beginning of time.

Positioning a sturdy length of a 2x4 beneath the stubborn stone, I used a fragment of another rock as a fulcrum and pushed down with all my might. The lever creaked and groaned under the tension, the boulder shifted, inch by grudging inch. At last, it rolled aside, freeing the sprinklers. The flowers, no longer overshadowed, basked in the sunlight and the gentle spray of water. The petals turned skyward with what felt like a big thank you.

This lesson, plucked from the heart of nature, reminded us that no problem is too great to overcome, and often, the solutions lie in the simplest of tools, waiting for us to apply them.

Social and emotional learning is a tool like a lever that makes everything else easier. As we embark on our Fifth Key, equipped with this transformative lever, we find ourselves at a crucial juncture.

Having achieved significant strides thus far, we're now faced with an essential challenge: how do we keep this positive momentum going? How can we create a system that is not only effective in the short term but also sustainable in the long run? This chapter explores these critical questions, with the goal of establishing a resilient and enduring foundation for the continued success of social and emotional learning.

Our first step in designing a cycle of success is to align our resources. When resources—such as funding, staff training, materials, and time—are properly aligned with a SEL program's goals, effectiveness is enhanced. Adequate funding ensures that the necessary materials and tools for SEL are available, and well-trained staff can more effectively implement and sustain programming. Furthermore, aligning time and resources is vital for integrating SEL schoolwide.

When these resources are unaligned, SEL programs struggle due to a lack of support, materials, or time. Of course, this leads to suboptimal outcomes. On the other hand, effective resource alignment ensures that SEL initiatives are not just aspirational but are woven into the fabric of the school's everyday operations, thereby maximizing their impact on student well-being and development. When this occurs, then gone are the days of disjointed solo acts; instead, everyone is attuned to a unified objective. In such an environment, where individuals and resources seamlessly click, communication flows effortlessly. This synergy not only fosters stronger teamwork but also elevates the overall energy and effectiveness of the school or classroom.

SEL is like a lever that makes everything else easier.

Now, imagine the school's activities and routines as a group of arrows. They were previously scattered but now are converging with purpose and direction.

Align the Arrows

Picture, for a moment, those arrows pointing everywhere, like a faulty compass. It's a bit like trying to follow multiple GPS directions simultaneously that show two opposing routes, and things become confusing, right? That's what happens when everything is unaligned in a school setting. It's difficult to figure out where the main goal is when everything (and everyone) seems to point in a different direction.

Now, envision a scenario in which all the arrows point in the same direction. It's as if all navigation apps are giving you a singular, cohesive route to your destination. When you realize you only need one app, you can trust it and can lean in its direction.

When there's alignment in a school's objectives and actions, the path to success becomes clearer and easier to travel. There's less ambiguity, fewer conflicts, and a greater sense of harmony. Staff, students, and parents understand the mission and can work collaboratively towards it, ensuring the journey is a smooth and purposeful one.

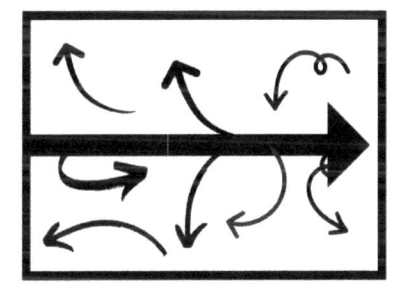

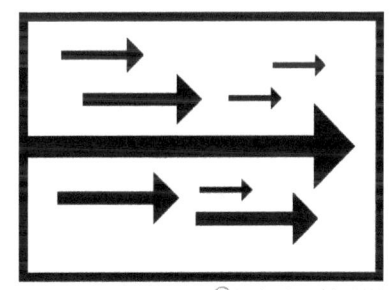

Disconnected Initiatives   **Aligned Resources**

© Penley Consulting 2023

When arrows aren't aligned, it gives mixed signals. Those signals aren't just puzzling; they eat up precious time and energy. Instead of everyone moving together toward a shared goal, an incongruous environment can feel more like bumper cars—everything bounces off in its own direction, or worse, bump into each other! For a school to *really* get where it wants to go, it's essential to ensure all those arrows and actions point the same way, aligned with one another.

Here is an example of how this came into play for our school. We were contacted and asked to participate in a new initiative, a book drive, with the Portland Trailblazers. Though this book drive would have some benefit for the school as a whole, it also meant we would have to roll out something new that would take resources such as time and energy. It also was not aligned with the SEL initiative. Though we appreciated the ask, we ultimately had to say, "No, thank you."

Think of SEL as your *big* arrow and all the other things you do as smaller arrows. The little ones should help propel the bigger one along. So, if something is not aligned with your big arrow, politely say, "No. Thank you."

Resource Decisions Support SEL

Once we've slowed down, examined the arrows, and consistently redirected them in the same direction, it's time to look at resources. If SEL is the focus, we must support it! Allocating assets in a manner that supports schoolwide goals is fundamental for any educational institution's success. By prioritizing and aligning goals, schools ensure that all initiatives, programs, and curricular activities are bolstered by support, optimizing the chances of achieving the outcome. **This can lead to a positive school culture where all can thrive.**

Such decisions not only provide the necessary infrastructure for teaching and learning but also convey to the staff and students that the school values a harmonized approach to education. The school is like a big team: each person has their role, whether teaching, managing, learning, or supporting. Now, if you want that team to succeed, you've got to make sure everyone has the necessary gear and equipment. If not, the game can't be played optimally. Essentially, this is the message we provide when we say that schools need to make decisions about time, staffing, and resources that back up the whole team.

When everyone—from teachers to administrative staff—observes that the school's resources are distributed in a manner that champions schoolwide SEL, morale is boosted as people feel a sense of a unified community and focus. It also means that collaboration is encouraged, ultimately leading to a more productive and positive educational environment.

But what does it look like to utilize your resources in a way that bolsters SEL?

Example at the classroom level: If we believe that the peace corner is an important strategy and tool for student emotional and behavioral regulation, we must fund it with school-issued resources. We can't expect teachers to supply funding for supplies out of their own pockets. Following the Peace Corner training, a school must provide the necessary supplies for it to be a successful addition.

Example at the school level: If you are implementing a Mindful Moment schoolwide, each school space should be provided with a chime to use. This will remove a barrier of implementation and help ensure fidelity.

To give you some fresh ideas as to how to examine resource alignment, let's look at a checklist. I mean, don't we all love a good checklist? I know I do!

Unlocking SEL's Resource Alignment Checklist Example

Resource	Aligned?	How is the resource aligned to our SEL Goals?
Title 1 Budget	✓	Money is allocated to PD trainings.
PTA funds	✓	Money is used to to purchase a student SEL curriculum.
Fundraiser	✓	Money is allocated to supply the Peace Corner.
Summer School	✓	SEL lessons are reinforced during after school programming.

Arrow Alignment Example

In the cozy confines of our school, there existed a cherished tradition: Reading with Grandparents. This special reading program was less about the books and more about the bonds it fostered. It was a place where grandparents, with their wells of patience and stories, became mentors to our youngest learners, children in grades K through 2 who faced challenges in reading.

Twice a week, these sessions painted a picture of shared discovery: grandparents would pair up with students, creating a nurturing space for practicing fluency as they listened attentively to the child's reading. Then, switching roles, they would read aloud, guiding young minds through the intricacies of comprehension. This exchange was a symphony of intergenerational dialogue marked by the joyous anticipation visible in the beaming smiles of grandparents as they entered the building. It was a sight to see as they often walked hand in hand down the hallway toward their reading nooks.

However, a poignant interaction revealed a gap we hadn't foreseen. One day, a grandparent approached me to ask about the term 'mindful moment'—a concept a child had mentioned. It was a moment of clarity, an acknowledgment that we had missed a step in engaging this vital part of our school's extended family. Our grandparents were adrift in a sea of unfamiliar terms and practices central to our SEL initiatives, a cornerstone of our school's ethos that had yet to be shared with them. **We had not aligned all our arrows!**

Determined to rectify this oversight, we organized an event that was more than just a mere meeting; it was an invitation to how we do schooling. We welcomed our grandparents to a thoughtfully arranged breakfast, where the aroma of coffee blended with the warmth of our gratitude. We celebrated them, expressing our deep appreciation. And over the course of a dedicated hour, we introduced them to the fabric of our SEL program, unraveling the threads of the language and practices that supported our children's holistic growth. It was an initiative to not just inform, but to harmonize our efforts, ensuring that every person within our school knew the gentle art of fostering mindfulness and emotional resilience in our students. Yes, this meeting took our time, but it was a piece of the puzzle that needed to be put in place so we could continue our journey to school transformation.

For our SEL initiatives to truly take flight, they require alignment, funding, and resourcing. Without proper support, initiatives are like kites on a still day—full of potential but lacking the lift of momentum. It's the commitment to fund and resource SEL that breathes life into the practice, sending it soaring to lofty heights where it can make a meaningful difference.

> ***Without proper support, initiatives are like kites on a still day—full of potential but lacking the lift of momentum.***

Resource support gives initiatives the lift of momentum.

🎯 PRINCIPAL POINTS

*Aligning your arrows can be one of the most challenging yet important things you do as a principal. For years, we did too much as a school. I didn't understand the **law of diminishing returns,** that adding new things can create distractions and split energy, taking away from the focus of SEL. In other words, we could never be great at anything because we spent too much time trying to be good at too many things. Do less to be better at more. This is a key characteristic of great leadership.*

💡 TEACHER TIPS

Look for ways to align resources with SEL within your classroom. For example, if you were to receive PTA funding for some new classroom supplies, how could you purchase items that may make the environment more SEL friendly? Perhaps you purchase flexible seating, inclusive books, or soft lighting to help support a positive learning environment.

Chapter Summary

If you are an educator who is seeking to foster a positive school/classroom culture, you can do it by aligning your school's resources with SEL programs. Each component is a crucial part of your school's ecosystem, like puzzle pieces that must fit together flawlessly. Each part is integral to the whole.

Effective resource alignment is not merely an aspirational goal. It can be a practical, embedded practice that enhances your school's everyday functions and directly impacts student well-being. The school moving together in a unified direction can ensure clarity, reduce conflict, and promote a collaborative, harmonious journey for all.

📢 Call to Action

- **Examine the arrows:** Are you ensuring all school arrows are pointing in the same direction?

- **Pause before resource decisions:** Ask yourself, "Is this supporting the SEL initiative?"

Chpt. 25: Leveraging Staff Meetings

"The hard truth is, bad meetings almost always lead to bad decisions, which is the best recipe for mediocrity."
- Patrick Lencioni

Impromptu Easter Egg Hunt

On a beautiful spring Tuesday afternoon, our school's staff trudged into the meeting room. It was time for our weekly professional development. Despite the loveliness of the season, there was a collective sense of lethargy weighing down the room. Another staff meeting had arrived, and with it, the usual expectation of agenda items and discussions.

That's when inspiration struck me. We needed a bit of fun to shake off the doldrums. I had just the plan in mind, and it involved Mr. B, our dynamic 4th-grade teacher known for his love of a good time and his infectious energy.

With a twinkle in my eye, I pulled Mr. B aside and posed a question: "Would you like to dress up as the Easter Bunny and bring a little magic to our staff meeting?"

"Sure, where do I sign up?" His enthusiastic reply was all I needed to hear. Amid a discussion on curriculum development, our staff meeting was suddenly interrupted by a giant, fluffy Easter Bunny bounding into the room.

Laughter and cheers erupted as Mr. B invited everyone outside for an impromptu Easter egg hunt. Teachers sprinted from their seats like children on a playground, eager to discover the hidden eggs that contained not only sweet treats but also coveted gift cards. It was a moment of pure joy and a reminder that a little spontaneity and humor could make even a staff meeting an event to remember.

Staff meetings don't have to be painful, boring, disjointed extensions of the school day. There can be a different way. When I was a teacher, the agenda seemed to be a random collection of announcements and directives, with little relevance to our daily challenges or professional growth. The sessions dragged on, with many of us discreetly checking our watches, waiting for the merciful end.

Upon becoming a principal, I was determined to disrupt this narrative. I wanted there to be a new STANDARD, that meetings were enjoyable, engaging, and used to leverage us toward this school transformation.

Before long, meetings became more like interactive workshops where people were invited to lean in and bring their whole selves. We would start with a quick connection activity such as asking about favorite movies to get the synergistic energy flowing. Next, we practiced intentional breathing through a mindful moment. For many of us, it might have been the first time that day we'd slowed down and allowed our mind and body to be in the same place.

Only then would we get into the meat of the meeting, where teachers shared successes, or collaborated on challenges, engaging in professional development that was directly relevant to their work. This new standard not only reinvigorated our team but also played a crucial role in transforming our school into a dynamic and innovative learning environment.

As we consider *designing a cycle of success,* we must be intentional, strategic, and entertaining with our staff meetings. A staff meeting isn't just a meeting: it should be an energy amplifier, not an energy vampire. It's a time for like-minded folks to unite and turn ideas into actions, fostering a vibrant and collaborative atmosphere that breathes life into educational goals and strategies. This type of energy is what it takes to move the needle for school change.

> *A staff meeting isn't just a meeting. It should be an energy amplifier, not an energy vampire. It's a time for like-minded folks to unite and turn ideas into actions.*

Set a Staff Meeting Standard

Let's start with logistics. What are the details of staff meetings? We are looking for **consistency** here, which means same day, same time, and same location. This allows for the guesswork to be removed and focus can be on the meeting itself. Next, is the **agenda.** By setting up a clear agenda, our meetings get a regular beat and a predictable flow, making it easier for everyone to know what to expect and really delve into the discussions. And finally, don't do a lot of direct instruction. The new standard is **collaborative.** Creating a space in which teachers can speak up about what they need and throw in their ideas ensures every meeting is useful and engaging.

In lieu of ambiance and consistency, we always had our meetings in our beautiful library. Our custodian would go down and make sure to vacuum beforehand. There would be soft music playing. I would then go early and write the agenda on a whiteboard and add an inspirational quote. Our wonderful secretary took roll to keep everyone from having to wait in line and sign in. We started on time, though we allowed a good 30 minutes after the final bell to dismiss students and for teachers to get a drink and maybe go to the bathroom for the first time in a long time. And then we finished on time, or early, usually with a positive ending question such as, "What is one thing you are excited about?" This type of consistency allowed for us to co-create our staff meeting standard.

What about virtual meetings? Though we may be post-COVID-19, and coming together as a community is important, there is still a need for virtual meetings at times. Virtual meetings can offer flexibility and inclusivity, allowing team members from any location to connect easily. This setup saves time and resources and maximizes efficient use of working hours. Additionally, virtual meetings can enhance focus and productivity, with participants joining from their preferred settings. Advanced tools such as breakout rooms can promote real-time collaboration and interaction, making them a key element of a modern, adaptable work environment

Align Agendas With School Buckets of Work

We want to ensure our meetings are synchronized with the larger work. Aligning staff meetings with our school's key areas of focus ensures that every conversation and decision directly contributes to our strategic objectives. It creates a cohesive and purposeful approach to our work, where every team member understands how their efforts fit into the larger picture. This alignment not only maximizes the productivity of our meetings but also fosters a shared sense of direction and commitment to our collective goals.

As you may recall from our First Key, our strategic initiatives were called our Buckets of Work. We must allocate dedicated time during our staff meetings for each of these crucial focus areas. This ensures alignment with our overarching goals and promotes a coherent and unified approach. For example, for the Bucket of Work of equity, we would allow for one staff meeting a month to focus solely on equity.

Let's say a school's staff meetings are scheduled for each Tuesday after school. The training schedule could look something like this:

- 1st Tuesday-Student SEL
- 2nd Tuesday-Equity
- 3rd Tuesday-Behavior Support Strategies
- 4th Tuesday-Teaching and Learning Best Practices

Naturally, this begs the question: Who leads the training? Occasionally, administrators (budget and resources permitting) may see a need to bring in external experts who can offer some fresh insights. Coming from varied backgrounds and experiences, these professionals can infuse new methods, perspectives, and techniques that a school might not have been previously exposed to. For example, several times we brought in mindfulness experts from the local university to deepen our learning.

However, most of our trainings were done internally as it is vital to recognize that within our schools' classrooms exists a treasure trove of knowledge and experience. We utilized seasoned teachers, staff members with years of hands-on experience, and even students who could offer a unique, ground-level perspective.

By tapping into this reservoir, all schools can foster a culture of peer learning, mentorship, and collaborative growth. Each staff member was on a team aligned with one of our Buckets of Work. Those teams presented at our meetings. This model of shared leadership helps elevate both staff investment and voice.

Meetings are Held in a Mindful Way

In addition to sharing the leadership, we wanted to ensure the meetings were conducted through a lens of mindfulness.

Let's look at four ways we did this.

We made sure the **space** was clean, calm, and welcoming to shift the energy from a more frenetic pace to a calmer one with seating and aesthetics for the adults. We incorporated a **check-in routine** giving each member the opportunity to voice their current state of mind, fostering a culture of openness and support. Then we did a **mindful moment** to allow time for educators to ground themselves with intentional breathing. Finally, the meetings were **ended in an optimistic way,** hoping to do a positive wrap up to the new learning.

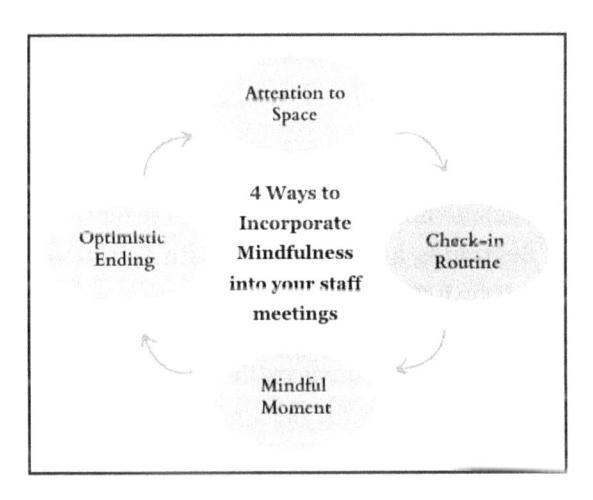

4 Ways to Incorporate Mindfulness into your staff meetings: Attention to Space, Check-in Routine, Mindful Moment, Optimistic Ending

Let's unpack the mindful moment for adults' strategy a bit more.

Imagine this scenario: You're in the middle of teaching a class full of energetic, enthusiastic young students. Your day is packed with engaging them in interactive lesson plans. You're carefully evaluating their assignments, managing behaviors, and providing personalized feedback to foster their growth. In this whirlwind of educational activity, you barely find a moment for yourself, often missing the chance to grab a quick coffee or even a brief bathroom break.

Then, as soon as your class ends, you must swiftly transition to a staff meeting. There's no downtime; as soon as you arrive, the meeting immediately delves into the critical task of something like analyzing student reading data. This part of your day is dedicated to scrutinizing performance metrics, discussing each student's progress, and strategizing ways to enhance their learning experience. It's a rapid shift from hands-on teaching to collaborative strategizing, all in a moment's notice.

You try to be present as you know the data of how a student is doing in reading is important, but all you can think of is either what you weren't able to cover or what you must get to tomorrow, all while trying to manage a personal state of exhaustion. You are tired, hungry, and in desperate need of a bathroom break.

Does this sound familiar to you? If it does, you're certainly not alone. Sadly, this is true across many schools today. The pace of the educational day can be frenzied. We need to interrupt this frenzy at the start of our staff meetings to allow for the humanity of our team.

Give our staff a few extra minutes to catch their breath by beginning meetings even five minutes later. Then, go into a mindful moment of intentional breathing. Beginning meetings with a mindful moment is like hitting a much-needed (and well-deserved) pause in a teacher's fast-paced day. Taking a moment to breathe and regroup at the outset shifts the entire meeting's vibe. **Beginning a staff meeting with an intentional pause is like a collective deep breath—a signal that says, *we are here in this moment together.*** This brief pause cuts through the noise and chaos and allows time to align everyone's mindset, fostering genuine active listening and collaboration. It transforms the meeting from just another task into a relaxed, productive space for real teamwork.

In crafting productive staff meetings, it's essential to consider not only what these gatherings should *encompass* but also what they should *avoid*. Here is a table that can help do just that.

Unlocking SEL's Staff Meeting Dos and Don'ts

Dos	Don'ts
Do a Soft Start. Make sure to honor the busy day many educators have had by starting with a personal check-in routine and grounding breathwork, a Mindful Moment.	Start with student data
Share the spotlight. Meetings should not be dominated by one-way communication from leaders.	A monologue by leadership
Staff meetings are for collaborative problem-solving, engaging, and community building. While details are important, staff meetings should not be solely dedicated to logistical details if they can be communicated by email.	Overly focused on minutiae, boring and unengaging
Solution focused. Meetings should not turn into sessions of unconstructive complaining but should lead more toward constructive, solution-focused progress.	A venue for venting frustrations
Celebrate what's right. It is important to balance the negativity bias of looking at what's wrong and celebrate and recognize what's going right.	Only focused on what's wrong

🎯 PRINCIPAL POINTS

If you want to capture the expertise of your staff as they present at the staff meeting, you must provide time for them to plan. You can't expect a full-fledged presentation if you aren't providing faculty adequate downtime to plan and prepare. An effective way to do this is to provide every 5th staff meeting as a team planning time.

💡 TEACHER TIPS

Don't be afraid to showcase your skills and lead a Mindful Moment. Embracing your expertise in mindfulness not only serves your personal growth but also enriches your community.

This initiative will not only ease the load on your administration, who will surely value the shared responsibility, but it also offers your peers a much-needed pause to reset and refocus. It's a gesture that can transform the tone of a meeting, promoting a more attentive and receptive atmosphere, which, in turn, can lead to more productive and meaningful engagements. Your willingness to lead in this way can inspire others to explore their own capabilities, creating a ripple effect of positive change within your school.

Chapter Summary

You can create staff meetings that embrace joy, mindfulness, and strategic alignment. Meetings should serve as energy amplifiers, utilizing connection activities and mindful moments to ground participants and encourage their full presence.

They should also be strategically aligned with your school's primary goals, or Buckets of Work, to ensure that every meeting advances the overarching vision. You can use consistency and structure to foster meetings that energize and propel school transformation. When we see meetings not as administrative necessities but as crucibles for collaborative innovation, everything changes.

📢 Call to Action

- **Decide on consistent logistics for your meetings**: Set a regular time, day, and location for the meetings.

- **Divide your school's work into buckets:** Streamlining the workflow into distinct buckets will help clarify and prioritize tasks.

- **Incorporate mindfulness and well-being**: Begin your meetings with a Mindful Moment to help everyone transition thoughtfully into the meeting space. This practice can help set a positive, focused tone for the meeting.

Chpt. 26: Monitoring the Process

"Trust the process."
-Anon

Power of the Process

When I first stepped into the role of principal, the halls of the school seemed to echo with a daunting challenge. I had to lead a community that I did not know, raise test scores that were in the tank, and carve out a path I had not yet learned to walk.

My early days were a whirlwind of trial and error, a balancing act between authority and approachability. Beneath it all was the sobering realization that the academic success of every child in my care hinged upon decisions I felt scarcely qualified to make. I often stood at the back of bustling classrooms, watched teachers at their craft, and wondered how to kindle the latent potential I saw. Leadership, I came to understand, was an intricate dance I had not yet mastered. Every misstep felt like a crushing misdirection of the future I was there to shape.

However, over time and with the impetus of the fire, things began to lift. After facing my initial failures, a truth settled over me like calm after a storm—**I needed a process.**

It became clear that leading with intention required an orderly, step-by-step approach to introduce and sustain our initiative of SEL. We started by defining 'what' we wanted to do: to weave SEL into the fabric of our everyday learning for both students and staff. Then, we had to determine 'how' we would do it: through regular training for teachers, a soft start to our day, integrated and explicit SEL lesson plans, and dedicated time for students to practice these skills.

Monitoring came through observations, feedback, and surveys, capturing the heartbeat of SEL's impact in classrooms. And tweaking—it was understood to be part of the journey, not a sign of failure. We prepared to adapt, using data and the lived experiences of our teachers and students as guides.

Slowly, the pieces began to fit together. Over time, I saw a picture form, a picture of a school where academic success was cradled in the nurturing arms of emotional intelligence.

As we move along the blueprint with SEL, we should notice some changes in our classrooms and school. Perhaps student referrals and suspensions have gone down, or maybe the vibe is simply much more positive. Just like in the First Key where we organized the work, at this point, we now want to be able to clearly define the process-what it is we are doing, and how to measure it. These steps move the work forward, from a one-and-done implementation to an ongoing cycle of success.

Create Your Process Pyramid

To clearly define something, we need to name it. I've aptly named the next graphic "Process Pyramid," a visual guide to the intricate dynamics of school operations.

At the pyramid's apex is social emotional learning. It serves as the overarching perspective for all educational activities. Just beneath it lies the SEL/Leadership team, a dedicated group meeting weekly to steer the school's direction, manage the calendar and events, and ensure alignment with the team's cycle of success. Following this, the process cascades down to staff meetings, a vital space for celebrating achievements, fine-tuning strategies, and tackling challenges. Lastly, at the pyramid's base, we categorize our efforts into four distinct 'buckets,' effectively structuring our approach to achieve our goals. Creating something like this as a framework for your school's goals and tasks can serve as an anchor, ensuring a clear, cohesive, and streamlined approach.

This Process Pyramid not only guides daily operations but can also embody our core values and vision, fostering a unified and effective educational environment. It is the way the successful work flows.

Process Pyramid

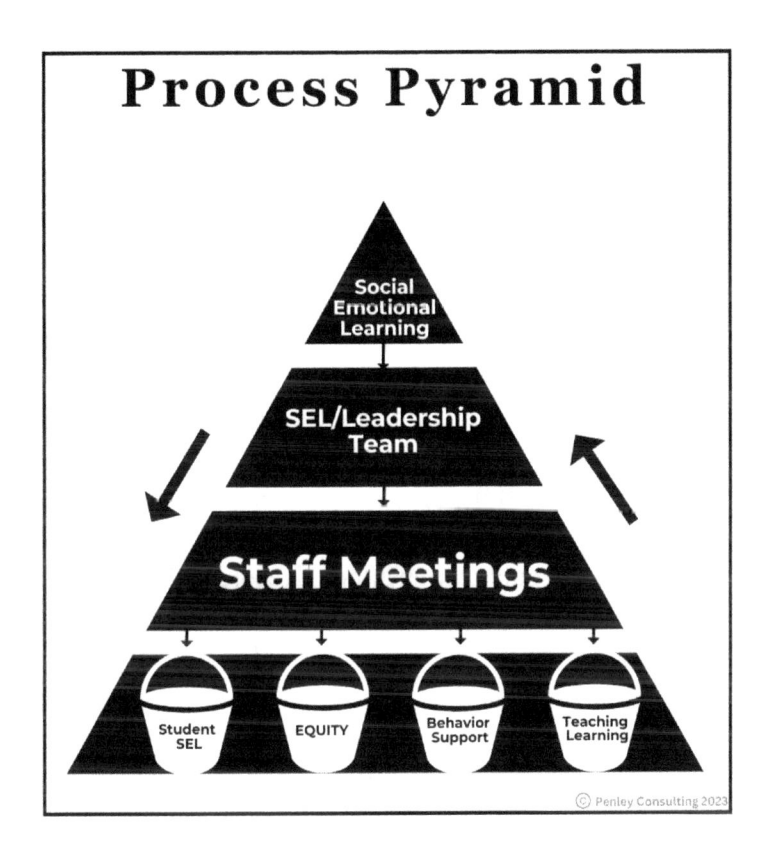

Monitor Progress

Activating the Process Pyramid sets our educational workflow in motion, leading directly to monitoring of SEL implementation. This critical assessment, both through direct classroom observation and feedback from surveys, helps us pinpoint where our SEL strategies are thriving and where they need bolstering. This continuous stream of data informs our approach, providing a compass for ongoing adjustments and improvements. Let's look at two ways to monitor the progress: informally and formally.

Track Progress Informally

Monitoring student progress informally is incredibly beneficial. Adopting this qualitative approach can reveal insights that more formal techniques might overlook. This type of progress monitoring offers real-time feedback, enabling educators to tailor their teaching strategies to the unique and evolving needs of their classroom. Such spontaneous checks not only contribute to a deeper understanding of student progress but also help foster a stronger teacher-student relationship.

By identifying and addressing learning gaps as they emerge, educators can demonstrate a deep commitment and proactive engagement in each student's individual journey toward success. Informal moments cultivate more authenticity, real conversations and a deeper understanding. **In essence, informal progress monitoring can serve as both a diagnostic tool and a relationship builder**.

Casually (yet effectively) noticing and tracking the development of students' social and emotional skills outside of the framework of formal assessments. Teachers could keep an informal record of these observations, perhaps in Google Drive, using them to tailor their teaching approaches and provide targeted support where needed. This kind of monitoring allows for a more nuanced understanding of each student's social and emotional growth, contributing to a holistic educational experience.

Following the gathering of the informal SEL information, it can be helpful to bring the conversation to your colleagues through either a staff meeting or a grade level/content meeting. Take some time to interpret your findings, looking for patterns to inform your SEL teaching and leadership moving forward.

Let's look at some ways to informally monitor SEL:

OBSERVE CASUAL HALLWAY INTERACTIONS: Notice how students interact with each other and manage their emotions in everyday situations. Pay attention to how students handle stress or setbacks, providing insights into their emotional well-being.

DO CLASSROOM CHECK-INS: Ask some important questions such as: what do you notice in your classroom? Are students behaving in a kinder manner? Are you feeling more regulated? Do the interactions reflect a sense of calm? Is there an increased enthusiasm to participate in class?

LOOK FOR THE SEL FOCUS SHOWING UP IN REAL-TIME: Look for ways the current SEL focus shows up in real-time. Perhaps you are talking about gratitude. You could look for ways you hear students saying thank you and show appreciation.

USE CHIT CHATS: Use regular, informal check-ins with students to discuss their feelings. Utilize challenges to gain valuable insights into their social and emotional development, looking for whether students feel a sense of belonging and safety.

BE CURIOUS: Ask students, colleagues, and administration how they think SEL is going. Where are the wins, and what are the barriers to implementation? How could the team raise the level of implementation even further?

Track Progress Formally

By now, you've decided which SEL student curriculum you're going to use and are explicitly teaching SEL-centered lessons. But how will you know if it is working in a more official capacity? Monitoring and reflecting on the effectiveness either schoolwide or in the classroom is an important step to ensure effective SEL implementation.

When we think about progress monitoring, we're talking about administering an SEL assessment multiple times throughout the year. We want to know if students are having a positive or positively affected response to the school's SEL program. If the data shows that is happening, it's time to celebrate. And if it is not happening, we need to make some adjustments.

In my experience, we did this in two key ways:

First, we conducted routine surveys of students through a Google Form. Surveying students about how they feel in the classroom is of paramount importance for several reasons as it allows educators to gauge the emotional and psychological well-being of their students. This is intrinsically linked to their academic performance and overall learning experience. Understanding students' feelings sheds light on factors that might be hindering their learning, be it anxiety, discomfort, or lack of engagement among others. By obtaining direct feedback, teachers can make necessary adjustments to the learning environment, teaching methodologies, or classroom dynamics.

Second, we held quarterly reviews as a leadership team to do a more formal deep dive into the data of surveys and informal conversations with teachers. We set aside 2-3 hours each quarter to review data, celebrate wins, discover challenge areas, look for trends, and recommit to our next quarter's focus.

A Monitoring Example

It was during our SEL/Support Team quarterly meeting that we did a deep dive into our data. Two things stood out. First, we had drastically decreased our referrals. We took some time to celebrate this achievement noting what SEL lessons were taught that quarter and noticing that all our classrooms were starting their day with both a Soft Start and a Mindful Moment. We couldn't wait to share the news with our staff.

However, along with that great news were some concerns. Though our overall attendance rate was high, we had nearly 30 students who had an attendance rate below 80%. The team sprang into action, personalizing outreach to support each affected student. We created a list of each student whose attendance rate was below the 80% mark. Then, we divided them up, placing each student under the care of support team members. Each one of us took our list of students to connect with, check in on, and help support them in increasing their attendance. We all left the meeting determined to make a difference with our students.

◎ PRINCIPAL POINTS

In addition to surveying the students, we also want to survey the staff. By doing this, we're essentially taking the pulse of the adults. It's our way of asking, "Hey, how are things on the ground with SEL? What's going well?

Where are the gaps?"

This kind of feedback can be a goldmine! It helps us catch potential issues early on, celebrate the things we're doing right, and adjust where and when they're needed. Plus, it sends a clear message to the staff that their perspectives matter and are valued. It's a two-way street, better communication leads to a happier, more effective team, and who doesn't want that?

💡 TEACHER TIPS

I've discovered that forging connections with students through casual interactions has been remarkably effective. Whether it's inquiring about last night's game or joining in playground activities during recess, these relaxed moments create a welcoming space for trust to blossom and dialogue to unfold naturally. Engaging this way not only nurtures a supportive rapport but also provides insightful glimpses into how SEL principles manifest in their daily experiences. These informal exchanges are more than just touchpoints; they're valuable opportunities to understand and support students' social and emotional journey.

Chapter Summary

It's important to establish a structured approach to implementing SEL within a school's fabric. It's necessary to start with a clear definition of the 'what' and the 'how'. Monitoring and adaptation form the backbone of the process, employing both observations and feedback to measure SEL's impact.

Remember, tweaking the approach is a natural part of the journey. Let data, both formal and informal, serve as your guide. This is the best way to ensure that SEL becomes a supportive framework for the academic success of your school, a success that's nurtured by emotional intelligence.

📣 Call to Action

- **Create your own Process Pyramid:** What would you keep, and what would you change?

- **Informally monitor your students' SEL:** Engage in conversation, do classroom check-ins, and be curious.

- **Review the data**: Take time to review the SEL data and adjust as needed.

Chpt. 27: Planning for Mistakes

*"You can't let your failures define you.
You have to let your failures teach you."*
-Barack Obama

From Conflict to Collaboration: Bridging Teacher Differences

Ms. Thompson and Mr. Anderson were both seasoned middle school teachers. Though they generally held mutual respect and admiration for each other's pedagogical approaches, their perspectives didn't always align. A point of contention arose when Mr. Anderson addressed a tardy student with a particular tone. Unbeknownst to him, the student's delay was due to Ms. Thompson holding them back in her class. Mr. Anderson felt disrespected as if his class didn't matter and understandably so. However, from Ms. Thompson's perspective, the students just needed a little more time to complete what they were working on.

The tension between them grew. They exchanged heated emails and tense body language as they passed each other in the hallway. Over time, it became apparent that the issue had to be addressed.

As a school, we could do one of two things: we could ignore it and hope it went away, or we could discuss it and try to find a positive middle ground. As the principal, I had heard about what happened. Fortunately, I had a good working relationship with both adults and knew they were strong teachers who each wanted to do what was best for their students.

One day, after the bell rang, I walked down to their hallway. I spoke with both parties individually to hear their side of the story. After listening intently, I realized I valued both of their opinions, and it was also clear that the two teachers both had the emotional maturity to find common ground. I asked if they felt comfortable speaking to one another and coming to their own common solution.

"Yes," they both replied. And that's exactly what they did.

In the end, their disagreement brought about collaboration as they worked toward a solution. Though they never became great friends, they did grow from the experience and create an even stronger working relationship.

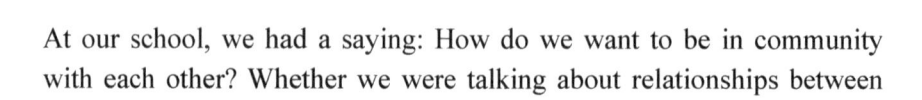

At our school, we had a saying: How do we want to be in community with each other? Whether we were talking about relationships between individual students or those between staff members, the answer is the same—**We want to be a community built on kindness and respect**.

This powerful question resonated deeply. It urged us to actively shape the kind of community we wanted. We each had a responsibility to do just that. The question prompted introspection and meaningful dialogue about mutual respect, collaboration, and shared goals. It became the cornerstone of cultivating a school environment where everyone thrived, united in purpose and community spirit.

This drove home the point of how we wanted to handle situations that occurred between the adults in our building. We wanted to be in a **community** where adults talked things out with each other with a sense of kindness and respect, looking for common ground.

It's important to remember that mistakes are going to happen. It's just part of the deal, no matter how awesome our teachers and students are. The good news is that if we plan for these slip-ups, we can come up with smart, proactive ways to handle them and learn from them. It's all about embracing our human side, with all the emotions, experiences, and little flaws that come with it. When we expect and get ready for these oops moments, we build a school that's stronger, more flexible, and way more supportive of everyone's growth.

A Note on Intersectionality

Due to diverse student and staff populations, schools can be a breeding ground for discussions of intersectionality. When educators use an intersectional lens, we are reminded that we are multifaceted humans, just like our students. Understanding this can help us remember that overlapping identities can influence how people interact with each other and show up in the classroom. Sadly, it can also influence how some are treated in the school system and how they can access educational resources. Why does this matter? Recognizing the intersectionality of both staff and students can ensure a more nuanced and equitable approach to supporting both academics and wellness.

Educators must take the time to know more about their students, their

> *Recognizing intersectionality can serve to ensure a more nuanced and equitable approach to supporting both student academics and student wellness.*

situations at home, what students are facing as a result, their particular combination of identities, and how these can affect their ability to show up in a classroom. When this happens, the classroom itself can become a place of belonging.

When schools acknowledge intersectionality, they can more effectively support students, creating policies and learning environments that consider diverse needs. This holistic approach can lead to increased empathy, reduced bias, and a stronger classroom and school community. This type of stance toward inclusion promotes the success of all students, particularly those who are most at risk of being underserved by traditional educational models. This boosts empathy and cultivates a more positive environment for all students, regardless of their race, socioeconomic status, gender, sexual identity, disability status, or cultural background.

As adults, we also have overlapping identities with race, gender, sexual orientation, socioeconomic background, disabilities, and more–that come into play and influence workplace dynamics and how we show up in the classroom. For example, a female teacher of color may encounter different or stronger biases or microaggressions than their white or male counterparts or an LGBTQ teacher may be afraid to share photos of her wife. **Recognizing intersectionality within the adult population is an emerging trend of SEL in schools and is vital to fostering a healthy, safe, and strong community.**

In a microcosm of school life, it is almost inevitable that we will encounter interpersonal challenges. Schools are generally small, contained spaces, but because of the large number of people involved in the school's inner workings, it's entirely natural and normal that people will 'bump' into each other from time to time.

These interactions, though sometimes challenging, are a vital part of the dynamic and complex fabric of school life. They present opportunities for learning, growth, and understanding diverse perspectives if we keep in mind the original question: How do we want to be in community with each other?

A Bit about Restorative Practices

What do you think of when you hear the term restorative practices? It suggests a process of restoring the healthy school and classroom communities cultivated by SEL. Restorative practices, rooted in principles of justice and empathy, are proactive approaches to student management. It focuses on repairing harm and restoring relationships when conflicts or wrongdoing occur.

SEL should precede restorative practices for two reasons. First, with SEL, we are working to create a more positive school culture, which would, in turn, decrease harmful events. Second, in order to practice restorative practices, there must be something positive to restore.

Instead of solely emphasizing punishment, restorative practices help individuals understand and address the underlying causes of misbehavior. **How to repair harm is essential for relationships, healthy schools, and prosocial classrooms.** When students behave in a way that is harmful to others, we must address the damage caused and take steps to amend it. It's crucial to re-establish trust and allow time and space for mutual understanding. This process promotes personal growth and responsibility and can help the victim find closure. The goal is to support all parties in building empathy.

By bringing together those who have caused harm with those who have been harmed, we foster accountability and provide opportunities for meaningful conflict resolution. **The approach underscores the belief**

that individuals can grow and change and that fostering positive connections and community is integral to this transformation. Through restorative practices, schools create environments where everyone feels valued, heard, and accountable to one another (Villani & Henry, 2023). Restorative practices go beyond the individual level and are crucial for the cohesion and unity of the broader classroom and school community.

When harm is acknowledged and efforts are made to rectify harm, these measures prevent the escalation of conflict and become a building block for the sense of community and trust building we seek in schools.

Restorative practices can vary at different locations, but, for our school, we focused on a two-pronged approach:

Build community circles into the fabric of the classroom.
To build proactive skills, many of our classes did community circles in the morning. This would most likely occur during the soft start. A topic example may be steps to apologize. The class would then discuss how apologies make them feel. Then they would discuss steps to apologize in the community circle. Following this time, the teacher would look for ways to incorporate this into daily lessons in real-time.

Repair harm with intention.
Repairing harm is one of the basic tenets of restorative and social and emotional learning. If someone or something has been harmed, we want to make amends. Making spaces feel safe is one way we also build belonging.

For example, if a student graffitied the school, they may have to help clean it up, paired with an apology to the custodian. Or if they made fun of someone, they could be offered the chance to hear how it made the other person feel and write a letter of apology.

Repairing harm is crucial in educational settings: When students learn to address and repair harm, they develop emotional intelligence and build their compassion skills. Understanding the impact of their actions on others and taking steps to make amends promotes a deeper sense of responsibility and serves to build a healthier classroom as well as a stronger sense of belonging. Restorative practices aren't a free pass for bad behavior; they are a bridge to better choices and stronger communities.

Ms. Thompson and Mr. Anderson stood at the precipice of a bad situation. They could have chosen a road that led to irreparable harm. Yet, rather than succumb to a path of lasting damage, they drew upon their inherent integrity and the proactive strategies we have instilled as a school community. Armed with the necessary tools and a shared resolve, they chose to engage with one another constructively. This chapter is a testament to the power of turning toward each other in times of error, maintaining openness, and being motivated by a collective aspiration to contribute to a thriving and positive community where each person is willing to do their part.

🎯 PRINCIPAL POINTS

It's important to recognize that planning for mistakes and incorporating restorative practices is not about eliminating accountability or penalties. Rather, it's about creating a culture where fewer mistakes occur and when they do, they are viewed as opportunities for learning and growth. In this environment, when students make mistakes, they are held responsible in a way that aims to understand the root cause of their actions and encourages them to acknowledge the impact on others.

The focus is on repairing harm and restoring relationships rather than simply punishing. However, within violent situations and to maintain a safe learning environment for all, there may need to be a period during which the student is suspended. By balancing accountability with restorative efforts, schools foster a sense of responsibility and empathy among students, which in turn helps to build a more respectful and cohesive school community.

💡 TEACHER TIPS

As a teacher, you might find it challenging to take time for repair when harm has occurred in your classroom, given the many demands of your role. Yet, this repair is crucial for nurturing a positive learning environment. Here's what you can do: Set aside dedicated time for restorative conversations, allowing both you and your students to understand each other and the situation. Incorporate regular check-ins, providing students with the opportunity to voice their feelings and thoughts. Use active listening during conflicts to affirm students' emotions and perspectives. Guide your students in collaborative problem-solving, teaching them constructive conflict-resolution skills.

Also, consider establishing a Peace Corner in your classroom, a quiet space for students to self-regulate and reflect. By weaving these practices into your daily routine, you can ensure that when harm happens, the path forward is one of healing and mutual respect.

Chapter Summary

You can take proactive measures in your school to cultivate a community built on understanding and shared responsibility. Of course, mistakes are inevitable but can be transformative when addressed constructively. Restorative practices make all the difference. They are not about absolving accountability but about creating a culture that views errors as opportunities for learning and growth.

By planning for mishaps, you can encourage a mindset where the community collectively supports each other, ensuring that challenges lead to stronger relationships and a more resilient school culture.

Call to Action

- **Embrace a culture of openness:** Encourage your school community to view mistakes as opportunities for growth.

- **Consider utilizing treatment agreements**: Actively work towards building a school community founded on mutual respect and kindness.

- **Integrate an intersectional approach:** Commit to understanding and addressing the multifaceted identities of students and staff.

Chpt. 28: Celebrating Wins

*"The more you praise and celebrate your life,
the more there is in life to celebrate."*
-*Oprah Winfrey*

Basketball and Belief: The Marysville Lions' Revival

During one year as principal, our girls' basketball team faced a potential hiatus due to their coach's absence. Although I had retired my whistle years prior, having previously coached high school girls' basketball in North Carolina, the thought of our team dissolving due to not having a coach was unthinkable. Despite my transition into administration, I felt compelled to step in. Plus, I just missed coaching.

What makes this story even more interesting is our team was mostly winless in previous years. Season after season, we struggled to even get a victory. The determination was there, but the mixture of inexperience, lack of resources, and inconsistent coaching had hindered the team's progress.

Yet, from the very first practice, I was taken aback by the sheer talent I saw. The girls were naturally athletic, but they lacked formal training and an understanding of basketball techniques and strategies. More importantly, they were missing the discipline and structure often associated with varsity middle school sports.

We began to work hard with daily practices. These highly energetic sessions served as both a chance to grow in our discipline and to strengthen the team's chemistry. A funny thing began to happen. As our practices continued, a new emerging belief took root in the girls. They, and I, began suggesting that we might not only be competitive, but we might secure a few victories this season! With audacious optimism, we set our goal: Win half of the games we play.

As the days turned into weeks, a palpable sense of camaraderie developed among the team. The girls connected, forming bonds stronger than any I'd seen in the team before. And then it happened–our first victory in years. If you saw the girls jumping and screaming in elation, you might think they'd won at the finals of the WNBA, not a regular season middle school game.

Remarkably, by the close of the season, the Marysville Lions boasted five victories. We finished with an even record: 5 wins and 5 losses. And while we might not have won the conference title, in my heart, every single one of those girls was a true champion. Their journey was a vivid testament to the wonders of teamwork and to the magic that unfurls when individuals believe in one another.

This journey underscored an invaluable life lesson for me: the immense unifying power of celebrating victories, whether big or small. Each win became a reinforcement of the potential within us when we persevere and come together as a unit.

Every celebration uplifted the girl's spirits, nurtured their confidence, and propelled us, as a team, forward. It was much more than just a morale booster. Recognizing and reveling in these successes taught me that every milestone, no matter its scale, deserves its moment in the sun. It's those moments that forge resilience, inspire future endeavors, and remind us of the beauty in our shared the beauty in our shared journey.

In Designing a Cycle of Success, we don't want to stop with discussing ways to repair harm. We also want to notice what is going well and celebrate those wins. Celebrations are important for fostering a joyful and motivating learning environment: one school teachers want to work at, and one that students want to attend.

Too often in schools, we are deficit-minded, asking questions like *what went wrong?* Where do we need to focus on improvement? Because of this, we spend very little time thinking about what went right. **These moments of celebration can invite us to take a moment to pause, be mindful, and appreciate the good in life. In other words, it's a time to savor the good stuff. It's not like hard things aren't there, it is just that**

we want to take joy along for the ride.

It reminds me of a research study that examined the use of rewards. In the study, young dental patients were rewarded with stickers and other small treats for their cooperative behavior. Using this technique, the number of disruptive behaviors was reduced from 90% to less than 15% (Allen & Stokes, 1987). WOW! That's the power of celebrating small wins!

Achievement is Recognized

Recognizing achievement in schools is a cornerstone of fostering a positive and vibrant learning environment. When students see their diligence and accomplishments acknowledged, they're much more likely to continue putting forth their best efforts. Such recognition not only boosts their self-worth but also sends a clear message about what the school values.

When we take a moment to celebrate at school, magic happens. Schools suddenly feel more like close-knit communities, buzzing with collaboration and respect. And let's be real, who doesn't love a good celebration? Celebrating wins and recognizing achievements makes learning more fun. Celebrations are more than just throwing a party. When we recognize our students' achievements, it's like telling them, "Hey, we see you, and you're awesome!" It is this general, positive vibe that makes students feel valued and pumped to be the best versions of themselves.

There are a million ways to celebrate students. If you're looking for some, here are a few that worked for me.

Unlocking SEL's Ways to Celebrate in Schools

Classroom Examples	School Examples
• Offer specific physical praise, such as," I like the way you took your time with that work!"	• Host monthly assemblies highlighting good choices
• Celebrate daily small moments with a classroom whoosh	• Post student character traits winner on the bulletin board
• Write a student a positive note	• Create Hall of Fame walls
• Call the parent to let them know their child is awesome	• Hold a talent show to encourage taking risks and pursuing passion
• Display work in the classroom or halls	• Have a classroom kickball competition just to have some fun together
• Implement a weekly wind down–a classroom reward of 30 minutes of game time for meeting homework or behavior goals	• Bring in a photo book
	• Pass out ice cream treats
• Watch funny videos	• Have popsicle days just because it is hot outside

Look for Ways to Laugh

As we look for ways to celebrate, don't forget about laughter. **In the high-stakes environment of today's schooling, laughter can be a refreshing reset.** Laughter holds a special significance in schools where atmospheres can sometimes be weighed down by pressure and anxiety. Laughter can break down barriers, ease classroom tensions, and create a sense of camaraderie among teachers and students.

When students and educators share light-hearted moments, they're not merely enjoying a break from routine; they're actively creating a stronger learning environment. Encouraging laughter in school is the way to create more engaged learners, closer relationships, and a more positive educational experience. It is simply one of the best ways to create a happy school day.

But what does the research say about laughter?

A good laugh has impressive short-term effects. Laughter induces physical changes in our bodies, including:

> **Getting better oxygen:** Laughter enhances your intake of oxygen-rich air, stimulates your heart, lungs, and muscles, and increases the level of endorphins released by your brain.

> **Relieving our stress response**: A rollicking laugh fires up and then cools down your stress response. It can also increase and then decrease your heart rate and blood pressure. The result? A positive, relaxed feeling.

> **Soothing tension:** Laughter stimulates circulation and aids muscle relaxation, both of which can reduce some of the physical symptoms of stress (Mayo Clinic, 2023).

🎯 PRINCIPAL POINTS

Celebration is paramount for principals, not just as a gesture but as a foundational aspect of a principal's positive leadership. By celebrating, principals not only acknowledge the hard work and achievements of their students but also foster a more positive school culture. Celebrations create a sense of community and belonging, motivating both students and staff to strive for excellence. They reinforce the values and goals of the school, reminding everyone of the collective efforts needed to achieve success.

💡 TEACHER TIPS

Celebrating our own wins as teachers is incredibly important. It's easy to get caught up in the daily grind and focus solely on the challenges and setbacks. However, taking the time to acknowledge and celebrate our successes helps us stay motivated and reminds us of the positive impact we're making. These celebrations, whether they're about small classroom victories or significant milestones, serve as a reminder that our hard work and dedication are paying off.

Chapter Summary

Celebrating wins is vital for creating a joyful and motivating school environment. Celebrations acknowledge achievements and foster a positive culture where both teachers and students feel valued. Often, schools focus too much on what went wrong, leaving little room to appreciate successes. By celebrating, schools can pause and savor good moments, bringing joy to the journey.

Recognizing achievements boosts students' self-esteem and reinforces school values. Celebrations transform schools into close-knit communities filled with collaboration and respect, making learning enjoyable. Various ways to celebrate include specific praise, positive notes, and displaying student work. Schoolwide events like assemblies, talent shows, and fun activities foster a sense of community. Laughter also plays a crucial role in creating a happy school day by breaking down barriers and easing tensions, enhancing the overall learning environment.

📣 Call to Action

- **Celebrate achievements in your school or classroom**: Create a culture where students, teachers, and staff are acknowledged and appreciated for their hard work and accomplishments.

- **Savor the positive moments:** Take a moment to pause and appreciate the small victories, acts of kindness, and moments of joy in your school environment.

- **Foster laughter and positivity:** Promote a positive, lighthearted atmosphere within your school. Encourage laughter, humor, and shared moments of enjoyment among students and educators.

Fifth Key Reflection Questions
Designing a Cycle of Success

Question	Answer
Do you feel your resources are aligned? Do they support SEL?	
How are your staff meetings currently running? Are they solution-focused, collaborative, and mindful? Do they align with your buckets of work?	
How do you currently progress monitor SEL?	
What happens when mistakes are made at your school? What does it look like between adults? How is it different with students?	
What are the 3 R's from Dr. Perry, and how do they relate to SEL?	
What role does celebration have in your school or classroom?	

For resources from the book, go to
www.unlockingsel.com/blueprint

Final Thoughts

Hope

As we draw the final pages of *Unlocking SEL* to a close, we reflect on a journey that beautifully aligns with this sentiment: "Life is a balance of holding on and letting go." This book, rich in resources, personal insights, and practical strategies, has been a testament to such balance.

"Life is a balance of holding on and letting go."
— Rumi

I hope that as you turn each page, embracing new insights and releasing any previous misunderstandings, you feel a stronger connection to the narrative, to me, and to the fundamental principles of social and emotional learning. This journey through SEL is about harmonizing the embrace of new understandings with the release of what no longer serves, enhancing our collective quest for growth and connection.

As you've traversed this book, I hope it's clear that SEL transcends the boundaries of a mere program or syllabus. On the contrary, **SEL is a comprehensive educational philosophy, one that equally cherishes and cultivates the emotional and social dimensions of learning.**

Our journey through the keys of SEL began with the *First Key: Build the Foundation*. This was essential groundwork, the sturdy base upon which all our future efforts would rest.

Next, we progressed to the *Second Key: Center Adult SEL*. This is where we learned that adult wellness is not merely a peripheral aspect of school change. Rather, adult SEL is the driving force propelling SEL forward, far more than just a mere component.

Then, we delved into the *Third Key: Come Into the Classroom*. This taught us "The Big 8," a set of eight strategies that, when implemented, can catalyze significant shifts in classrooms and schools.

Our journey expanded with the *Fourth Key: Scale Schoolwide*. Here, we widened our view to understand how to create an environment that nurtures the growth and well-being of both students and staff.

Finally, we reached our *Fifth Key: Design a Cycle of Success*. This is where we learned to transcend the typical lifecycle of fleeting initiatives. By establishing a cycle of continuous and evolving strategies, we can ensure that the changes brought about by SEL are not transient but lasting and impactful.

My hope is that *Unlocking SEL* becomes an indispensable guide for university education departments, blending the pursuit of emotional intelligence and social competence with academic excellence, mirroring the evolving landscape of modern education. Universities can utilize it to equip future educators with an integrative approach to teaching, cultivating classrooms that are academically challenging and nurturing in equal measure.

Moreover, the SEL Blueprint can offer universities a well-defined, research-backed framework for weaving SEL into the very fabric of educational culture and practice, serving as a vital roadmap for those in training. As a bridge that connects theory to tangible classroom impact, it aims to equip educators and administrators to significantly enrich students' learning experiences.

As I reflect on my own journey through education, I am even further convinced that the inclusion of SEL resources like this could have greatly enhanced the breadth and depth of my learning. My dream is to see it help others.

As we turn the last pages, I'm filled with hope that these concepts have resonated with you, intertwining practical guidance with a spirit of empathy. As we bid farewell, may you feel equipped, inspired, and ready to animate the principles of SEL within your educational realms. Because when you do, you'll nurture a legacy of impactful teaching and learning that can affect generations to come.

In closing this book, I am filled with optimism. Ultimately, my greatest hope with the writing of this book has been to offer not just a **how-to-guide for SEL, but one infused with humanity.** A guide that resonates on a personal level, bridging practicality with the human touch. I aim to inspire educators to see the profound impact SEL can have on creating compassionate, resilient, and thriving school communities. As we part ways with the last chapter, I hope this book has met that mark, leaving you empowered and inspired to bring SEL to life in your educational journey.

Rebuild Update

Our rebuilt school wasn't just about emerging from adversity; it was about sculpting a future rich with promise. The restless thoughts shifted from *How did we endure?* to *What comes next?* We sought not just to be a testament to resilience but to become a beacon of progress.

And indeed, we did just that. Three years on, in 2012, we stepped across the threshold of our lovingly restored Marysville. I still recall the morning we came back with vivid clarity: though I had hardly slept, a surge of anticipation swept that aside. As we crossed into the spaces we once knew so well, now transformed and renewed, a sense of accomplishment swelled within us. We had come full circle.

That morning, as our community walked through the doors of the reborn Marysville, the air was thick with emotion. It held a collective sense of achievement. Our journey had been arduous, but the sight of freshly painted walls and the sound of laughter ringing through hallways once silent was a powerful affirmation of our collective spirit. It was a moment steeped in symbolism, a fresh start etched not just in the newness of our surroundings, but in the resilient hearts of everyone who had a hand in rising from the remnants. We had not only rebuilt our school; we had rekindled the very essence of our community and crafted a legacy. Each new step in the building felt like a stride toward innovation, resilience, and excellence. We were finally home. It was a Marysville Miracle.

In 2017, KOIN news in Portland, Oregon did an update on "Marysville School: Rising from ashes through mindfulness."

Scan QR code for the story.

Afterword

When I first walked into Marysville K-8 school in SE Portland, it didn't take long to realize there was something really special happening within the walls of the schoolhouse. Hearing Principal Lana Penley tell the story, it was clear that the opportunity to rebuild the school in the aftermath of a school fire provided fertile ground for the school to regenerate and to heal. With heart and determination, Lana set forward on a journey that would not only restore Marysville's sense of community, but it would set the school on a trajectory for success.

An outlier among other neighboring Title 1 schools, Marysville's school culture became marked by high engagement, strong staff retention, joyful children, strong academic outcomes, and involved community. News of Marysville's magic started spreading, and soon, Lana and her team were leading school learning walks and helping to inspire others to adopt mindful practices as the anchor for belonging, safety, learning, and positive culture. Lana's story and leadership remind everyone that there is no more powerful tool than social and emotional learning practices to transform a school.

Robert W. Roeser, PhD
Professor of Human Development and Family Studies
Bennett Professor of Care and Compassion in Education
The Pennsylvania State University
State College, PA

Appendix A:
Lana's Professional Development Offerings

Lana's ability to engage and inspire her audience makes her sessions not just informative but also highly interactive and enjoyable. Her trainings are tailored to meet educators' and schools' unique needs, focusing on practical, implementable strategies that directly benefit classroom practices.

Through working with Lana, your school will gain access to cutting-edge techniques and insights, fostering an environment of continuous learning and improvement. See below for Lana's three main types of professional development offerings:

KEYNOTES: Discover the transformative power of SEL with Lana as your keynote speaker. Her engagements are more than just talks; they're a confluence of actionable insights and uplifting inspiration designed to leave audiences both equipped and energized for change.

SEL SCHOOLWIDE SERIES: Embark on a transformative 5-part SEL journey tailored to your school's unique landscape. Under Lana's guidance, your team will dive into both adult and student SEL strategies. This program is celebrated for its profound impact, with many calling it a catalyst for educational revolution.

MINDFUL LEADERS NETWORK: Join Lana in a dedicated 3-part series crafted for educational leaders, focusing on mindfulness as a cornerstone for stress management. Through practical strategies rooted in Lana's experiences, leaders will gain invaluable tools for personal and professional well-being.

Appendix B: Resource Reminders

A Few Reminders

✯ To learn more from Lana right away, go to www.unlockingsel.com/jumpstart for her online mini course-SEL Jumpstart.

✯ Join our Facebook groups: For teachers @unlockingsel
For leaders: @unlockingselforleaders

✯ Go to www.unlockingsel.com/blueprint for resources to complement your experience, scan the QR code.

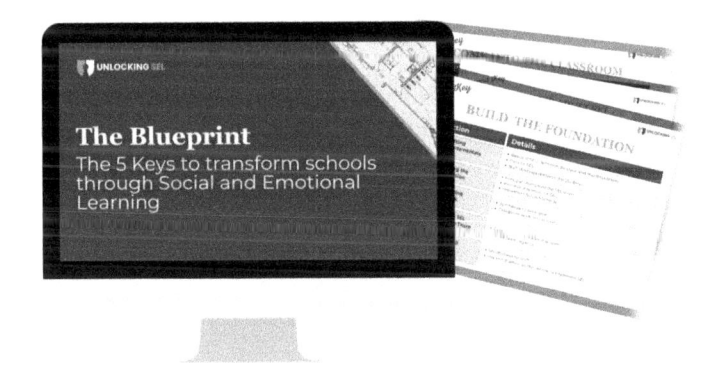

Appendix C:
5 Habits of a Mindful Educator

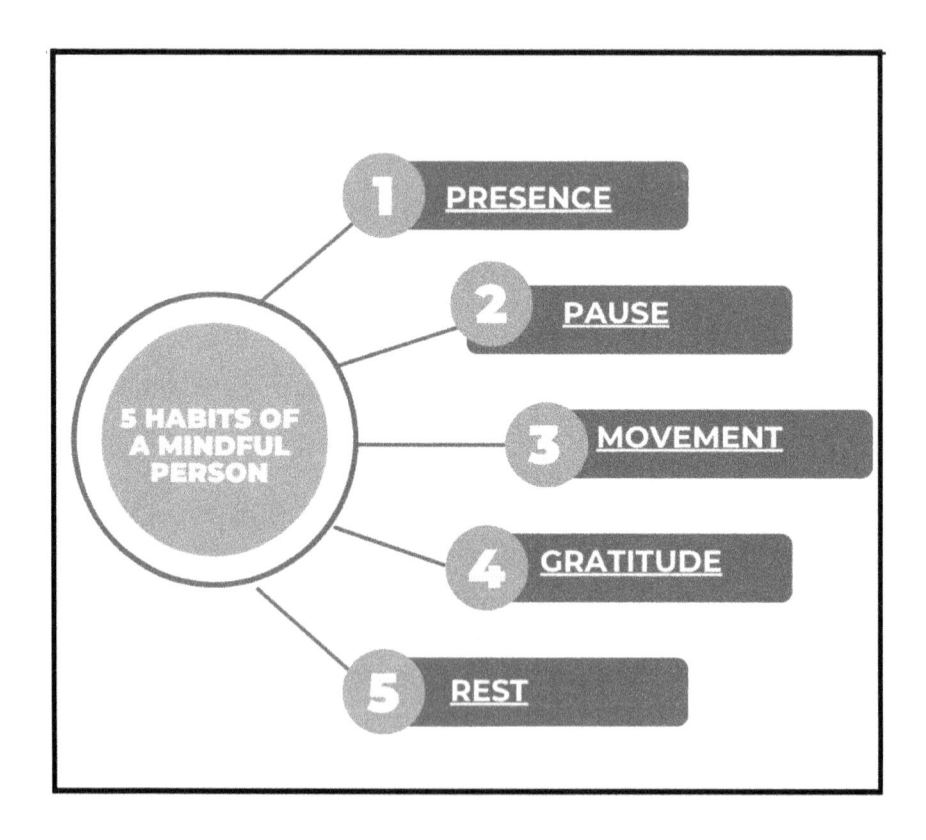

5 HABITS OF A MINDFUL PERSON

1. PRESENCE
2. PAUSE
3. MOVEMENT
4. GRATITUDE
5. REST

Appendix D: The Big 8 Classroom SEL Strategies

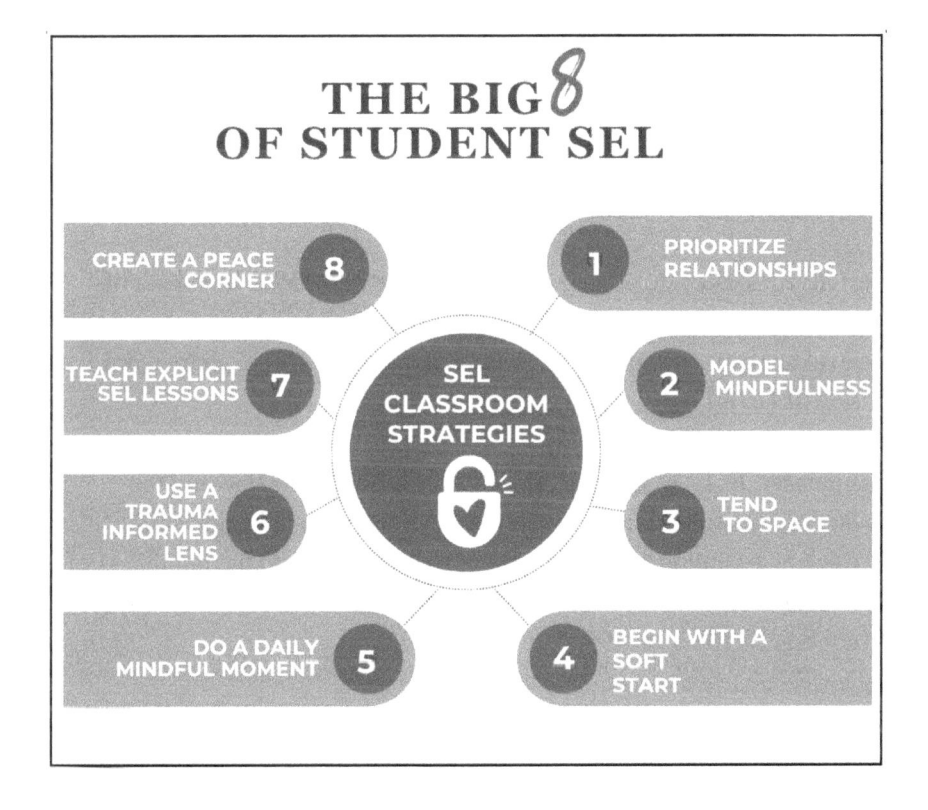

THE BIG 8 OF STUDENT SEL

SEL CLASSROOM STRATEGIES

1. PRIORITIZE RELATIONSHIPS
2. MODEL MINDFULNESS
3. TEND TO SPACE
4. BEGIN WITH A SOFT START
5. DO A DAILY MINDFUL MOMENT
6. USE A TRAUMA INFORMED LENS
7. TEACH EXPLICIT SEL LESSONS
8. CREATE A PEACE CORNER

References

Allen, K. A., Kern, M., Rozek, C. S., McInerney, D., & Slavich, G. M. (2021). Belonging: A review of conceptual issues, an integrative framework, and directions for future research. *Australian Journal of Psychology, 73*(1), 87-102

Allen, K. D., & Stokes, T. F. (1987).Use of escape and reward in the management of Young Children during dental treatment. 20.4. (1987) (5.5)

Barrett, P., Davies, F., Zhang, Y., & Barrett, L. (2015). The impact of classroom design on pupils' learning: Final results of a holistic, multi-level analysis. *Building and Environment, 89,* 118–133. https://doi.org/10.1016/j.buildenv.2015.02.013

Baumeister, R. F., & Robson, D. A. (2021). Belongingness and the modern schoolchild: On loneliness, socioemotional health, self-esteem, evolutionary mismatch, online sociality, and the numbness of rejection. *Australian Journal of Psychology, 73*(1), 103–111. https://doi.org/10.1080/00049530.2021.1877573

Benton, T. D., Boyd, R. C., & Njoroge, W. F. M. (2021). Addressing the global crisis of child and adolescent mental health. *JAMA Pediatrics, 175*(11). https://doi.org/10.1001/jamapediatrics.2021.2479

Brunting, Susan. (2023). *SEL policy at the state level.* CASEL.

Bushweller, K. (2022). *How educators view Social-Emotional Learning, in charts.* Education Week. https://www.edweek.org/leadership/how-educators-view-social-emotional-learning-in-charts/2022/11

Carsley, D., Khoury, B. & Heath, N.L. (2018). Effectiveness of mindfulness interventions for mental health in schools: a comprehensive meta-analysis. *Mindfulness* 9, 693–707. https://doi.org/10.1007/s12671-017-0839-2

Chen, J. A., Stevens, C., Wong, S. H. M., & Liu, C. H. (2019). Psychiatric symptoms and diagnoses among U.S. College Students: A comparison by race and ethnicity. *Psychiatric Services (Washington, D.C.)*, 70(6), 442–449. https://doi.org/10.1176/appi.ps.201800388

Cipriano, C., Strambler, M., Naples, L., Ha, C., Kirk, M., Wood, M., Sehgal, K., Zieher, A., Eveleigh, A., McCarthy, M., Funaro, M., Ponnock, A., Chow, J. J., & Durlak, J. (2023). *The state of the evidence for Social and Emotional Learning: A contemporary meta-analysis of universal school-based SEL interventions.* https://doi.org/10.31219/osf.io/mk35u

Cloke, H. (2023). *What is Malcolm Knowles' Adult Learning Theory?* Growth Engineering. https://www.growthengineering.co.uk/what-is-malcolm-knowles-adult-learning-theory/

Cobb, F., & Krownapple, J. (2019). *Belonging through a culture of dignity: The keys to successful equity implementation.* Mimi & Todd Press.

Dadds, M., Ham, D., Montague, R., & Shochet, I. (2006) *School connectedness is an underemphasized parameter in adolescent mental health: Results of a community prediction.*

Durlak, J., & Mahoney, J. (2019). *The practical benefits of an SEL Program.* https://casel.s3.us-east-2.amazonaws.com/Practical-Benefits-of-SEL-Program.pdf

Durlak, J. A., Weissberg, R. P., Dymnicki, A. B., Taylor, R. D., & Schellinger, K. B. (2011). The impact of enhancing students' social and emotional learning: A meta-analysis of school-based Universal interventions. Child Development, 82(1), 405–432. https://doi.org/10.1111/j.1467-8624.2010.01564.x

EdWeek Research Team. (2023). *Is teacher morale on the rise?* EdWeek. https://fs24.formsite.com/edweek/images/WP-Merrimack-Is_Teacher_

Morale_on_the_Rise.pdf

Epperson, A. (2021). *How often should you praise students?* PBIS Rewards. https://www.pbisrewards.com/blog/how-often-should-you-praise-students/

Fundamentals of SEL. (2023). CASEL. https://casel.org/fundamentals-of-sel/#:~:text=SEL%20is%20the%20process%20through,and%20make%20responsible%20and%20caring

Gaffney, C., Mattingly, E., & Pettway, A. (2016). *Teaching at the intersections.* SPLC. https://www.learningforjustice.org/magazine/summer-2016/teaching-at-the-intersections (5.4)

Goleman, D. (1998). *Working with Emotional Intelligence.* https://stephanehaefliger.com/campus/biblio/017/17_39.pdf

Goodenow, C., & Grady, K. E. (1993). The relationship of school belonging and friends' values to academic motivation among urban adolescent students. *The Journal of Experimental Education.* 62 (1): 60–71.

Greenberg, M. T., Brown J. L., & Abenavoli, R.M. (2016). *Teacher stress and health effects on teachers, students, and schools.* Edna Bennett Pierce Prevention Research Center, Pennsylvania State University. https://prevention.psu.edu/wp-content/uploads/2022/09/rwjf430428-TeacherStress.pdf

Hanson, R. (2021). *Taking in the good stuff - Dr. Rick Hanson.* Dr. Rick Hanson - Learn the Practical Neuroscience of Lasting Happiness. http://www.rickhanson.net/taking-good-stuff (5.5B)

Horowitz, J., & Graf, N. (2019). *Most U.S. teens see anxiety, depression as major problems.* Pew Research Center's Social & Demographic Trends Project. Pew Research Center. https://www.pewresearch.org/social-trends/2019/02/20/most-u-s-teens-see-anxiety-and-depression-as-a-major-problem-among-their-peers/

https://casel.org/systemic-implementation/sel-policy-at-the-state-level/

Ito, Y., Browne, C., & Yamamoto, K. (2022). The Impacts of Mindfulness-Based Stress Reduction (MBSR) on mindfulness and well-being for regular and novice meditators. *Mindfulness*. https://doi.org/10.1007/s12671-022-01888-6

Khoury, B., Lecomte, T., Fortin, G., Masse, M., Therien, P., Bouchard, V., Chapleau, M., Paquin, K., & Hofmann, S. (2013). Mindfulness-based therapy: A comprehensive meta-analysis. *Clinical Psychology Review*, *33*(6), 763–771. https://doi.org/10.1016/j.cpr.2013.05.005

Korpershoek, H., Canrinus, E., Fokkens-Bruinsma, M., & De Boer, H. (2019). The relationships between school belonging and students' motivational, social-emotional, behavioural, and academic outcomes in secondary education: a meta-analytic review. *Research Papers in Education*, *35*(6), 641–680. https://doi.org/10.1080/02671522.2019.1615116

Lam, A.G., Sterling, S., & Margines, E. (2015). *Effects of five-minute mindfulness meditation on Mental Health Care Professionals.* https://www.semanticscholar.org/paper/Effects-of-Five-Minute-Mindfulness-Meditation-on-Lam-Sterling/7a7529a9e6401679016ab78f398eaaf4487aff84

Lee, Ingrid Fetell, Lee. (2018). *Where joy hides and how to find it.* TED. https://www.ted.com/talks/ingrid_fetell_lee_where_joy_hides_and_how_to_find_it?language=en

Lister, Josephine. (2018). *Can we design our schools to inspire joy and increase learning?* Hundred. https://hundred.org/en/articles/can-we-design-our-schools-to-inspire-joy-and-increase-learning

MAEC. (2021). *MAEC-Restorative Practices.* MAEC, Inc.https://maec.org/wp-content/uploads/2021/05/MAEC-RestorativePractices-2021.pdf (5.4c)

Martin, A. J., & Collie, R. J. (2019). Teacher–student relationships and students' engagement in high school: Does the number of negative and positive relationships with teachers matter? *Journal of Educational Psychology*, *111*(5), 861–876. https://doi.org/10.1037/edu0000317

Maynard, N., &Weinstein, B. (2020). *Hacking school discipline: 9 ways to create a culture of empathy; responsibility using restorative justice*. Times 10 Publications. (5.4c)

Mayo Clinic Staff. (2023). *Stress relief from laughter? It's no joke*. Mayo Clinic. https://www.mayoclinic.org/healthy-lifestyle/stress-management/in-depth/stress-relief/art-20044456 (5.5C)

NCES Staff. (2022). *Press Release - Roughly half of public schools report that they can effectively provide mental health services to all students in need*. NCES. https://nces.ed.gov/whatsnew/press_releases/05_31_2022_2.asp

Next Generation Learning Challenges Staff. (2020). *Building a sense of schools as communities of care*. NGLC. https://www.nextgenlearning.org/articles/schools-as-communities-of-care

NIMH Staff. (2017). *Any anxiety disorder*. NIMH. https://www.nimh.nih.gov/health/statistics/any-anxiety-disorder

Paley, A. (2022). *2022 national survey on LGBTQ youth mental health*. The Trevor Project. https://www.thetrevorproject.org/survey-2022/

Perry, B (2013). *https://www.neurosequential.com/*

Peterson, S. (2018). *School personnel*. The National Child Traumatic Stress Network. https://www.nctsn.org/audiences/school-personnel#:~:text=Research%20suggests%20that%20approximately%2025,children%20who%20have%20experienced%20trauma.

Perry, B. D., & Winfrey, O. (2021). *What happened to you?: Conversations on trauma, resilience, and healing*. Flatiron.

Press release - Roughly half of public schools report that they can effectively provide mental health services to all students in need, (2022). https://nces.ed.gov/whatsnew/press_releases/05_31_2022_2.asp

Research on mindfulness. Mindful Schools. (2023, August 18). https://www.mindfulschools.org/about-mindfulness/research-on-mindfulness/

Qualtrics Staff. (2022) *Only half of high school students feel a sense of belonging at their school, Qualtrics research shows.* Qualtrics. https://www.qualtrics.com/news/only-half-of-high-school-students-feel-a-sense-of-belonging-at-their-school-qualtrics-research-shows/

Rands, M. L., & Gansemer-Topf, A. M. (2017). The room itself is active: How classroom design impacts student engagement. *Journal of Learning Spaces, 6*(1), 26–33. https://files.eric.ed.gov/fulltext/EJ1152568.pdf Relationships: A review of selected research underlying the framework. *Search Institute.*

Research on Mindfulness. (2019). Mindful schools. https://www.mindfulschools.org/about-mindfulness/research-on-mindfulness/#reference-1

Roehlkepartain, E. C., Pekel, K., Syvertsen, A. K., Sethi, J., Sullivan, T. K., & Scales, P. C. (2017). *Relationships first: Creating connections that help young people thrive.* Minneapolis, MN: Search Institute.

Sato, K., Kuroda, S., & Owan, H. (2020). Mental health effects of long work hours, night and weekend work, and short rest periods. *Social Science & Medicine, 246,* 112774. https://doi.org/10.1016/j.socscimed.2019.112774

Scales, P. C., Roehlkepartain, E. C., & Houltberg, B. J. (2022). *The elements of Developmental Relationships: A review of selected research underlying the framework.* Minneapolis: Search Institute. www.searchinstitute.org

Scanfield, V., Davis, L., Leah Weintraub, & Dotoli, V. (2018). *The power of common language.* ASCD. https://www.ascd.org/el/articles/the-power-of-common-language

Schreiber, A., Miller, B. A., & Dressler, K. (2022). *An introduction to restorative practices.* National Center for School Safety.https://www.nc2s.org/wp-content/uploads/2022/07/An-Introduction-to-Restorative-Practices.pdf

SEL Policy at the State Level. (2023). CASEL. https://casel.org/systemic-implementation/sel-policy-at-the-state-level/

Shin K. M., Cho S. M., Shin Y. M., & Park K. S. (2016). Effects of early childhood peer relationships on adolescent mental health: A 6- to 8-year follow-up study in South Korea. *Psychiatry Investigation.* 13(4):383-388

Substance Abuse and Mental Health Services Administration. (2014). *SAMHSA's concept of trauma and guidance for a trauma-informed approach.* HHS Publication No. (SMA) 14-4884. Rockville, MD: Substance Abuse and Mental Health Services Administration.

Superville, D. R. (2022). *New Survey: How the pandemic has made school leadership more stressful.* Education Week. https://www.edweek.org/leadership/new-survey-how-the-pandemic-has-made-school-leadership-more-stressful/2022/01

T. D., Boyd, R. C., & Njoroge, W. F. M. (2021). Addressing the global crisis of child and adolescent mental health. *JAMA Pediatrics,* 175(11). https://doi.org/10.1001/jamapediatrics.2021.2479

Tapia-Film, C., Moreno-Barahona, M., Garza-Teran, G., Corral-Verdugo, V., &Fraijo-Sing, B. (2020). School environments and elementary school children's well-being in Northwestern Mexico. *Frontiers in Psychology.* https://www.frontiersin.org/articles/10.3389/

fpsyg.2020.00510/full

Taylor RD, Oberle E, Durlak JA, Weissberg RP. Promoting Positive Youth Development Through School-Based Social and Emotional Learning Interventions: A Meta-Analysis of Follow-Up Effects. Child Dev. 2017 Jul;88(4):1156-1171. doi: 10.1111/cdev.12864. PMID: 28685826.

Transformative SEL - Casel. (n.d.). https://casel.org/fundamentals-of-sel/how-does-sel-support-educational-equity-and-excellence/transformative-sel/

Villani, S., & Henry, S. (2023, August 24). *Getting started with restorative practices.* MAEC, Inc. https://maec.org/restorative-practices/

Walker C., & Greene B. (2009) The relations between student motivational beliefs and cognitive engagement in high school. *Journal of Educational Research.*

Will, M. (2022). *Teachers are not OK, even though we need them to be.* Education Week. https://www.edweek.org/teaching-learning/teachers-are-not-ok-even-though-we-need-them-to-be/2021/09#:~:text=Sixty%20percent%20of%20teachers%20say

I close with my favorite poem, Mary Oliver's "Wild Geese", as it has threads of SEL. The poem encourages embracing one's self highlighting the importance of empathy and shared human experiences. It promotes mindfulness by describing the continuity and beauty of the natural world, fostering a sense of belonging and connection. Additionally, the imagery of wild geese heading home symbolizes resilience and hope, aligning with SEL's goal of helping people navigate challenges all while maintaining their optimism for a kinder world.

Wild Geese

You do not have to be good.
You do not have to walk on your knees
for a hundred miles through the desert repenting.
You only have to let the soft animal of your body
love what it loves.
Tell me about despair, yours, And I will tell you mine.
Meanwhile the world goes on.
Meanwhile the sun and the clear pebbles of the rain
are moving across the landscapes,
over the prairies and the deep trees,
the mountains and the rivers.
Meanwhile the wild geese, high in the clean blue air,
are heading home again.
Whoever you are, no matter how lonely, the world offers itself to your imagination,
calls to you like the wild geese, harsh and exciting-
over and over announcing your place
in the family of things.

Mary Oliver

Printed in the USA
CPSIA information can be obtained
at www.ICGtesting.com
LVHW022012280924
792408LV00004B/914